LAPCHICK

LAPCHICK

The Life of a Legendary Player and Coach
in the Glory Days of Basketball

GUS ALFIERI

The Lyons Press
Guilford, Connecticut
An imprint of The Globe Pequot Press

The Lyons Press is an imprint of The Globe Pequot Press.

10 9 8 7 6 5 4 3 2 1

Printed in the United States of America

ISBN 13: 978-1-59228-869-4
ISBN 10: 1-59228-869-3

Library of Congress Cataloging-in-Publication Data is available on file.

"Sometimes I rub my eyes in wonder.
This game of ours—the players, the auditoriums—
it all seems too good to be true."

—Joe Lapchick,
in an interview with sportswriter Lennie Koppett,
February 1963.

This book is dedicated most lovingly to
my wife, Janet, for all the sacrifices
she had made in our marriage.

Table of Contents

Acknowledgments

Lapchick would never have been written if it weren't for the inspiration of Joe Lapchick. There was no doubt that his fatherly shepherding drew me to the project.

I always had a strong curiosity about Lapchick, who had been my basketball coach at St. John's University more than forty years ago. One evening I came across his old letters in my attic. They were fascinating, and as I read them, I realized I had been too young to have understood their significance. The letters sparked a curiosity to know him better.

The first stop I made for inspiration was to Lou Carnesecca, who had been his assistant and was genuinely excited about my idea. He directed me to the necessary sources and lent me his time and encouragement.

When I began the project, Dr. Richard Lapchick allowed me access to his father's papers, which included extensive newspaper clippings, photos, and sports memorabilia, and helped sort the chronology of his father's career. Barbara Lapcek and Joe Lapchick, his two other children, were also of great assistance. Each helped me see their father in a different light. My research revealed that Joe Lapchick had to be the most quoted sports figure of his time, or at least in the realm of basketball. Writers sought him out for insights and leads to their stories. He was always available, and they loved him for this. The result was that Lapchick's position on a great many topics has been preserved by a variety of newspapers.

I conducted more than 250 interviews, from Wilt Chamberlain, Bob Knight, and John Wooden to Benito, his favorite waiter at Leone's, to Lapchick's Yonkers next-door neighbor. The initial help and kindness of Helen Kutsher, matriarch of the famous New York resort, will never be forgotten. She was another example of the "class" Lapchick admired his whole life.

Much of what Lapchick had to say was recorded by the print media. He was not an author, journalist, or political figure, and he kept no diaries or logs. Interviews with those who dealt with him on a daily basis did that. Sportswriters like Lennie Koppett, Jerry Izenberg, Sam Goldaper, Lennie Lewin, and cartoonist Bill Gallo helped.

Richard Lapchick revealed his father was "an incredible letter-writer." I was able to learn much about him from the many letters he loved writing. In an age that relied on letter-writing more than the telephone, Joe Lapchick enjoyed sitting down at home, in his coach's office, or in distant hotels and writing to his many friends. Whenever I concluded an interview I would ask for his letters, and I gathered many. Lapchick's large and clear handwriting made them easy to decipher.

Bill Himmelman, the NBA historian, educated me on basketball's pioneer days. His fingertip access to past figures of the game made many interviews possible. Todd Caso from the NBA Entertainment Center generously gave his time and necessary research material. The Basketball Hall of Fame, in Springfield, Massachusetts, was helpful with my research. Its archivist, Doug Starke, worked to satisfy my requests.

Thomas Flynn, president of the Yonkers Historical Society helped me reconstruct Joe Lapchick's youth, while John Favareau, the Gettys Square librarian, supplied added records and documents about Yonkers and its famous citizen. Through their efforts, I tracked down community neighbors who remembered the Lapchick family, even one who recalled delivering newspapers to them.

A significant part of the book focuses upon the years I played for Coach Lapchick. The personal experiences of my St. John's teammates and I form the foundation of our playing days with him. They helped me reach many of my conclusions. Dick Engert and Alan Seiden had fine memories. The St. John's years were helped by Lou Roethel, Joe Daley, Tony Jackson, Bob Genirs, Walter Brady, Pete Carroll, Ken LaMotte, Dick Duckett, Hughie Kirwan, John Ryan, Bob McIntyre, Ken Wirell, and managers Ken McGinniss and Vinnie Colluro. Mike Parenti was kind enough to discuss a difficult period in his life.

Jerry Houston, cocaptain of the 1964–65 St. John's team, Lapchick's last, was instrumental in unfolding the events of Lapchick's spectacular coaching climax. After Lapchick's death, Houston remained a close family friend. He made Coach Lapchick's retirement period come alive. The book could not have been authentic without the help of the NBA's Alumni Department's head Zelda Spoelstra. Her personal experiences with Mr. Lapchick and knowledge of the early NBA as President Maurice Podoloff's aide provided a rich flavor of both. She not only helped research material, but put me in touch with many legendary figures for the project.

I would not be writing this acknowledgment without the efforts of my literary agent, Philip Spitzer. He not only provided the final professional shape to the book, but he also shared my passion for the subject and recognized that it not only chronicled Joe Lapchick's life, but also "The Glory Days of New York Basketball." His knowledge of sports as well as the literary marketplace proved to be an unbeatable tandem. Like a talented sculptor, he envisioned what the completed manuscript would become. I never felt Philip Spitzer was selling a book but was sharing our passion for sports with the world.

Newsday's award-winning investigative reporter and successful biographer, Tom Maier, shared his understanding of the literary marketplace. It was his persistence that helped my manuscript receive a proper presentation. His teacher-pupil direction was fully appreciated.

Encouragement and editing direction came from Jack Clarke, Edith Duncan, Mike Candel, and Basil Palmeri. They provided the daily reading of my manuscript. Jack Clarke inspired by reminding me of the fundamentals of writing, while Edith Duncan was a tough, bulldog taskmaster who constantly demanded my best. Candel, formerly of *Newsday*, offered the analytical mind of a sportswriter along with the instincts of an athlete. Basil Palmeri's editing turned the manuscript into a more polished work, while offering a continuous stream of encouragement when I could have easily lost my way.

"Late entries" Walter Bode and Paul Golub helped get the manuscript into the "red zone," ready to score. Each made major suggestions that helped maneuver the study in the right direction.

The late Jack Gimmler, St. John's trainer and sports wit, provided honest, straightforward explanations filled with enthusiasm. Bob Knight added details and insights that helped me understand Lapchick's mentoring ways. The late Eddie Donovan and Johnny Bach also revealed the pattern of his teaching.

Ivy Summer, who played for Lapchick at St. John's and was instrumental in the 1944 NIT championship, provided warm memories of the period, as did Hy Gotkin, Dutch Garfinkel, Fuzzy Levane, and the late Harry Boykoff.

Normie Ochs added anecdotes as well as an analysis of the period. Ochs, who played for St. John's and Columbia in the 1940s, was part of the life of the famous McGuire family and Rockaway's historical setting. His patience and many helping hands made the book a reality.

Joe Lapchick's Knicks years included interviews with Carl Braun, Ernie Vandeweghe, Vince Boryla, Dick and Al McGuire, as well as Ray Lumpp, George Kaftan, Harry Gallatin, Buddy Ackerman, and the late trainer Don Friedrichs.

Boston Celtics Bob Cousy told compelling stories of the early pro era that demonstrated Lapchick's character, while Carl Bennett, Fort Wayne Pistons general manager, provided firsthand information about NBA integration.

Joe Jares, Murry Nelson, Bob Wolff, Larry Pearlstein, Alex Hannum, Bill Tosheff, Earl Lloyd, John Shanley, Fred Podesta, Jack Curran, and Bernie Reiner were others among many who contributed to the book.

In my darker moments, my coaching friend Stan Kellner kept the flame lit, nudging me to be "proactive," as he preached, to accept nothing less than a published book.

I want to thank The Lyons Press staff and especially my editor Dr. Rob Kirkpatrick, who saw what I envisioned in the Lapchick book and made it become a reality.

Last, I want to acknowledge the support and understanding of my wife, Janet. She had to listen to my laments and frustrations and never had the chance to hang up or leave the room. Her cross was perpetual, and loyally carried.

Foreword

My most vivid memory of the legendary basketball coach Joe Lapchick was watching him being carried off the court by his St. John's players in Madison Square Garden. His team just defeated powerful Michigan, the number one team in the country, by one point in the final of the 1964 Holiday Festival. Joe was in his mid-sixties and enjoying the attention and the partisan crowd's affectionate response. The pioneer coach was proud of the victory, but his announced retirement made it that much sweeter.

Afterward, as he accepted the winner's cup to cheers and photographers' flashing lights, I thought of what this legendary figure meant to basketball. The next day the newspapers called the come-from-behind victory his greatest moment, but most readers had no idea Lapchick had one more miracle left in him.

I first heard about Joe Lapchick in the 1950s as a youngster in Crystal City, Missouri, when I began to take basketball seriously. I attended basketball camps run by my NBA heroes like Ed Macauley and Jerry West, who taught me fundamentals I never forgot. I watched Joe Lapchick's New York Knicks play the St. Louis Hawks in Kiel Auditorium. I knew all the pro names, and he was well-known at the time.

When I attended Princeton, my coach, Butch Van Breda Kolff, talked about Joe Lapchick, his coach when he played for the early Knicks.

"Coach Lapchick taught pride and class," Van Breda Kolff said. He described the tall, lean coach as "tough, but fair."

Most significantly, Lapchick pioneered NBA integration when the Knicks signed Sweetwater Clifton, one of three blacks who entered the NBA in 1950. Again, Joe Lapchick demonstrated fairness, regardless of race. As a man of character, Lapchick treated his tall forward fairly in a world still unequal for blacks, making Clifton's transition seamless. As a pro player, Lapchick traveled throughout the country during the 1930s playing many games against all-black teams. He admired their ability at a time in America when it was unpopular to interact with minorities.

Because of my play in the Holiday Festival, I was voted the best visiting college performer by the Metropolitan sportswriters and invited to accept the award at their annual March dinner. When I arrived that evening at the Hotel Americana in New York City, I saw a large group of sportswriters busy interviewing Joe Lapchick. It didn't take long for the honorees to realize we would take a backseat to the dinner's main focus: Bill Russell, Coach Jack Ramsey, and I were happy to be part of Joe Lapchick's retirement party given by his many sports-media friends.

After Lapchick finished his interview, he walked over to greet me. As we talked, I realized we were about the same height at 6'5". Neatly dressed with a blue suit, white shirt, and striped tie, he looked every bit the success he had been his entire life. He talked softly and listened carefully, making me feel as if I were the only person in the room.

As speakers came forward, and Joe Lapchick's life unfolded before the five hundred guests, I realized how much the sports world loved and admired him, and would miss him. He was a gentleman who was always concerned for his friends and the integrity of the game that he loved. As I listened to the speakers, I identified with Lapchick's passion for the game, which sent chills up my spine.

"Joe Lapchick was a great Celtic," one sportswriter reminded the audience. As an Original Celtic, Joe Lapchick was considered the best professional big man of the 1920s. I learned that the Celtics were the New York Yankees of the era and looked upon as World Champions. Another sportswriter spoke of Lapchick's thirty years as coach of St. John's and the Knicks. Old pro players told humorous stories, while others spoke of how he had reached out to help them.

But there was humility to this man that I appreciated. When I entered the banquet room, I overheard some of his interview where he talked about his limited formal education and how retirement would now allow time for the handicraft work that he enjoyed. There was nothing lofty or self-inflating about him. He was a regular guy unimpressed with his stature and impressive in his simplicity. As I tried to encapsulate what made him successful, I sensed that his experience to intuitively know people coupled with the advantage of being a pioneering professional player made him an effective coach. He instinctively understood that coaching required solidarity and that successful coaching grew from player camaraderie. There were few better at creating team chemistry than the tall coach.

Al McGuire was once asked what made Lapchick a successful coach. "Joe Lapchick didn't know basketball," McGuire leveled at the shocked sportswriter. "He felt it . . . like I did." Joe Lapchick was a natural because basketball was in his blood. No one would have to spend time teaching him about the game. His first reaction was often correct about it.

I curiously kept track the rest of the season, to see how he would complete his career. In the last game, his St. John's team sent their coach out a winner by defeating a strong Villanova team in the final of the 1965 National Invitation Tournament. After the game he was quoted saying, "What a way to go," while sportswriters reported the victory was his fourth NIT championship. It was a fitting tribute to a good man. Few coaches ended their career winning a major championship. Joe Lapchick was a man who devoted more than fifty years to basketball as a paid player and college and professional coach, had been inducted into the Hall of Fame twice, and was admired by the basketball world.

In a sense, Joe Lapchick was every American's success story, proof that in our country opportunity and hard work pay off. Lapchick demonstrated that a man could educate himself, learning to match his skills with the nation's best. His life encompasses much of the early history of basketball, and yet his work is still very much a part of the modern game. He believed enough in the basic decency of Americans to help champion the introduction of blacks into pro basketball and endured frightful encounters for this fundamental belief in equality. This sorry but extraordinarily important chapter from basketball's history is explored thoroughly in Gus Alfieri's account of Coach Lapchick's life.

Yet with all his honors, Joe Lapchick's most striking quality was that he was a man of character, someone respected by his peers. I've learned, partly from Lapchick's example, that neither money nor hype can add this quality to a person's reputation. It must be earned. It is a legacy that every basketball player—every American—should strive for.

—Bill Bradley

Preface

Iwas fifteen years old and a freshman at St. Francis Prep in Brooklyn in the early 1950s when I got to know Joe Lapchick while watching the former Original Celtic on my fifteen-inch black-and-white Zenith television. He was standing tall, all 6'5" of him, and erect by the New York Knickerbockers bench with his hands on his hips staring at referee Sid Borgia after what must have been a bad call. I loved the Knicks and basketball, and the tall, lean coach was part of my world. I seem to have complete recall of my first meeting with Coach Joe Lapchick. I passed him as I entered the 69th Armory in New York City. I was a little awed when I first spotted him. He had just completed a practice, and I was entering the armory to play a prep-school game.

Then, in the fall of 1956, he was rehired to coach the St. John's Redmen, and I was a sophomore scholarship player his first year back. I paid particular attention to how he coached, and I found him to be an interesting man, someone I wanted to understand better. I played three seasons for Coach Lapchick and then spent the last eleven years of his life keeping in touch and communicating with him by letter, phone calls, or social meetings. I kept all my correspondence with him and realized that when they were read in their entirety, there was much that was still unanswered about him. So I set out to find the missing pieces.

His three children were extremely helpful, and after I had visited in Boston with his youngest, Dr. Richard Lapchick, I was off and running in my hunt for answers. Joe Lapchick's other two children, Barbara Lapcek and Joe Lapchick, each helped me to see their father in a different light.

Joe Lapchick had seen and done it all in the fifty years that he traveled through the world of basketball. After studying his life and knowing him as one of his players, and as a former coach, I was able to understand how the sport became the natural pastime for kids all over the world. Even though basketball has become international, its roots are found in America's soil, and Joe Lapchick will always be the experienced lens through which all can examine, study, and enjoy the fifty years of basketball he lived.

Prologue

Joe Lapchick looked upset, almost as if he felt an odd sensation in the pit of his stomach as he watched his St. John's Redmen warming up in Madison Square Garden. The team was playing the 2:00 P.M. game against Brigham Young in the first round of the 1956 Holiday Festival. The repeated rumors were that the St. John's Redmen were dumping games. The team had been sluggish in yesterday's Christmas afternoon practice, but perhaps that had been too much holiday cheer. Today, Lapchick watched them carefully from the bench, sipping a cup of water. There was no spirit, no energy on the court, just lethargic layups to Gladys Gooding's organ music.

At 6'5", Lapchick was the pro game's first successful big man, and his play with the Original Celtics is historic. He was a legendary basketball figure and twice inducted into the Hall of Fame, first with his team and then as an outstanding pro player. Less than a year ago, at a hasty press conference in the Garden, the Knicks front office had announced that Coach Joe Lapchick had "resigned." In fact, the Knicks had forced him out, but he had quickly found a new home, returning to St. John's University for a second tour of duty. He was happy to be at St. John's, in the Garden coaching again, but he didn't like what he found. Unknowingly, he had walked into a scandal.

His suspicions had been aroused during last week's loss to Utah, a team St. John's should have beaten. One sportswriter said the Utes seemed "more determined" during their 79–71 win, but Lapchick wasn't convinced. Dick Young of the *Daily News* targeted one postgame statistic that stuck in Lapchick's craw: Alan Seiden, a 5'10" sophomore guard, had out-rebounded the team's big men.

It wasn't only one play that was wrong, but an overall lack of effort. To Lapchick, a winning team was like the fingers on a hand: they all had to work together. This team lacked chemistry. The sophomores—Seiden and Buddy Pascal—seemed like orphans from a Dickens novel, hungrily waiting for someone to feed them the ball. Hustle was Lapchick's coaching trademark. He knew how to motivate, press the right buttons for players to give their best. Lapchick was familiar with the fresh, clean smell of success; he sensed it miles away. Now he only inhaled the daily stench of deception.

Lapchick's gut instincts were borne out when BYU sprinted to a 12–0 lead. St. John's missed its first six shots and didn't score in the first five minutes. As he kneeled by the bench, he focused on his big seniors, 6'7" Mike Parenti and 6'5" Bill Chrystal, the tarnished gold-dust twins. Both had great skills but now only loped through practice and games. Worse, their tepid approach was contagious. Parenti watched flat-footed as Brigham Young forward John Benson beat him to the ball and scored a layup, points Lapchick could only classify as garbage points.

He took special notice when Seiden raced downcourt, only to have Chrystal whip him a crosscourt pass that wound up in the coach's lap. After several other misguided plays, Chrystal allowed his man to dribble past him for an easy hoop, almost as if he were inviting the Cougar to score. But there was one play that had to ring the old pro's bell.

St. John's guard Dick Duckett was nursing the ball up court after a Cougar score when he hand-signaled Seiden to set a screen for Chrystal, hoping to free him for a score. But when Chrystal came around the pick, he allowed BYU's Lynn Rowe to cut between, intercept the pass, and sprint home for an easy basket. Boos poured from the crowd. What further infuriated Lapchick was that Chrystal never moved a muscle to stop Rowe.

Lapchick immediately called time-out, and it didn't take much imagination to see smoke exploding from his ears. He looked around as the starters gathered in the huddle. No one was paying attention, and the two big men didn't look into his eyes. "What kind of a play was that, Bill?" Lapchick asked the senior.

"I don't know, Coach. Guess I didn't pay attention," he muttered carelessly in his own defense. Lapchick didn't like fussing over mistakes publicly, but this was different. Chrystal looked as if he didn't give a damn. Lapchick waited until after the next series and then sent in a substitute for Chrystal. The Redmen guards, Duckett and Seiden, didn't fare much better, giving up 47 of the 89 points BYU scored. The malaise had contaminated the whole team. St. John's lost 89–75, and Bill Briordy of the *New York Times* felt, "St. John's blew baskets that you could make."

As an Original Celtic who had barnstormed the country, and as coach of the New York Knicks, Lapchick had seen pros dogging it, but Parenti and Chrystal looked as if they were doing illegal business. At eight-and-a-half-point favorites, the seniors had a margin of error to work with and still cash in their gambling chips.

Old pros like Lapchick knew how a game was fixed: play poor defense, miss free throws, keep the ball away from teammates with hot hands, and who knows the difference? Done with skill, it was hardly noticeable. The fixer could even score, but he also had to make key mistakes—like dribbling off your foot, which St. John's players did often. But how could kids understand the harm they were doing—deceiving a university and thousands of its fans?

Joe Lapchick had grown up with basketball, and basketball had grown up with him. During his Celtics days in the Depression, he traveled back roads to spread the new game. It was fun but difficult to scratch out a living. He took the initiative and learned to manage the team, getting players from one town to another, buying beat-up, secondhand Pierce-Arrows and Cadillacs big enough to hold everyone, making sure everyone gave his best. The history of basketball is indebted to the tall, thin coach. His fifty-year career mirrors the game's rise from kids playing with stuffed soccer balls to today's international competition. He had worked to win honorably his whole life, and in his twilight years he ran into a bunch trying to lose. It was a nightmare, but it was real. And there was little he could do. He had no evidence, nothing he could use to confront the suspects.

After the loss, Lapchick shook hands with BYU coach Stan Watts and headed for the dressing room. Ike Gellis, the *New York Post*'s sports editor, caught up with him. Gellis, gruff as a dance-hall bouncer and looking like an angry, miniature bulldog, hooked an arm under Lapchick's and blurted out what troubled him.

"It doesn't look good," Gellis whispered to his friend in the runway. "Parenti and Chrystal are in the tank," he insisted.

"Do you know for sure?" Lapchick pleaded, as he weaved toward the locker room, sucking on a Lucky Strike, despite the facts all seeming to verify the sportswriter's suspicions.

"Nobody, and I mean nobody, plays that bad, especially after the showing they made two weeks ago against Rhode Island." St. John's, picked eighth in the country during the preseason, had clobbered Rhode Island, setting a Garden record by scoring 115 points. Everyone had looked good, from seniors to the sophomore kids, but it all seemed to disintegrate between then and the Brigham Young game.

"Joe, they took last week's Utah game off the boards. What does that tell you?" When bookmakers suspected a fix, they refused to take bets on it, or they took it off the boards.

The weary coach went home thinking about Gellis's words. He couldn't shake them, or thoughts of his team's inconsistent play, but his troubles didn't end in the Garden. Sitting in his attic study, the phone rang, and his wife, Bobbie, answered it.

"It's for you, Joe. He didn't give his name." The coach turned off the radio, slid down the stairs, and picked up the phone.

"Hey, Lapchick, your team is in the sewer, and you'd better do something about it!"

"What do you mean?" he wanted to know.

"They're dumping! I lost a bundle last night on the Brigham Young game. Wake up, we know about it on the street!"

The phone on the other end slammed down, leaving Lapchick holding the receiver. Bookmakers on the street were as good a barometer as there was, and the first line of defense.

Dumping college games was nothing new and was talked about since 1945 when Brooklyn College tried unsuccessfully to fix a game in Boston. Lapchick heard rumors of other fixed games. It was whispered about among coaches, but other than Brooklyn College, nothing ever made the newspapers, and there were never any charges.

In 1951, college basketball was rocked by a point-shaving scandal, which implicated many players and schools. The point-spread craze caught players from Eastern and Midwestern schools fixing games. The shock changed the history and innocence of sports forever in America. Five years had passed and New York basketball was trying to recover, but what was being whispered about his team could cause a new scandal to explode in his face.

Since the early 1940s, a new system of sports gambling involving point spreads had become popular: you didn't bet on whether the team would win or lose, which was often pretty obvious, but by how much they would win or lose. If you bet on a team that was an 8-point favorite and they won by 10, you'd win. But if they won by 6, you'd lose. As a result, gamblers appeared to have a better chance of winning and betting boomed. The problem was that now it was easier for players to orchestrate a winning bet, and there was money in it for them.

He paced the attic, measuring the floor over and over again, until he decided he needed air, a walk to clear his head. Joe Lapchick was a tall man easily recognized in his hometown of Yonkers, New York, but on this night, he had no interest in being sociable.

"Hi, Joe. The team didn't look so hot last night," next-door neighbor Berj Kalpak called over. The coach looked up, smiled, waved, and moved on to Tibbetts Park. Team practice was becoming uncomfortable. Dick Duckett, the floor leader, seemed lost, while Parenti and Chrystal played indifferently. The old pro was obviously worried about his team.

Lapchick was familiar with how the horror show started in February of 1951, when the scandal ripped the foundation from under college basketball and reduced Garden crowds to only three or four thousand. Clair Bee and Nat Holman, well-known New York coaches, were destroyed. Holman and Bee didn't fix games, but it happened on their watch, and now they were gone. How far was Lapchick from meeting their fate?

Lapchick had no one to discuss his dilemma with, and he was confused. He loved sportswriters, including Gellis and Murray Janoff, but could he be sure they wouldn't whistle? The president of St. John's, Father Flynn, should be told, as should Walter McLaughlin, the athletic director, but Lapchick feared being blamed. If he benched starters, there would be questions. The press would want to know, "Why Parenti and Chrystal? Weren't they the hub of the team and its best players?" Sportswriters' questions never end.

Lapchick had a family, was in his fifties, and pondered what to do. He was a man of character who backed his word. Everything that was good in Lapchick's life came from the sport. All his friends and honors, challenges and fond memories, were rooted in basketball. He had the pleasure of being a pioneer when the game was in its infancy. He was a sportswriter's dream with good stories about the inception of roundball that helped them meet deadlines. He was proud of his accomplishments, but now he was mired in the greatest worry a coach could have—a team dumping games. But even when a fix is suspected, it's difficult to substantiate.

As he walked and struggled with the agony and frustration of not being able to freely discuss what he knew, he couldn't help drifting back to early, happier days, when as a ten-year-old in Yonkers he was introduced to a new game that had worked its way down from New England.

Chapter 1

From
Hollywood
to Holyoke

"**P**ass the ball, Joe," his teammate, Michael Turczyk from Nepperhan Avenue, called out. The blond Joe Lapchick was exceptionally tall for a ten-year-old, and as he held the homemade ball over his head out of reach of the smaller competitors, he surveyed his options. Out of the corner of his eye he spotted Dave Kurbask, flipped him the ball, and Kurbask shot it over the ledge of the entrance to Joe's tenement. "Two points," his teammates yelled as Turczyk retrieved the ball.

Like many immigrant kids from the Hollow of Yonkers, New York, in 1910, a sprouting Joe Lapchick had shifted his attention to basketball, the new exciting street game. When equipment was unavailable, he and his friends imaginatively improvised games in front of his Mulberry Street tenement. They used a cap filled with paper and stuffed into an old discarded soccer ball to give it a round shape. Throwing it onto the short entrance roof scored points.

The same beat-up soccer ball was used for another version of the new game on the main streets. The makeshift game was played, "circulating around ice wagons," Lapchick recalled, "and passing the ball to teammates." A score resulted "when we maneuvered and could toss the ball between the legs of the walking horses." It was a new game that quickly became popular in the Northeast and would eventually leave its impact on America.

O

In December 1891, James Naismith and the other professors at the YMCA training school in Springfield, Massachusetts, had difficulty with the onset of winter running indoor physical education classes. After two colleagues failed to tame a restless class of eighteen rugby-football players, Naismith had an idea he thought might work. The game was not to be a variation of football but was to have its own identity. "In the fall," Naismith wrote, "we decided that there should be a game that could be played indoor during the winter seasons." By making the ball large enough to discourage running with it, Naismith felt the game would favor skill rather than rugby violence.

Basketball was designed as a game of finesse, centering on shooting a ball at a goal with a scoring system involving a goal through which the ball could pass. To prevent interference with a scoring attempt, Naismith placed it above the players' heads, so that they would not gather around it, and made it horizontal. Naismith believed this innovation was the new principle that was needed. As a former football player, he felt it best not to have players run with the ball, and the seeds of a passing game were born. Unlike soccer, a player's hands could control the ball. Naismith's game was shaping up.

No mention, however, is made in Naismith's original thirteen rules for dribbling the basketball or requiring a center jump after a score, facets of the game that would be added later. A field goal that was originally 1 point would later be valued at 2 points, and a 1-point free throw was added for an infraction of the rules. The center jump would become of great importance and favor tall players like Joe Lapchick.

When Naismith asked for two average-sized boxes, all the building superintendent could come up with were a couple of peach baskets, which narrowed at the bottom. "I found a hammer and nails," Naismith said, "and tacked the baskets to the lower rail of the balcony, one on either end of the gym." At the beginning the ball was caught in the basket, but by 1912 the bottom was opened for it to fall through. The height of the balcony accidentally fixed the basket at ten feet, making it forever sacred and even surviving the ravages of today's seven-footers.

The first game was played in the school's basement on a court 35 x 50 with eighteen students forming two nine-man teams. They played in long pants with long-sleeve jerseys, and most of them sported stylish walrus mustaches like their professor's. The first ball was a regulation-size soccer ball. One goal was scored, with the game ending 1–0. One student suggested it be called Naismithball, but the good doctor rejected that notion and instead permanently baptized it "basketball."

The number of players varied from seven to eight and even nine, but eventually settled on five per team. At first, playing time was two fifteen-minute halves, with five minutes in between. When balcony spectators interfered with the ball's flight, a backboard was added. Its popularity was immediate, and with support from YMCAs and athletic clubs, basketball became the most popular indoor sport in the country. As players became more skilled, the simplicity of scoring points encouraged exciting play, which in turn helped attract a fan base. The game offered plenty of exercise while requiring neither space nor expensive equipment. You played in hot or cold weather, urban or rural settings. It attracted Midwestern wheat farmers as well as Eastern street-smart city kids. Playing areas were easily created, both indoors and out. A hoop could be nailed to a barn door as well as a tenement building. Athletes from all social classes played, and a solitary player could have fun shooting a ball for hours. Native Americans would play basketball on college campuses, as well as immigrants who became more Americanized playing in the Eastern cities. It was a sport for Americans developed by Naismith—a Canadian—in America.

In the East, New Yorkers in urban playgrounds in particular adopted basketball as their city game. It became a trademark identified with the modern player that features ballhandling, defense, and percentage shooting, and it became the stamp of metropolitan New York's play.

But before it hit New York City, it worked its way down from New England into Westchester County's many sports clubs and church recreation centers, which encouraged the young to taste the new sport.

○

On April 12, 1900, on Holy Thursday, a bright-looking blue-eyed boy, Joseph Bohomiel, the first of seven children, was born at 324 Nepperhan Avenue near the Hollow of Yonkers, New York, to Joseph and Frances Lapchick. His mother liked the Czech name Bohomiel, "God's love," which showed religious respect.

Joe's parents were Slavic; his father a Czech out of Bohemia, his mother born in Russia. On a warm summer Sunday, Joe and Frances

Lapchick wrapped their firstborn in a blue cotton blanket and made their way across Walnut Street to the Catholic Slovak church. Holy Trinity—with its tall steeple, slanted roof, and Romanesque arches, where the young couple had married a year earlier—baptized their son.

Joe's parents were part of the Hollow community that included Slovaks, Poles, Ukrainians, and Russian working-class people. Joe Sr. was a big, strong-looking man with huge, powerful arms and a pair of hands toughened from his agrarian youth in Bohemia. At one time he worked on a trolley, then as a hatter, and by 1913, he had joined the Yonkers police force. Young Joe would resemble his mother's narrow frame, blond hair, and high cheekbones while inheriting the athletic advantages of his father's large hands and long arms.

Religion was a force that bound Slovak immigrants, shaping their appreciation of life's blessings while helping them endure economic hardships. The nationalistic church was the pillar of life for most Slovak Catholics in Yonkers, as well as the Lapchicks. Yonkers would turn out to be a good place to raise their children.

By the early part of the twentieth century, America had grown from an agricultural society to the world's leading manufacturing nation, with Yonkers reflecting its transition. Its hilly landscape projected majestic energy that is still present today and was an idyllic setting for immigrant Americans adjusting to a new world in a new century. The thriving industrial community's catalyst to economic growth was its access to the Hudson River. Besides hat manufacturing, the world-famous Smith Carpet Factory, which employed more than seven thousand, and the Otis Elevator Company provided work for the overflow of immigrants.

○

Basketball appeared in Yonkers around the turn of the century. It wasn't long before the tall youngster heard friends talking about it in Public School 20. The game seemed easy enough, and Joe Lapchick became interested. He waited impatiently for school to end and rushed to Doyle Park to play with real basketball rigs cemented into the ground and practiced until the older fellows chased him. But there was another place for him to play during the winter.

Coach Oscar W. Kalkhof liked donating his time two nights a week to help Pastor Charles Cate of the Immanuel Chapel Presbyterian Church on Nepperhan Avenue. The pastor had the idea a few months earlier to open the church basement for neighborhood boys to play basketball.

"Three cents for the hour, please," Coach Kalkhof asked a tall, thin boy the others called Joe. The tall Czech reached into his pocket and found he had enough for two hours. He dropped the pennies into a church collection basket by the entrance. The pastor made the youngsters pay to cover the expenses of heating and lighting the dim makeshift gymnasium with its two baskets.

Joe was ten years old and became attracted to a game that favored his height. After playing informal games for about a half hour, Coach Kalkhof lined up the eighteen boys and gave them a lesson in fundamentals. Since Kalkhof was a YMCA recreation director and a basketball official, he started with the rules and followed with some basics. He taught that they should stay between the man they were guarding and the basket, and not to punch an opponent. The coach demonstrated how to shoot and pass with an even, two-hand follow-through. He was a meticulous instructor, whom Joe credited as his first coach.

By the time Joe was twelve, he'd grown to 6'3" and weighed 140 pounds, extraordinary height for the times. His size did not go unnoticed. As basketball blossomed in Yonkers, youth programs began to compete for the big Czech. The Holy Trinity Midgets from Joe's parish church had a starter team coached by a burly Smith carpet weaver named Johnny Mears.

"Would you like to play?" Mears asked.

"Sure," Joe answered.

The Midgets gave young Joe his first taste of organized ball. He later joked he was "the biggest midget around." He smiled recalling his "great floor game," spending much time falling on it. The youngster was ungainly, but his early clumsiness motivated him to improve and pay attention.

After his family moved from the Hollow, Joe, who was approaching thirteen, continued playing with the Midgets. The team had given him a clearer sense of basketball and made him realize how much he had to learn. Like most youngsters who grew rapidly, there was awkwardness to his game that made him stumble and lose his balance, often landing on the floor as the others raced up court.

Unhappy with his clumsiness, Joe began a nightly, self-imposed training program on the cinder roads in the back of the carpet mill until he mastered his coordination. He ran at full speed, stopped suddenly, pivoted, changed direction, ran backwards, and shadowboxed. There were no coaches to correct errors or motivate him, only his determination and athletic instincts to guide him. He enjoyed working by himself, something he would do the rest of his life when he wanted to improve. With hard work he got better.

Like most of Yonkers's working class, Mr. Lapchick believed that after grammar school his children should find steady work. When Joe completed eighth grade, he took a job with the Ward Leonard Electric Company in Bronxville at fifteen cents an hour on a ten-hour day.

As young Joe continued to play and grow, his talents became better known in Yonkers. The Hollywood Athletic Club on South Broadway and Hudson Street had wonderful facilities and one of the best youth teams, which often traveled to other towns to play. Joe was looking to expand his skills and dreamed of playing for them, a team with magic about it. He had no idea it would springboard him into professional basketball and change his life.

○

"The Czech kid is really good," George Pettus, the Knights of Columbus basketball coach, insisted. Lou Gordon, sporting goods proprietor and manager of the Hollywood AC, looked up. "How good?"

"Well, he's the tallest kid I've ever seen. The other night I saw him block a shot and tip it to a teammate before it went out of bounds." Gordon hadn't heard of too many shots being blocked in a Yonkers game. "Where does he play?" he wanted to know.

"I saw him in town against a good Bantams team with Billy Grieve, and he was the best." The Bantams were an up-and-coming semipro team starting to catch on and playing games upstate. "He can pass, make free throws, but most of all he can control center jumps," the excited coach related. Gordon thought while he rubbed his chin. The rules called for a center jump after a score, and the big kid could control ten to twelve a game, which added to a team's offense.

"What's the kid's name?" the sporting goods owner asked. "You know him, Lou. He's the big foreign-looking kid who hangs around the store three, four times a week; his name is Joe Lopchick or Lapchick. It's always misspelled in the papers. He's from over by the carpet mill, and he's got to be every bit of 6'5" or 6'6"." Gordon made a mental note to pay attention to his tall customers in the future.

A few days later on a sunny Saturday afternoon in October, a tall and thin blond teenager made his way over to the heart of Yonkers's shopping area and Lou Gordon's Sport Shop. Young Joe Lapchick was familiar with the store. After work and when not playing, he often walked to the Palisade Avenue store to listen to Yonkers sports talk. When he entered, he spotted the latest Louisville Slugger ash wood baseball bats and smelled strong cowhide from a shipment of Reach gloves in the rear of the store.

Joe particularly liked the galvanized rubber aroma of the latest Spalding basketball sneakers, which he could only dream about. They were fancy with black stripes over the white canvas tops. He liked the suction cups, which prevented slipping on the dusty courts he played on. The black ankle patches identified the manufacturer, but to young athletes they made the $1.95 sneakers with the white laces more attractive.

Joe knew sneakers didn't last long playing with the Trinity Midgets. The ones he wore had a large piece of folded newspaper inside that covered the half-inch hole boring through the rubber sole of his right sneaker. As the oldest of seven children, his factory wages were needed to help his family. For now the sneakers remained a dream.

"Like those sneakers?" Lou Gordon asked. "You're the Lapchick boy," Gordon concluded before the shy giant could answer. Towering over his inquisitor, Joe could only nod his head and look away. But Gordon wanted to talk to the youngster and decided to discuss what had to be his favorite subject.

"I hear you like basketball." Joe looked up from the sneakers, saw a dark-haired man with a medium build, and again nodded. The store owner noticed the threadbare condition of his sneakers. "Would you like a pair of those sneakers?" Gordon offered with a smile. There was no hesitation now. "Yes sir," he answered. "Well, Spalding gave us a few sample pair of that new model, and if I have your size in stock, you can test-wear them for us."

Joe couldn't take his eyes off the new pair of Spaldings under the arm of the owner as he returned from the stockroom. "Thank you, Mr. Gordon," the boy's good manners kicked in as he accepted the large box. But as he turned to leave the store, Gordon asked one last question.

"Joe, would you like to play for the Hollywood AC?" Two Christmases in one day was more than the tall youngster could handle. Joe turned, faced the smiling owner, and more than nodded. "Yes sir, I sure would." Gordon explained that he was the manager of the team and told him to report next Saturday morning to Coach Jim Lee for a tryout. "Coach Lee will take care of you."

Joe was shocked. The Hollywood team picked scholastic stars, and he might not have much of a chance. Besides their overall talent, he would battle local star center Jimmy Herald, whose experience exceeded his.

"Do you think I have a chance?" the soft-spoken youngster asked.

"Sure, sure you do, Joe. Show up at the gym, and I'll tell Mr. Lee you're coming."

As Joe walked home with the brown box of Spaldings firmly tucked under his arm, he passed the club's tall building with its lofty reputation on South Broadway and Hudson Street. He hoped to make the team and a name for himself. As the eldest, it was his responsibility to lead the younger Lapchick children.

Sporting his new Spaldings, Joe arrived at the Hollywood gym thirty minutes before the 9:00 A.M. tryout. The magnificent gym was on the first floor, along with its locker room and more than four hundred lockers for its members. Joe had never seen an athletic facility that provided so much for its patrons. Bowling alleys, billiards, showers, and a pool were some of its offerings. As he entered the gym, a gentle-looking man with a shock of red hair and a confident manner greeted him.

"Hi, I'm Coach Jimmy Lee, and you must be Joe Lapchick," he said as he extended a hand. "Take a locker and warm up." Unknown to the young center, an introductory note was sent to the coach. "Here's the Hollys' new center," Gordon predicted.

When the team assembled, Lee ordered two lines for layups and barked corrections as he and two assistants helped scrutinize the players. Joe looked embarrassed after a missed layup and absorbed the sting of a coach's constructive criticism, but the young Czech learned quickly and worked to improve.

After two weeks of intense practice, Joe found his name on the list pinned to the gym bulletin board. Much to his surprise he made the team, beating out the local star. He was thrilled to receive a uniform. In his new purple jersey with "Holly" written diagonally across the chest, a script bar under it, and purple knee-high socks with white stripes, he was ready to play.

Making the Hollys was the first major accomplishment in Joe Lapchick's basketball career. Lou Gordon's sneakers and the Holly team were warm memories for him. Gordon's suggestion changed his life. The confidence Lapchick gained also led him to the Bantams, another power-ful Yonkers team, which opened doors to budding pro promoters. How-ever, he never forgot the sporting goods owner's kindness and guidance. Lapchick started attracting attention as a fifteen-year-old playing for the Hollys and the powerful Bantams, and gradually he began to play for pay.

After an outstanding game where he had scored five field goals and four free throws of the Hollys 25 points, the local newspapers snapped his photo. Standing straight, arms folded behind his back, wearing heavy-duty knee guards, Joe Lapchick, with a serious but proud look, was ready to make a name for himself.

Seeing him play simultaneously with the Bantams and the Hollys caused a *Yonkers Herald* sportswriter to wonder which team Big Joe would choose when they clashed. The sportswriter suggested he had to choose because he was "too good to sit out a game and deprive fans of his skills." The sportswriter then thanked the young Czech for "putting Yonkers on the basketball map."

While playing night and weekend games in 1916 with the Bantams, Joe experienced his first taste of professional play when he earned $3 for a game. The team set dates and fees, and players were usually paid by "passing the hat" after games. On other occasions, home teams charged a modest fee at the door to cover expenses.

Representing Ossining and playing their home games in Yonkers's Columbus Hall, the Bantams traveled to nearby Beacon, Wappinger Falls, and Hudson, where he netted $15 and then $18 in successive years. Enjoy-ing local popularity, he was thrilled someone would pay to see him play.

While gaining experience and a reputation, Joe maintained his job as a machinist in a local factory and caddied in the off-season. When he had time, he pitched sidearm for the Federal Sugar Refinery. His life was filled with sports.

Lapchick's excitement for basketball, however, did not initially meet with parental approval, and he was forced to hide his uniform. His father's stern foreign upbringing made it difficult for him to understand why his son ran around in short pants and an undershirt. "Joe, is that what you wear when you play?" The affirmative reply further confused his father, who considered the outfit unmanly.

The expanding economy along with the nation's rising sports interest helped Lapchick's career to blossom. When his income surpassed his fa-ther's, he no longer hid his uniform. Mr. Lapchick saw matters differently.

Joe's brother, Bill, verified this feeling. "Up to then, my father had been puzzled and a little disturbed. But when he saw the money roll in, he changed his mind."

○

Prewar professional basketball was part of a free market system that created a bidding war for top talent, which catapulted young Joe Lapchick into the enviable position of having teams chasing him to play. What followed was a whirlwind of neighborhood teams vying for "the tall Yonkers kid," who moved freely into "play for pay" basketball circles.

Unlike baseball with its reserve clause that denied players a choice of teams once they signed a professional contract, basketball's competitive market caused game fees to skyrocket for quality players. Joe was tall, fast, and talented. "I was getting a local reputation," he remembered, which led to games during the 1916–17 season with the best teams in New York City.

Increased demand caused Lapchick to play on four teams simultaneously. With center jumps after every score, he controlled the taps and rebounds vital to a team's success. He began to realize that his size, once an embarrassment, was now helping him to high earnings.

At eighteen, while playing for the Hollys in Manhattan against the well-known and talented Whirlwinds, Lapchick caught the eye of the opposing manager. For $7 a game, a factory worker's weekly pay, Lapchick made frequent trips into New York.

Lapchick's salary continued to rise. With teams playing twice a week, and it being impossible to satisfy each manager, he jumped center for the highest bidder. By playing one team against another he increased his earnings dramatically. Like most pros, Lapchick switched teams for $5 more from another manager. There was no team loyalty, and money was the only bargaining chip that influenced their decision.

The going rate for quality players started at a dollar a minute, but it didn't take long to figure his true value. At this point, Joe Lapchick was a top professional consumed by how well he could score points and play defense, the criteria that measured a star's performance.

Gradually he got to know the game's best players, who met at Grand Central Station in Manhattan, determined to create a bidding war for their services. Well-known performers like Honey Russell, Benny Borgmann, and Elmer Ripley showed Tall Joe the ropes. Grand Central became the marketplace where they telephoned regional teams about their fees. From there they boarded trains to the best payday. As word of Lapchick's value made the rounds, he parlayed his skills into more money than he had ever seen. He learned how to promote himself.

O

"Any talented players in Yonkers?" Holyoke Reds coach Tom McGarry asked his star guard, Dave Wassmer. Like every other team in the Western Massachusetts League, the Reds were searching for a big man. "Everybody is talking about this big Czech kid," said Wassmer, who then described the tall, lanky 6'5" center making a name around Westchester. "I think he can help."

Semipro basketball involved a roller coaster of teams in Eastern leagues springing up overnight, struggling, and disappearing as quickly. But in spite of the game's instability, Joe Lapchick's size was his meal ticket. He was nineteen and more than 6'5" when he joined Holyoke. Newspaper accounts heralded his effectiveness when he set a league record the first game by canning all eleven of his free throws. The record "gave me a reputation," Lapchick recalled. "Now I was a full-fledged pro." But the industrial town was not prepared for the excitement stirred by Lapchick's size.

Unusually tall, Lapchick was treated as if he were part of a traveling circus. The Holyoke townspeople gawked as he walked the streets after a game, calling him gypsy, freakish. People over 6'6" were rare, and seven footers didn't exist. With time he learned to handle the taunts of hecklers.

By 1919, Lapchick, who now earned $15 a week as an apprentice machinist, was making $10 a game, four to five nights a week. He and his family began to live better. By the early 1920s, in addition to Holyoke and occasional games with Hollywood, Lapchick played for Schenectady and Troy in the New York State League and for the well-known Whirlwinds. The exposure with them led him to the Brooklyn Visitations in the Metropolitan League, who played Sunday nights when other teams were idle. His bargaining eventually increased until it reached $90 to $100 a game no matter how many minutes he played.

Teams fought to pay him more money than he or any member of his family earned. What he demanded he got. "I was making so much money I became a big shot," he recalled with a smile. He bought a gray deluxe

DeSoto roadster with a rumble seat and parked in front of the Knights of Columbus Hall, threw his bag in the air, and escorted the Yonkers youngster who caught it into the game free. He learned this trick from Larry McCrudden and Ray Wertis, local stars who had extended the same courtesy to him. Now he was the star.

When the season ended, Lapchick returned to golf and baseball, which were still off-season passions. Shortly after his nineteenth birthday, he received a serious baseball offer. "I liked to pitch," Lapchick recalled. As a tall, strong sidearm pitcher, he had something to offer. The Brooklyn Dodgers and their manager, "Uncle Wilbert" Robinson, were interested and sent a scout to check him out. When the reports were favorable, Robinson offered him a Dodger contract.

Lapchick considered the offer a high point as well as a crossroad. After some thought he turned down the Dodger offer and stayed with basketball, even though it was in its infancy. "I had been doing well playing in New England and upstate New York," he reasoned. During this transitional period he had advanced from semipro Yonkers teams to a championship with the Holyoke Reds.

O

"Inter-State League 1921–1922 Champions," the caption on the photo reads. Six durable-looking players and a manager immortalized the Holyoke Reds championship. A bloated-looking leather basketball, huge by today's standards and resembling a summer beach ball, rested between the feet of two players. Few of today's NBA pros could palm this "pumpkin." Each player wore large, heavily padded knee guards, as if they were ready for combat in some futuristic war, and sported worn leather hightop shoes similar to those a boxer would wear. They were all neatly dressed in a dark-colored, woolen V-neck sweater with a large red "H" sown on the chest, and not a hair out of place.

Like most team photos, shorter players benched up front. The guards seemed uncomfortable with their hands, not knowing where to place them. The tallest two players standing in the rear sandwiched the manager, Tom McGarry, who was nattily dressed and seemed proud of his team's success. To the left, a huge, small-mouthed, lantern-jawed 6'4" bruiser dripped confidence. Hair parted down the middle and eyes straight ahead with a look that dared the photographer to make an error. On McGarry's right stood the tallest but youngest-looking. Joe Lapchick must have been distracted as the camera clicked. With his body tilted left he looked right with a genuine smile that radiated satisfaction. This was his first professional championship, and the Big Czech looked to be enjoying it.

○

One of Joe Lapchick's unforgettable early professional experiences was playing for McGarry's Reds. There wasn't much to encourage team managers because early pro basketball didn't attract baseball crowds. Besides being unprofitable, the pro game in the early 1920s was slow moving, brutal, and primarily played by working-class athletes. While the game struggled with its social image, promoters paved its future.

A newspaper printer by trade, McGarry typified the times. Like most managers, he operated the team "out of his coat pocket." The Reds' small crowds forced the team to exist under minimal semiprofessional standards. They enjoyed no sponsors and survived by promotions and passing the hat. The Reds were one of the first teams to sponsor dances between and after games to draw crowds.

While the team struggled financially, McGarry's reward was wrapped in pride. Turn-of-the-century political bosses suffered a similar exhilaration. They, too, enjoyed standing on street corners puffing their chests when "their man won." McGarry, like the young Czech, was a basketball pioneer and loved every minute of it.

The game's rowdiness made caged playing areas popular and necessary. While the rope or wire cages kept the ball in play, it also restrained hostile fans from inflicting punishing pranks on visiting players. The twelve-foot-high cages, however, began to lose their popularity by the mid-1920s, but not before permanently labeling players *cagers*.

Despite McGarry's charming Irish wit, which he used on opposing managers, many games ended with heated confrontations requiring a quick backdoor escape. When the Reds won on the road, it was not unusual to need a police escort out of town. During a game against Chicopee, an intoxicated fan was heaping verbal abuse on Lapchick to the point that Lapchick threw the ball into the fan's face. He was thrown out of the game, but not before he scored 9 vital points in the victory.

○

By 1922, after Lapchick had been pounded in games by the aging Horse Haggerty of the Original Celtics, rumors circulated that their owner, Jim Furey, was interested in the tall Czech. Haggerty, one of the game's most physical players, was thinking of retiring to a small farm in Reading, Pennsylvania. With Haggerty hanging up his sneakers, it was Lapchick's time to join the Celtics. But to make sure, Joe wanted to discuss his future with Dave Wassmer, a Yonkers friend and Holyoke teammate.

"I think I'm going to sign with the Celtics," he admitted to Wassmer, as he lit a new Turkish blend Fatima cigarette. "I only went to grammar school," Lapchick said. "Basketball's what I'm built for. I'm 6'5" and I love the game, and besides, Mr. Furey promised me a guaranteed contract."

"Maybe you're right, Joe," Dave answered.

Basketball was in Lapchick's blood, and he wanted to test himself against the best in the game, a chance he was going to get.

Chapter 2

Joe Lapchick, Original Celtic

The Original Celtics were "the greatest basketball squad ever assembled," according to the consensus of the times. They were the first team to operate as a unit with none of their members playing for other teams. They always "threw to color, always to green," the color of their uniforms, as Joe Lapchick liked to say, and were the first to make real use of peripheral vision. As basketball struggled to establish itself while being overshadowed by baseball, football, and boxing, the Celtics changed the way the game was played, becoming the standard to follow.

Early pro basketball was noted for roster changes that make today's free agency look like team stability. Better players regularly negotiated to simultaneously play with three or four teams in different leagues, with the highest bidder retaining their services. There were no rigid rules committing players to one team. Some star performers even switched teams at halftime of a game.

The Celtics changed this approach. They were the first to alter the way professional teams were formed. Team manager Jim Furey signed talented players to exclusive contracts, which welded his Celtics together, giving them an advantage over their more loosely assembled opponents.

Their uniqueness involved teamwork, something ordinarily not found in pro basketball. The game required five players to succeed with one ball, to work smoothly like the fingers on a hand, and teams that recognized this concept won. The key to Celtics success was its passing game, learning to "let the ball do the work."

As they played together, they added new techniques that made them more effective. When the Celtics introduced switching on defense, which involved two defenders trading assignments when crossing, it confused opponents. Schoolboy coaches would come to Celtics games prepared to copy their clever center jump plays that often led to quick scores. But it was more than original formations.

Celtics passing became widely known and emulated throughout America in the 1920s. Much of what they did spun off passing, and it was their ballhandling that separated them from the rest. Dutch Dehnert's pivot play, which relied on slick passing and cutting, revolutionized every level of the game. It created an offense everyone in basketball imitated. Teams attracted to smooth play later adopted the Celtics ballhandling style. The Celtics were the ones written about and copied when the game was trying to become established.

The Celtics reached more people in demonstrating new concepts, and they did it in championship style. They were the first pro team to call itself World Champions, and they backed it up. In the 1920s, "Celtics" was synonymous with clever, opportunistic play.

Celtics basketball was propelled by a cohesive, confident style of play, the same sureness that separated the Yankees from the rest of baseball. The Celtics knew they were good, and when their opponents tried cracking their system, most failed. They were winners, and that confidence poured out of them, smothering their opponents. The perception of Celtics ability worked in their favor. Opponents were often beaten before the shamrocked team took the floor.

The Celtics were similar to a touring troupe of vaudevillians on the Orpheum Circuit, visiting every small town. They became legendary by barnstorming America, spreading the game into backwoods gyms from Biloxi, Mississippi, to the winter wilds of Wisconsin and back down to Miami, Florida. They would travel anywhere to put on a show and were proud to demonstrate their talent. These basketball pioneers were the closest thing to a household name in professional basketball. Lapchick, Nat Holman, and Dehnert did not have the name recognition of Babe Ruth or Red Grange, but if someone ordered the best in basketball to stand up, the Celtics wouldn't hesitate making their way to the podium.

Joe Lapchick, the tallest Celtic and center-jump specialist, became the most recognizable Celtic. Later as a college and pro coach, he won the hearts of millions of people who got to know him. He would, however, shape his future by the years he wore the shamrock green of the Original Celtics. Although a tight-knit group enshrined in basketball's Hall of Fame, several Celtics besides Lapchick became known beyond their playing days. Holman, a slick shooting guard, went on to fame as a college coach at CCNY, while Dutch Dehnert, immortalized by his pivot play, remained in basketball as a coach and adviser.

○

Dehnert, like most New York City youngsters, learned to play in the streets by scoring points in makeshift baskets. Sometimes the street's livery horses became moving obstacles for Dehnert and his friends to sidestep. "When the horses stood still, we had to go under their legs," he recalled. The wagon owners got angry when the horses were startled. Garbage cans and homemade cloth basketballs seemed unlikely vehicles for the future Original Celtic to learn the game.

Out of the settlement houses in the Chelsea section of Manhattan came the Hudson Guild, a neighborhood basketball team later called the New York Celtics and started by Frank "Tip" McCormack in 1912. The name originated from an Irish west side playground on Twentieth Street called Celtic Park.

At first, the Celtics attracted mostly Irish Americans, but with time the team became an ethnic mosaic of working-class youth. The excitement sports generated gradually replaced the attraction of neighborhood youth to local gangs, poolrooms, saloons, and brothels, which parents appreciated. The Celtics eventually outgrew playgrounds and became professionals. When McCormack returned from World War I in 1918, Jim Furey had become the team's manager and coach. A squabble with McCormack forced Furey to rename his team Original Celtics.

Furey's innovative step of signing quality players to exclusive contracts with guaranteed salaries separated the Celtics from other pro teams of the time. The maneuver required financial backing, which, despite his job as head cashier with Arnold Constable, a large New York department store, he had. None of the players questioned Furey's bankroll, but the truth was he was dipping into his company's money.

But since Furey frequently stocked up on other teams' players, many regional leagues refused to play the Celtics. To survive, he barnstormed the country as an independent. Playing as many as ten games a week, Furey covered expenses while spreading the team's reputation.

As the Celtics developed their invincibility in the 1920s, several regional professional leagues struggled to stay alive. The turnover was frequent, with new teams springing up only to fold within months. But there was a steady stream of new owners attracted to sports management and willing to trade money for the prestige and excitement of backing a professional team. Some resembled stock market devotees of the time who invested on a whim. They came from a variety of backgrounds, from promoters like Tex Rickard, who built Madison Square Garden, to middle-class businessmen, gangsters, entertainers, or just plain sports lovers like Furey, who wanted the action with a small-time sports franchise.

Requiring little space, basketball fit well with New York's asphalt base. Despite the new sport's lack of well-known figures, it survived in metropolitan centers. With only a few exceptional teams and a handful of outstanding players like Nat Holman, Johnny Beckman, Benny Borgmann, and later Joe Lapchick, the roughneck profession received little press recognition and had yet to capture the public's imagination.

Lapchick's exceptional size helped make him popular in the Northeast and contributed to his rise in professional basketball. As Lapchick's game improved, Furey offered him an exclusive contract at the end of the 1922–23 season, which he gladly accepted. "My heart was jumping so hard," Lapchick said, "I could hardly sign the contract." Whether based on size, ability, personality, or a combination of all three, Lapchick was hailed the best big man of his time. Sportswriters reported that he could handle the ball, play defense, and shoot free throws all while demonstrating court sense. But as successful as Lapchick was going to be, his inexperience at first upset Celtics team rhythm.

The big Czech struggled most with defensive switching, which involved guarding the closer offensive player when opponents crossed. Switching with a teammate saved energy but confused and frustrated the rookie. Unfamiliar with the play, he always got in somebody's way and accidentally screened teammates. The young player didn't initially realize what a disadvantage he faced breaking in with an established team.

According to teammate Pete Barry, Lapchick at first was not well received by his Celtics teammates. "Whatever the reason, we met to decide on replacing him." Cliff Anderson, a 6'4" center who had played for CCNY was available, and some of the Celtics thought he was more mature. "I remembered one thing they were forgetting . . . and when it looked like Anderson was in, I said 'Jim, who was our leading scorer for the season?' Furey gave me a look. I pressed him. Finally he said, 'I guess it must have been Lapchick.' With that, I busted up the meeting and Joe stayed."

Basketball was the Celtics' life, their livelihood, and they played with passion. As pros, they didn't hold back criticism. If anyone fouled up, he heard about it. "When a fellow made a mistake," Lapchick remembered, "the rest of the Celtics hollered at him and chewed him out until he got it right. No floor instructions, just hints." There were no coaches providing detailed corrections, only players offering their instinctive suggestions to one another. Learning became trial and error with players coaching each other. Lapchick gradually learned from his mistakes.

Fortunately, he listened to veteran Celtic Johnny Witty. "We know what you can do with the ball," Witty reminded the young center. "It's how good you are without the ball that makes you a basketball player." The old pro taught Lapchick the importance of moving without the ball, a Celtics creed that stands today. With time, Lapchick learned. Once he won the center position the following year, his career skyrocketed.

The unsettled nature of professional basketball did not seem to affect the Celtics, who drew big crowds and paid their stars the highest salaries. Beckman, Holman, and Lapchick each pocketed more than $10,000 a year. In 1925, top players received $1,500 a month playing four and a half to six months a year, with the monthly salary being more than a Midwestern schoolteacher made in a year. "I played in a doubleheader in Cleveland," Lapchick recalled, "where the Cleveland Rosenblums and the Celtics drew 22,000 people. The paid admissions exceeded $18,000."

Whether they were the best or not, they were perceived as such and became the sport's standard-bearers. Although most of the Celtics had little formal education, they sensed their historical importance as they traveled the country and formulated a style of play that became the model for others.

O

The word *pride* was never written on Celtics jerseys or listed in their bylaws, but they all recognized its importance. Celtics pride drove them to play and teach their best when visiting little towns, to leave a positive understanding of a game that was becoming popular. It forced these dedicated men to play while hurt, sick, and, when barnstorming during the Depression, often underpaid, because basketball was in their blood, and they could not disappoint a gym filled with wide-eyed fans.

Lapchick described pride as "winning without gloating and losing without whining." It had much to do with the Celtics success, which left a deep impression on the young center. Celtics pride generated a special code that governed player conduct. The team resembled a nomadic fraternity, one with deep-rooted values that shaped Lapchick's future life.

The Celtics spread the gospel of basketball all over the country in the 1920s, playing 125 to 150 games a season and winning more than 90 percent of them. It was the Celtics who later cracked open the South for basketball, playing college teams like Georgia Tech, Alabama, Mercer, and Rice Institute.

Lapchick enjoyed talking about the old days. It didn't take much for him to offer a glimpse of what the Celtics were like. He often discussed with sportswriters the pioneer days of professional basketball played throughout America for big paydays, as well as in off-the-road Depression towns for survival money. He saw it all and seemed to be repaying the sport that shaped his manhood. Sportswriters realized that he had access to a period of sports history few knew or could frame in proper perspective. As an informal cultural historian, Lapchick could weave together Celtics life that told of the growth of basketball and its hardships.

Lapchick demonstrated Celtics pride whenever he appeared in public. Older son Joe Lapchick remembers his father's Celtics as "neat, happy, manly older guys." Holman was "a handsome, dapper, smooth guy. They were men's men." Joe touched on their meticulous public appearance when describing them. Whenever cameras clicked, they were in dress uniform: suit, topcoat, white shirt and tie, gloves, scarf, and neatly snapped-down fedora.

Lapchick knew he would always be recognized because of his size and made sure his public appearances were up to his standards. Even when casually dressed, he demonstrated concern. Posture to Lapchick was also related to appearance and was a lifelong discipline. He trained himself to walk up straight with shoulders back in a military fashion and not stoop.

O

Whenever sportswriters had to meet a deadline, Lapchick liked telling how Dutch Dehnert in 1925 would slip into the pivot—the area between the foul lanes—and ballhandle spectacularly as Celtics crisscrossed past him looking for a pass. In his prime, Dehnert was one of the game's better-known players, and he knew how to thrill crowds. Posters later nailed to local general stores and barbershops urged fans to "See The Original Pivot Play, Starring The One And Only Dutch Dehnert."

During a one-sided game—one the team called a "walkover"— Dehnert, to add excitement, took a position fifteen feet from the basket and spontaneously returned passes to teammates who cut to the basket for easy layups. Out of that inspired moment the pivot play was born, and it grew into one of the game's fundamental offensive maneuvers identified with the Celtics.

"Dehnert walked under the basket, turned his back to it," Lapchick remembered, "and began to kid the other team by receiving a pass and throwing it back," like youngsters playing keep away. After several passes and cuts, the defense became frustrated, and a Celtic was unguarded for an easy basket. The maneuver, later called "The Wheel Play," was repeated with the same results. "We saw what Dehnert conceived as a joke was a powerful offensive threat," Lapchick related.

Sports history has credited Dehnert with its conception, but its origin has been disputed. Whether Dehnert and the Celtics invented the maneuver or not is less important than that they demonstrated its effectiveness throughout the country. Pivot play undisputedly influenced how the game was played nationally, and it became one of the most celebrated aspects of Celtics basketball, a keystone of the team's success in the 1920s.

"Let the ball sing" triggered Celtics ballhandling magic. They whipped the pumpkin—the name used in the past for the larger ball— around Dehnert pinwheel fashion and cut to the basket. Eventually someone unguarded received a return pass for a layup. This was Celtics basketball, a style that encouraged school coaches to bring their teams from miles around to see championship ball at its best. "When high school and college players were in the stands, it was like a shot of adrenaline to us," Lapchick admitted. "We said, 'Let's really turn it on tonight.'"

Celtics success stemmed from team chemistry. Since they traveled and played exclusively together, there were many opportunities to review their game and correct mistakes. The basketball court became a laboratory for new ideas. But they believed they improved team play best through "truth meetings." During these informal postgame sessions player faults were openly discussed, and by airing these mistakes, solutions were often found.

After a Celtics loss, Lapchick remembered, "Our dressing room was an awful place, like a den of starved wolves. Recriminations were vicious, profane, and sometimes physical." However, when the whistle blew the next night, the Celtics were ready and together.

What bothered the Celtics most was an opponent's lack of respect. No one wanted to win more, but when they were beaten they could accept it, shake hands, and look to another day. What they couldn't swallow was sassiness, as happened once in Louisiana.

The Celtics were on the tail end of a rugged trip, playing eleven games in ten days with clinics in between. By the time they played Yahoo Center, a team of tough semipros, they struggled to tie their sneakers. Early in the second half they fell behind, with Yahoo winning by a few points. The loss would have been acceptable if one of the Yahoo players hadn't made a wisecrack to Joe Lapchick as they shook hands. Lapchick didn't react to the slight, but walked over to the telephone and called Nig Rose, the team manager, who booked games out of Cleveland.

"Get us a game with those punks as soon as you can," Lapchick demanded. The Celtics doubled back to play Yahoo Center, but this time the old pros taught them a lesson. The final score was Celtics 61, Yahoo Center 18.

Besides the serious play associated with the Celtics, there was also the fun side of professional ball. To Lapchick, the Celtics were a rough, tough, hard-drinking bunch "full of fun and camaraderie." One night in upstate Hudson, New York, the team wobbled back to the hotel from some arduous "road work." En route, they passed a grocery with crates of milk piled in the doorway and a cake of ice set on top. Johnny Beckman, the team's humorist, grabbed the ice in his huge hands, carried it to the hotel, slung it on the desk, and asked the clerk to "check this." The startled clerk instead checked the Celtics out of the hotel. "Becky thought it was very funny, though," Lapchick recalled.

Dutch Garfinkel remembered a drinking story Lapchick told years after Dutch's playing days at St. John's. "The Celtics would check into cheap hotels, and they were always looking for booze." They ordered some liquor and asked that it be put in their hotel-room dresser drawer for after the game. They played the game but went back to find their room in a shamble. "The liquor had exploded," Garfinkel smiled. "It was corn liquor; it was a powerful concoction and it exploded."

Garfinkel's second Celtics tale had a funny but different twist. During the Depression, the Celtics were barnstorming in a Pierce-Arrow touring car driven by Nat Hickey, and after finishing a game they headed to Miami. As the team was dozing, Hickey spotted smoke coming from a front wheel. "It's freezing, a cold night, they're tired, and they look at the front of the car and see the brake lining on fire," Dutch related. "They didn't have any water and none was available. They finally decided to all stand around and piss on the wheel." After they put out the fire, they continued to the next town.

O

In the 1920s the Celtics resembled gladiators rather than ballplayers. Extra padding in their uniforms made them look battle-ready. Huge leather knee guards cushioned physical impact, while elbow, hip, and leg padding added to the protective appearance. Celtics Green dominated their gear. A woolen warm-up sweater had "Celtic" balanced on a white horizontal bar centered above a large green shamrock. The wool warmed the lightly dressed players in frosty armories, while fans often huddled with fur-lined coats and hats. The jersey-styled game shirt came in home white and a green road version. The V-neck whites had solid green ribbing across the chest with the same Celtics logo. The rounded neck greens reversed the pattern.

Light brown, corduroy-textured pants fastened by laces around the hips tried to protect them from the game's bruises. Short by today's "past the knees" standard, the pants were longer than those worn in the 1960s and 1970s. High-cut sneakers made from thin, poor-quality rubber with suction-cupped bottoms were standard equipment.

In comparison, Lapchick's Holyoke Reds from the early 1920s wore better sneakers. Since New England was the nation's footwear capital, each Red wore leather high-cut, durable, boxer shoes, which like Model T Fords or telephones of the period, came only in black.

Celtics sported flashy green-and-white warm-up jackets with "Original Celtics" trumpeted across the back. In their barnstorming days of the 1930s, they were pictured in newspapers across the country wearing black leather jackets, announcing them as "World Champions," the accepted leaders in their field.

As attractive as their uniforms were, and as neat as the Celtics generally appeared after games, their playwear was unusually messy and often unwashed. Most of the colors ran, and when mixed with perspiration stains, they smelled and looked ragged. The spreading green dye was also known to cause infections; these were cured by Beckman pouring whisky over them.

They wore their uniforms for weeks without laundering them simply because they never had time. Each man carried his own equipment in a small handgrip. The soiled, sweaty uniforms were stuffed in after each game, never to see daylight or feel fresh air until the following night, when they were pulled out of the bag for the next game. "Eventually somebody would think of ordering a new set, and the old ones would be discarded."

Celtics dress clothing in a way faced the same expedient treatment. All the players learned to travel light, a habit Lapchick later as a coach made an art form. Standard equipment was a suit of clothes, a uniform, and two dark shirts. They incurred no laundry bills. Their suits were pressed to maintain their public reputation as champions. The dark shirts, called "thousand milers," because of the distance they were worn, were brown or blue flannel and were expected to last over a long trip and then be thrown away, never washed. Handkerchiefs, socks, and underwear, purchased in five-and-dime stores, faced the same treatment when soiled. The Celtics had no time to clean clothing.

O

The rules, style of play, and approach to professional basketball at the turn of the century was an uneven affair that hindered its development and varied from region to region with many decisions left to local interpretation. Players, and often game officials, were unfamiliar with the rules, but this did not prevent everyone from tampering with them.

Yet, standards like the ten-foot basket, a Naismith accident, gained universal acceptance and have never been challenged. Early experimentation, however, included the game's length and the number of team players, but with the exception of women's rules, five remained the accepted number.

Lapchick described how early professionals dribbled apelike with a hopping two-hand, double-dribble motion. Originally only two shots were taken from the field: set shot and layup. The one-hand and jump shot were the later products of imaginative collegians Hank Luisetti and Kenny Sailors.

Another pioneer pro, Frank Baird of the Kautsky Athletic Club in Indianapolis, talked about the game's unwritten rules in the 1930s. "There was no rule book in those days. I never saw one." For self-preservation, there were three things a pro never did: throw elbows when rebounding, trip another player, or set moving picks or screens where a player's hips or back could be broken. Games were not closely officiated, but a violation of the unwritten rules, according to Baird, drew a serious response from an opponent, often causing the game to become more physical.

When new rules ended the center jump after every score in 1937, the Celtics insisted it continue because it allowed them to rest between baskets. As a compromise, they agreed to play one half without and the second half with the center jump.

The center jump encouraged a slowed-down, more methodical half-court style of play that favored defense and ballhandling. Unlike today's fast pace, the break in play after a score allowed a team to prepare defensively and reduce scoring.

Prior to the jump shot, players averaged 30 percent from the floor and 60 percent from the free throw line. In many cases, one player—called a standing guard—stayed back on defense and rarely joined the offense. There were few open shots taken because defenders stayed glued to a shooter with limited offensive weapons.

Pioneer basketballs contributed to low shooting percentages. "A ball having four pieces of leather sewn together with a slit in the center where they put the bladder in and the laces," remembered old-timer Joe Schwarzer of the New York State League, "had difficulty bouncing evenly." The leather monstrosity was also a problem when shooting. "You didn't want the laces to hit the rim," Schwarzer said. Pros shot the two-hander with the ball's laces facing the ground for better balance.

Basketballs varied in weight, size, and texture, from heavy to light to slick, with little uniformity among manufacturers. Most balls had little consistency and quickly became misshapen. "Some had laces stick out more than others," Baird remembered, "which caused many to become out of round." After much use, a lopsided ball encouraged passing rather than risking dribbling a ball with a mind of its own.

Team warm-ups were another pioneer problem. Unlike today, where basketballs are unlimited, pros often had one ball for both teams. Lapchick recalled, "warming up with the game ball for five or six minutes," and then giving it to the other team.

By the early 1920s, however, the ball became more standardized, measuring 9.55 inches in diameter, compared to today's 9-inch ball. "The official ball in the 1920s," Nat Holman explained, "weighed twenty to twenty-two ounces, just as it does today," but its circumference measured thirty to thirty-two inches, as contrasted with today's twenty-nine to thirty inches. (At the time, the Celtics' Horse Haggerty was reputedly one of just three pro players who could palm a basketball.)

The lack of consistency in the game's rules helped breed confusion. Besides regional interpretations, professional and college rules differed. The lack of uniformity hurt professional basketball's early development and encouraged rowdiness. Because college games were more closely supervised, they were less hazardous, while beer-drinking, blue-collar pro crowds often challenged an official's authority.

Officiating was a difficult job in pioneer pro leagues, with often only one referee working a game. Action was swift and calls were instantaneous and frequently incorrect, while poor lighting and cigarette smoke reduced accuracy. Limited knowledge of the rules by fans added to the problem. The lack of control often led to rough play and fan attacks on visiting players and referees.

Unlike colleges, pros had no disqualification rule, which meant play could get out of hand. Not until 1927–28, when the American Basketball League adopted a five-foul rule, could officials attempt to harness rough play. But even then the player had to have the ball before the referee could whistle the play, which substantially reduced the number of called violations.

What this also meant was that referees of Lapchick's era didn't look to call "off the ball" violations, which only added to the physical play. When the Celtics barnstormed in the 1930s, foul disqualifications were often ignored to allow fans to see the stars. Once, Celtics center Pat Herlihy committed fifteen fouls and played the whole game.

"Homers"—referees who favored the local team—added to the dilemma. Since the Celtics were primarily a "road team," poor officiating was a chronic issue. When local officials overdid their partiality, the visitors balanced justice. "We would put on what we called 'the press,'" Lapchick explained. As the referee tossed the ball at center court, a Celtics forward and guard slammed head-on and "sandwiched" the referee. After a press the official usually got the message, curbing any desire to please local fans.

In the 1920s, better pro leagues paid officials a respectable $25 per game. Money alone, however, was not an incentive for what traditionally seemed a thankless job. Why take abuse, which in Celtics times could be physical? Some referees enjoyed controlling a game, while others felt they were necessary for play. Whatever the attraction, it encouraged many former players to remain part of the game.

O

"The game centered around ballhandling and defense," Joe Lapchick insisted when asked to compare Celtics play to the modern game. Speaking at a sports banquet in the 1960s, Lapchick conceded the current basketball player was superior in every phase of the game except one. The Original Celtics were expected to handle the ball, and as their big man, Lapchick handled it effectively. At its peak in the 1920s, the Celtics' deliberate style encouraged polished play.

While the modern player's athleticism overcomes many defensive flaws, the old-timer was motivated to stop his opponent from scoring. The Celtics were dedicated to defense, an art often overshadowed in the modern high-speed game, while Lapchick saw an element of softness in the 1960s player, who seemed willing to ease up on defense.

"Cover that man, don't let him score," was enough of a challenge and didn't require modern repetitive drilling. The Celtics lacked formal coaching but helped teach and motivate each other to become world champions.

Celtic box scores and sportswriter game descriptions demonstrated their unselfish play. They learned that playing together and accepting specific roles made them winners and that the team was more important than any individual. There was little concern for individual statistics, something modern pro players use in their salary negotiations.

Holman and Beckman were offensive threats while Lapchick played defense, ballhandled, and controlled center jumps. Dehnert worked his pivot play and acted as the enforcer, protecting scorers like Holman and later Davey Banks. Pete Barry, the "jack-of-all-trades," was a reliable interchangeable part all winners need.

The Celtics went with the flow of the game. If a player was playing well, the others unselfishly helped maximize his output for the good of the team. Lapchick never forgot how Celtics chemistry made winners.

As in any team sport, injuries were a problem. No pro team could afford a medically trained assistant. Out of necessity, Johnny Beckman dispensed spontaneous remedies for injuries, often urging teammates to play through pain. He had little patience with whiners and maintained, "If you walk, you play."

One cold night, while driving between games in upstate New York, Lapchick was seated between Beckman and Chris Leonard, "who was complaining about a jock rash." When Leonard opened his pants to let some air in, Beckman, who had had enough of Leonard's moaning, poured gin over a towel, reached across, and slapped it on Leonard's exposed rash. The surprised player, according to Lapchick, exploded into the roof of the car, almost "making our sedan the first convertible."

Injuries weren't the only inconvenience. Most pioneer gyms were crude by today's standards, with many of them using chalked free throw lines and center jump circles. Pre-World War I games were often played in cages enclosed by metal or rope mesh and a netted hoop with or without a backboard. "The hoop extended eighteen inches from the post instead of the customary six inches," Holman explained.

The netted cage often inflicted punishment when visitors were forced into its rough roping. "The wire fences were as high as your hips. When you came down the floor, you took your shots and were jammed into those things; you saw blue," Holman said. Lapchick also remembered fans with nippers cutting the wire so it would be sticking out onto the court and would scratch the legs of visiting teams as they ran by. Then they pulled it in not to hurt the home team. Cages lasted well into the 1920s.

Many of Lapchick's treasured Celtics game programs announced contests played in cages, armories, dance halls, high school and college gyms, and, in a pinch, a makeshift warehouse, church basement, or even a Sayville, Long Island, garage. As late as the early 1930s, the average court measured sixty-five feet by thirty-five feet, with some gyms having backboards nailed to walls, which proved dangerous when a player drove to the basket. Many church basements had huge pillars over the floor with creative players running the defense into petrified screens. Besides stationary screens and low ceilings, many a gym's hot radiators and even wood-burning stoves became home-court advantages.

Celtics games in the early 1920s were booked as halftime entertainment for big jazz bands like Paul Whiteman's. When Lapchick was once asked why games had twenty-minute halves, he answered, "Because that was the time the big bands needed for their break." However, as the Celtics gained fame, bands fought to be on the same card with them. But there was a price paid playing in dance halls.

The floors were as slippery as an ice rink and proved dangerous. If players did not turn ankles, they were likely to get decked by aggressive defenders. Liquored patrons vented a steady stream of abuse while launching lighted cigarettes at referees and players. Manhattan Casino on Eighth Avenue and 155th Street in New York was a famous dance hall with slippery floors where basketball was sandwiched around dancing. Before, after, and often at halftime, patrons danced. "It was so difficult," Holman remembered. "I cut two holes in the soles of each basketball shoe and filled them with a petroleum jelly to reduce slipping."

Pioneer basketball players were smaller in comparison with today's athlete. In the 1920s and 1930s, few players were taller than six feet. Joe Lapchick, at more than 6'5", was considered the Wilt Chamberlain of his time. But taller players often proved awkward and ineffective. Lapchick was fortunate in that he refined his game while playing with the demanding Celtics.

One of basketball's serious growing pains was its slow pace. Fan interest drifted when a team in the lead could stall. Even a team with a slight lead and with the clock running down was guaranteed a victory by having its best ball handler dribble over the entire court, and when he was fouled successfully shooting free throws. The combination was deadly for the trailing team. The result was a dull finish. But help arrived in 1932, when a half-court ten-second line limit was introduced. The rule forced the team on offense to get the ball past half-court in the allotted ten seconds, which reduced the area in which a team could "freeze" the ball and gave a trailing team a better chance to get back into the game. In 1935, the three-second rule prevented the taller pivot players from camping out around the basket, while opening the offensive area for all the players.

Another action-reducer was the center jump after every basket. The National Basketball Rules Committee ended it in 1937 by allowing the ball to change hands after a score. The old rule favored teams with tall centers like Lapchick, who could win the center jump and maintain possession of the ball after scoring. With the clock running, play was continuous and encouraged fast-breaking that raised scoring, created action, stimulated fan interest, and forced players into better shape.

○

The consensus in the 1920s was that the Original Celtics were the best. Holman, Dehnert, Lapchick, Beckman, and Barry were favorites every time they stepped onto the court. They were from metropolitan New York and were making famous a style that grew from the streets of the city. When they packed their bags during the 1920s and traveled the country to play as many as 150 games a season, they were opening fans' and coaches' eyes to how basketball should be played. The team taught, and everyone from spectators to opposing teams learned.

Barnstorming into the 1930s, the Celtics began playing college teams as well as semipros, which resulted in top-flight basketball filtering into the Southern states of Florida, Georgia, Alabama, and Louisiana. The Midwest states of Indiana and Ohio, along with the northern states of Wisconsin and Minnesota, were other stops made along the way. No one was overlooked. They were on a mission they felt responsible to carry out.

Historically, the 1920s were golden. The glitter could be found in its jazz music and exploding Wall Street investments as well as its sports, which filled the American landscape. With money in their pockets and time on their hands, Americans turned to spectator sports. Baseball, boxing, and college football were well attended. Professional basketball tried pushing its way onto the sports pages; while far from dominant, basketball began to catch on nationally, with the Celtics most often mentioned.

But as professional sports like football and basketball commercialized, they faced an uphill battle when it came to social legitimacy. Pro athletes were generally perceived as uneducated and coarse types who played only for money. While Babe Ruth's heroics legitimized baseball and Jack Dempsey's mauling thrilled boxing, basketball had no icon to show the way. And yet, in spite of this, the Celtics excelled.

During the winter of 1925, Red Grange launched a barnstorming tour to test the country's interest in professional football. While The Galloping Ghost popularized the sport, George Preston Marshall, laundry tycoon and owner of the National Football League's Washington Redskins, convinced Chicago Bears' George Halas and Cleveland businessman Max Rosenblum to join the new American Basketball League, a more sure-footed venture that attracted teams from the East to the Midwest.

While the ABL struggled, Jim Furey and his Celtics played as an independent and beat all challengers. But by the 1926–27 season, when independent teams refused to play them, the Celtics joined the ABL. They dominated the second half with a 19–2 record and swept the Cleveland Rosenblums in three playoff games.

In 1928, the Celtics again won their league championship with a 49–9 record and defeated the Fort Wayne Hoosiers in the playoffs. The combination of these two ABL titles along with their barnstorming dominance made them the unofficial but undisputed world champions. Joe Lapchick was at the pinnacle of professional basketball and was earning more money than he could have dreamed possible growing up in Yonkers. While the money poured in, there were times when he wondered about meeting the right girl and raising a family.

O

Bobbie Sarubbi's family was well-to-do with her father operating an architectural construction company. She was tall but worried about meeting someone she towered over. Joe, on the other hand, had never gotten over the effects of being considered a giant. When around basketball people it was less of a problem, but when he returned home at the end of a season and exchanged his basketball uniform for the swimsuit he wore while working as a lifeguard at Tibbetts Park, he was among people who crowded his elbows.

A nervous Joe Lapchick was to pick Bobbie up on a blind date to the local movies. As she waited by the window for a black sedan to pull up, she hoped he didn't turn out to be another average-sized date that made her uncomfortable. But as the tall athlete ducked his head and slid out of the car, Bobbie let out a sigh of relief.

Joe liked Bobbie. "She was straightforward, honest, and intelligent." As they walked from the movie house to his car, he noticed she had a run in her stocking, and thought, "This is a kind of gal who I can relate to, my kind of down-to-earth woman."

Joe and Bobbie dated the rest of the summer and were married the following spring in 1931. They settled in Yonkers and started a family with

Joseph Donald in 1932, the first of three children. Barbara followed shortly after, while Richard would have to wait until the mid-1940s to make his appearance.

Each of the children did well academically and would become successful in their life goals. They would grow up to be well-mannered, upright citizens, well respected in their professions as well as their communities.

Joe Donald, who played football at West Point, would earn a doctorate at Harvard after his military service as a pilot and become superintendent in several school districts. Tall, elegant Barbara became a top fashion model after earning her degree from Barnard. She is the only one who has preserved the family's Czech tradition, spelling her name Lapcek.

Dr. Richard Lapchick is today a nationally known authority in athletic social issues. He is the author of more than a half dozen books and has received numerous honorary degrees. When NBA commissioner David Stern sent a group of star-studded athletes, headed by Patrick Ewing, and Alonzo Mourning to South Africa in the mid-1990s, Richard was their spokesman. When recent presidents wanted a clear grasp of a social issue involving sports, Dr. Richard usually got a call. Their parents could only speak with pride when their children's names came up.

Life had been fine for the Lapchicks in the 1920s, but like everyone else in America, they would face tougher times during the Depression, while they tried to raise a family on the salary of a barnstorming basketball player.

O

Looking back on the 1920s, the Celtics had amassed an outstanding record winning 714 of 795 games, 90 percent of them on the road, including a thirty-nine-game win streak. The 1922–23 season was their best with a 102–6 won-loss record. Their overall record of 714–81 was one of the most amazing in the history of professional basketball. Both press and sports historians considered the Celtics the best team of the 1920s. But the Celtics were disbanded in 1928 under clouded circumstances. Although rumor claimed it was because of their dominance, the real problem involved "mismanagement."

"CASHIER IS INDICTED AS $187,000 THIEF," the *New York Times* headlines screamed out on June 17, 1926. As head cashier for the prestigious Arnold Constable Department Store in New York, Celtics manager Jim Furey controlled the company's financial accounts. After twenty years of service, starting as an eleven-year-old mail-room clerk, he had earned the company's confidence. Unfortunately, he was accidentally exposed when a customer contacted the store complaining about a bill she already paid. To pay his team, Furey had been stealing from his employer.

Rumors reached store executives that he was living a life of luxury, "an unusual style for a man of his income." He was often seen "riding [in] an expensive automobile and was known to be well supplied with ready cash." After a company audit, investigators discovered Furey cashed and spent several large drafts. "We'd often go to the store where he worked," Lapchick recalled, "and he'd pay us for two or three games." Money never seemed an issue.

Nothing in newspaper accounts, however, tied Furey to the Celtics, except one article that mentioned Furey "was well known in athletic circles." He had nothing more to do with the team, except that after World War II he supposedly sold the Celtics name to Boston owner, Walter Brown.

Few readers would have connected the breakup of the Original Celtics with a 1920s front-page story about "the demise of one James 'Bugs' Donovan." In need of an investor because of Furey's "personal problems," the team attracted Jim Donovan, whose profitable bootleg operation provided ready cash. "I'll pay all your back salaries," Lapchick quoted about Donovan in a local Yonkers newspaper in 1935. The Celtics thought him "an engaging little chap, even though he didn't bother explaining what his 'outside business' was."

The bootlegger was thought to be in real estate, but shortly after he bankrolled the team, according to Lapchick, the investor was found shot. Donovan "was picked up full of lead and very dead." He'd been crossing New York's Tenth Avenue one night, "after quarreling with his erstwhile partner." The Celtics attended the wake finding "their former boss a mess." Lacking a backer, the Celtics were then traded off.

Lapchick, Dehnert, and Barry were shipped to Cleveland where they helped Max Rosenblum's Clevelanders win two ABL titles. Johnny Beckman had already been dealt to the Baltimore Orioles as player-coach, while Furey traveled in a different direction: he was sent to Sing Sing Prison, where he was sentenced to five to ten years for grand larceny. He would serve three of them.

○

A professional basketball player's life was a tradeoff between the joy of playing and its emotional and economic uncertainties. The values the Celtics learned and their sense of accomplishment made the sacrifices worth it. They knew that life as a professional basketball player, like the life of an actor, was precarious, and that management was somewhat shaky. Most early pros had little formal education or other marketable skills. Basketball was what they did for a living.

Knowing Celtics lifestyles, Lapchick was "surprised any of them lived to be seventy." They were young men, living on the road, in hotels, traveling by train or in touring cars, trying to make a living. They cursed, brawled in games, tried gaining every athletic advantage, and drank with the best of them.

The hardships of professional basketball in the 1920s and 1930s also pivoted around family life. Dehnert was rarely home, yet he fathered three children. When most Celtics ended their playing days, Dehnert remained in basketball, coaching, scouting, and traveling for another twenty-five years. Pete Barry bounced around in New York, never landing any sports jobs. Lapchick's three children saw little of their father, too. Bobbie was forced to make the best of it while her husband struggled to earn a living.

When the Celtics are discussed historically, they are the team of the 1920s that set the standards that others followed. It was their innovative style that influenced how basketball was played in the future.

With a 90 percent won-loss record through much of the decade and two ABL championships, and with Lapchick, Barry, and Dehnert winning two more with the Cleveland Rosenblums, the Celtics earned the title World Champions in the 1920s. But with the coming of the Depression, the remaining Celtics soon realized that the days of plenty were gone. Unlike in the past glory days, Joe Lapchick and his mates had to reach down deep to grind out a living no longer as the glorious Original Celtics, who could leave a $5 tip at the bar, but as barnstormers, itinerant professionals using survival skills to compete with the younger stars of the 1930s, especially the all-black New York Renaissance and Harlem Globetrotters. Joe Lapchick and the remaining Celtics were going to learn there was a price to pay for being pioneers.

Chapter 3
Barnstorming: The Not-So-Good Old Days

In the 1930s pioneer basketball was flat-footed and intense, while today's players demonstrate greater athleticism. "From a physical point of view, today's players are much better, but team play is not," former pro and UCLA coach John Wooden emphasized. "Today they're playing above the rim, and they didn't in those days," he observed about the 1930s. "Basketball played today by the very finest women's team is more like men played then." Women pay attention to fundamentals often lost in men's high-speed athletic play. For a lover of pure fundamental execution, women's basketball is a pleasure and a throwback to the way the game used to be played in Lapchick's time.

It was late in March of 1933 as the Rosenblum Celtics were winding down their season. They had just gassed up and hit the road to go to their next game. "We had played in Huntington, West Virginia, and were heading to Cleveland," Lapchick recalled. The old car by this point was limping along, barely able to function. "We hardly had a glimmer of headlights and no brakes to speak of." Late at night the driver, Nat Hickey, didn't anticipate any traffic and was breezing along at a fast clip hoping not to run into any breakdowns.

As they approached Massillon, Ohio, Lapchick noticed what appeared to be a fire dead ahead. The "fire" turned out to be a freight engine tugging a long line of cars across the highway, directly in their path.

Hickey, anticipating the inevitable collision with the barreling train, applied what turned out to be imaginary brakes with little effect on "old unreliable."

"Everyone in the car was in a panic," Lapchick remembered. Carl Husta opened the front seat door and bailed out. Hickey swung the car to the left, trying to cushion the collision by going over a twenty-foot embankment. As he made his move, Davey Banks, fearing the worst, flew out the side door and tumbled like a circus clown along the side of the road.

Lapchick was tightly wedged in the back seat between Dutch Dehnert and Pete Barry, surrounded by cases of beer. Fewer than a hundred yards from the train, the auto lurched down an embankment. Lapchick distinctly recalled Dehnert grabbing his arm and yelling, "Jesus, Mary, and Joseph, here we go!"

"Then the miracle happened," Lapchick smiled. The car rolled gently down onto a dirt road and came to a halt on a soft cow pasture that had been churned up into a sandy field. The team sat there for what seemed an eternity as silent prayers of thanksgiving raced to heaven. Barry looked up at the roof of the car and whispered, "Thank you God for your wonderful gifts." They all thought he should have been a priest.

O

Proof of the tortuous lifestyle appeared in a riveting letter written from the Edson Hotel in Beaumont, Texas, on January 30, 1935. Exhausted from travel and concern for his family, Joe Lapchick wrote to caution his wife, Bobbie.

"Played a game twenty-two miles out of here last night and got $6 each. Doesn't even pay our three-day hotel and meal expenses. That's about the fourth bad one since we left home. Don't expect any dough 'till next week."

For Joe, barnstorming obviously lacked the glamour players find in today's NBA or even what he was used to in the 1920s. There was no guarantee that there would be enough of a crowd to pay expenses when the Celtics arrived. Travel arrangements were tighter and had far inferior modes of transportation than today's professional play.

Many distant one-night stands were booked, and to make a living two games were often played the same day. "We leave Texas tonight for Sulphur, Louisiana, and I am not expecting that to be a good money game." In

Louisiana, they played in Monroe to another sparse crowd. Lapchick was concerned. After a day off, the Celtics "rode five hundred miles to Birmingham, Alabama, then to Chattanooga, Nashville, and Old Hickory, and last on the Southern tour in Memphis." When they left the South, they headed north "to Chicago, and after that only heaven knows." The tired barnstormer affectionately signed the letter, "Lovingly, Daddy Joe."

Webb Garrison, a North Carolina wordsmith, once described barnstorming in this way: "In the early days of traveling theater, third-rate companies didn't get the best facilities. Many had to settle for almost any empty building. Some held one-night stands in barns."

The word had a flighty, nomadic quality to it; barnstormers didn't let grass grow under their feet, always on the move while not commanding those best facilities. A passion seemed to drive them. The word is identified with early daredevil pilots in bi-wing planes traveling the country giving air shows and providing carnival thrills about the mysteries of flying.

Barnstorming also described pioneer professionals like the Celtics who brought basketball to towns that couldn't support their own leagues during the Depression. The Celtics were joined by the New York Renaissance and the Harlem Globetrotters, making up the three best teams that traveled America's big cities and blue-line back roads to provide quality basketball when it was an emerging sport.

"Sometimes I rub my eyes in wonder," Lapchick offered in retrospect. "This game of ours, the players, the auditoriums, it all seems too good to be true." His eyes saw basketball's recent growth and glory as well as its past hardships. "The contrasts are worth looking at as a reminder that the good old days weren't necessarily so."

Joe Lapchick spent most of the 1920s as an important player on the profession's best team. The Celtics were used to staying in luxury hotels and playing before large crowds. Lapchick, Nat Holman, and Johnny Beckman were three Celtics earning more than $10,000 a year, making them the highest-paid players in the sport. Lapchick's income placed him in the top 10 percent of Americans, earning more than eight times as much as an Indiana schoolteacher's annual salary of $1,200. It didn't take much to get used to buying new cars and fashionably dressing the part of a sports celebrity.

The economic turmoil changed the world Joe Lapchick was accustomed to. Reality arrived along with his deflated 1930 American Basketball League contract from business manager Nig Rose to play for the

Ceveland Rosenblums. It called for $1,000 a month and guaranteed only four months. "I'm sorry it cannot be the same as last year," the business manager apologized. "Still it is a whole lot more than other clubs can afford." Lapchick agreed and signed it, settling for less than half of his former salary. As the economy tightened, Max Rosenblum could no longer make payroll, and in early December he disbanded his team, signaling the end of the ABL. Lapchick faced a dilemma. He needed to provide for his family, but what he knew best was crumbling around him.

"'What if we form our own team and play around the country," he suggested to Celtics teammates Barry and Dehnert. Both agreed. Lapchick reasoned it was easier for a town to support a visiting team a few times a year than for a full season. Rosenblum agreed to help with bookings, and the Rosenblum-Celtics' "road show" was born.

Lapchick found a way to provide for his family during the hard times of the Depression by barnstorming with a collection of aging Celtics. Forced to economize, the Celtics toured the South and Midwest, hoping to play anyone for a day's pay. Celtics marquee value still attracted Depression-weary Americans willing to slap down 40 cents for good basketball.

From 1930 until he retired as a player in 1936, Lapchick organized the Celtics and took to the road from late November until April on eighteen- to twenty-game tours with usually six players. Gone were luxury Pullman cars and plush hotels; they were replaced by all-night travel in beat-up Pierce-Arrow town cars with luggage roped to the roof and averaging 125 miles between games. Despite being tired, sore, and often while nursing injuries, the Celtics walked into a crowded gym and pulled on their jerseys, suddenly healed and ready to go.

At first Rose doubled as road manager while Lapchick learned to speak to the press, organize clinics, and appear on radio in addition to being player-coach. He didn't realize it, but he was learning to think for a team. He now anticipated problems, coached more, and was attracted by the public relations end of the business. Gradually, he learned to be responsible for all the "on the road" business aspects and maintained a log of his transactions.

Tommy Humphries from Chattanooga, Tennessee, later headed "the front office" by booking games by penny postcards without a telephone. He received 15 percent of the booking fee. Their game fee was $125, but occasionally they collected as much as $1,000, with a top figure of $1,650 for battling the popular Rens in St. Louis. When times were bad, they took whatever they could get.

While Humphries booked "one-nighters," the players made their own accommodations, which often turned out to be their own jalopy amid several cases of beer, with the designated driver battling to stay awake.

The Celtics were aware that barnstorming was entertainment. They were the circus that came to town, the anticipated fun and excitement that made a Depression week bearable. As a new sport trying to attract fans, pride demanded they put on a good show.

Advance publicity in local sports pages bragged about Lapchick's "ability to shape his hand into a capital S while holding the ball," and Dehnert—"the Honus Wagner of basketball"—was blessed with immense hands and long arms for clever pivot play. To stimulate interest, they were photographed clowning in a gym or casually playing cards in a hotel room. While in town they gave clinics and were available to the press. The local teams provided game competition while the Celtics imparted skills and entertainment.

The Celtics knew how to please crowds by not running up scores and keeping local teams in the game. "If a team was reasonable," Lapchick pointed out, "and not be rough on us or take advantage of the fact that we were professionals, we'll let them down easy and make a good show of it."

When the team failed to keep less-talented opponents competitive, each player entertained with sidebars of talent. "Tall Joe" did tricks palming the ball, faking out opponents while Davey Banks dribbled between his long legs in a drive to the hoop. The two, billed as "The Celtics' Two Extremes," worked well. Banks, the Brooklyn sharpshooter, complemented the big center, and the routine became a part of Celtics play. When all else failed, Dehnert's pivot wizardry could still hypnotize crowds.

When the local talent was limited, Lapchick realized the importance of presenting them in a positive light. "We had to entertain the crowd so that they'd come to see us again." But occasionally, some college team got too enthusiastic, forcing the visitors to assert their superiority by "playing for blood," which wasn't fun for them or the crowd.

During a January barnstorming tour in 1934, the Celtics faced a fired-up Coca-Cola Triangles before a packed house in the Memphis Auditorium. In their enthusiasm to snap a Celtics seven-game win streak, burly Tommy Hughes elbowed tiny Celtics guard Davey Banks in the face, a play pros didn't tolerate. To demonstrate their displeasure, the Celtics decided to embarrass Hughes by setting double and triple screens that prevented Hughes from guarding Banks, who scored 19 points. As a result of the aggressive blocking, the Triangles' coach was forced to bench Hughes. The Celtics taught another lesson by defeating the Triangles, 35–23.

The strenuous game schedule necessary to make a living and traveling long distances in secondhand cars created problems. Acquiring a reliable used car for road needs with room for six players was always a problem. The Celtics' touring car, with its huge trunk, was often used for ten to twelve thousand mile junkets from the Southwest, into the Midwest, and back to New York. When not sleeping in their car, their daily hotel bill rarely exceeded $1.25. Food was relatively inexpensive, never presenting a problem. But their "luxury cruisers" often broke down, and repair bills frequently ate into food money. On many occasions their unreliable vehicle left them scrambling to keep their scheduled game.

There was one stretch when the Celtics played the Rens in St. Louis on January 31, another game in Evansville, Indiana, on February 1, followed by a date in Dayton, Ohio, on February 3. Seeing there was an open date on February 2, Humphries penciled in the Earle Cardinals in Memphis for good measure. But that wasn't enough.

Lapchick asked the booking agent to schedule a second game with Baldwyn in Mississippi, a team they lost to in mid-January. That night they pushed a broken-down Cadillac for miles and finally had to leave it behind and hitch rides to arrive just before game time. Exhausted, they reached for their adrenaline and came from behind only to lose by a point, 27–26.

The second game with Baldwyn on February 2 was necessary to satisfy their pride. After not having a day off since early December, the Celtics won comfortably. Before the trip ended, the Celtics played thirty-two games in twenty-eight days, including a triple-header in Nashville.

On another trip, the Celtics left New York on a cool November night in 1933 for Cleveland, a city where they had won ABL championships and were always warmly received. As they stopped in a hotel for the night, the temperature unexpectedly dropped below freezing. Since no one remembered to put antifreeze into the radiator, when Nat Hickey started the car the next morning, he discovered the motor had a split cylinder block. The Celtics thought they had solved their problem by trading the disabled car and $100 for what Lapchick described as "an ancient crate." The car placed a serious drain on the team's income. Hickey was unable to keep ahead of the car's problems, since the "bomb" needed the daily attention of a professional mechanic. During that miserable winter, the unpredictable vehicle constantly broke down, frequently making them push it to the next town to an off-key rendition of the "Volga Boatman." But in spite of its temperament, they never missed an engagement.

○

A prominent barnstorming attraction in the 1930s was the Celtics and the all-black New York Renaissance, known as the Rens. Both played local semipro and college teams and occasionally, to stimulate attendance, battled for mythical world crowns. They were evenly matched and the games well attended, but age was catching up with the Celtics.

"Much of the fun of the old days was gone," Lapchick admitted. With age and chronic injuries, playing basketball became "a hard racket." But as much as Lapchick complained, he knew basketball was in his blood, and all of his adult life was on the road with men who were closer to him than his own brothers. When he groaned over the hardships, he stopped and thought about life without basketball. "We love the game, we always have and always will," he said. But his love was often tested.

Buffalo promoter Ray Fischer begged for a Celtics game, hoping to rekindle local interest. The Celtics agreed to play the Bisons for $100, which they claimed was "their lowest figure." Payment was expected at halftime, but when the promoter was nowhere to be found, Lapchick got the message. Attracting only 120 spectators had something to do with his vanishing act. The Celtics had hoped to couple the Buffalo visit with a Monday game in Oswego to help pay expenses, but it backfired. It wasn't the first or last time shady managers shortchanged the Celtics.

○

The Saturday-night ride from the Chicago suburb of Whiting to Indianapolis was stormy. The 195-mile trip took three and a half hours in good weather but closer to five in January snow. The temperamental Pierce-Arrow knifed through heavy weather that promised no letup. It was Nat Hickey's turn again at the wheel. He liked chew-tobacco and spit its excess fluid through a hole he had carved in the floorboard. The drafty old black town car rattled along as the others dozed. The Whiting Owls had proved pesky—a scrappy bunch of ex-college kids trying to claim fame by playing a little too aggressively for the veteran pros' taste. The Celtics taught them a lesson—at a price. They were forced to show their might by using legal but physical "tricks of the trade." Screens into opponents were harder and elbows, like lethal weapons, flashed more quickly, often catching an opponent's more sensitive flesh, but in so doing the team was using up valuable energy. The aging team now needed a good night's sleep to recuperate.

Lapchick stared out a frosty window. He tried sleeping, but it was hard grabbing those fleeting moments. As he rested his eyes, the worn athlete seemed worried about where the big ride would end. His wife Bobbie and the kids needed care. His body was running on empty. The Southern trip always wore him down, and his legs weren't what they used to be. These days when he got a charley horse, he needed extra rest.

Joe Lapchick learned to manage the Celtics. There was talk about Lapchick coaching when he retired, but where? No one made any formal offer. Basketball was all he knew. Pros hired few coaches because most of the teams coached themselves, which gave the six or seven players a bigger cut of the pie. Also, it was difficult for him with his limited education to crack into the college ranks.

The snow was blinding Lapchick as the team car passed through another dark, silver-edged, silent early-morning village. The Celtics were to play the competitive Rens, a team that faced discrimination daily. Blacks were barred from playing on the same team with whites in the South and Midwest, but the Celtics could entertain crowds playing against them.

Indiana's segregation issues made it difficult for blacks. Celtics memories of bold posters in Evansville, Indiana, the last February admitted the arena had, "SEATS FOR COLORED." The sign, trying to rationalize its bias read: "There will be a section reserved for colored people, and they turn out in large numbers." The poster couldn't hide Hoosier intolerance. White fans didn't mind black ballhandling magic, but they didn't want to sit too close to them.

As Hickey entered the outskirts of Indianapolis, he steered to the YMCA on Senate Avenue, the "Colored YMCA," as it was known. The Celtics had no objection to colored folks. Modestly priced, the rooms provided needed rest for Sunday's game. Their visit to Indiana usually lasted a week, playing three to four games throughout the state, and it always included the Kautskys in Indianapolis.

Frank Kautsky was a short, stocky local grocer who loved sports enough to risk forming a professional team during hard times. With a supply of homegrown talent, he hoped to break even on his fantasy. Charles "Stretch" Murphy at 6'7" was an outstanding center. His spectacular rebounding and pitchouts had triggered Purdue's fast break. But Kautsky's prize was the other former Purdue star, three-time All-American John Wooden.

John Wooden could have played with the Celtics or the Chicago Bruins, but he chose to stay near home. Nig Rose tried stealing him with an attractive Celtics offer. He would have been a great draw throughout the Midwest. "I was offered $5,000," Wooden said. He, however, returned to Indiana's Central High in South Bend to teach, coach, and play locally, and he was fortunate to receive $1,800 a year, a top teacher salary.

He accepted the Kautsky offer of $50 a game plus expenses, averaging forty to forty-five games a season. The team traveled as far as Pittsburgh, and after Sunday road games, Wooden drove all night, covering 130 miles back to Indianapolis to make Monday classes.

"Professional basketball in those days," Wooden recalls, "was hectic and harrowing." Stories told about the early NBA couldn't compare to the years he carried his own gear, liniment, tape, bandages, and basketball. Wooden usually traveled with several players by car and often arrived just in time to play. He also recalled the hardship of travel in wintertime. "With car heaters that weren't as they are today, it was very difficult, but fun." He didn't do it for money. "You loved the game, and played and enjoyed it."

He recalled the hardships surrounding a game in Pittsburgh. "It was a long trip, roads and cars weren't that good." He traveled with a teammate named Bill Perigo, and because of weather conditions, they were running late.

"Bill went to call and I went to get something to eat; a fellow asked where we were headed. I told him Pittsburgh, to play. He said we wouldn't make it with the way the roads were. We said we would. Then he said, 'That's what those two fellas in the morgue said.'"

○

It was a Celtic-Kautsky Sunday afternoon sellout; Indiana fans loved their basketball. By game time the sun had melted the remaining snow. The

Celtics pushed past early birds waiting by Tyndall Armory's entrance on Pennsylvania Street, wanting close-ups of "world champions," while youngsters gathered looking for autographs. Lapchick scribbled a large, clear version of his name. Dehnert and Hickey repeated the ritual. Popcorn and hot dog aromas competed at the doorway with pregame cigarette smokers setting the game's ambience.

Herb Schwomeyer was sixteen and working the concession stand to earn college tuition. He liked his job. He saw boxing and wrestling bouts two nights a week while he sold popcorn and Coca-Cola. His concession manager sold no alcohol, but fans privately drank. No Coke bottles were given to customers to prevent them from being thrown at visiting players.

Anticipation cut the air. The Celtics defeated the Kautskys last year, but the Hoosier home crowd sensed victory. An amateur preliminary game received mild attention, and increased pregame tension.

"The armory's gym was on the second floor," Frank Baird sketched from memory. Fans in the balcony paid 25 cents, downstairs 40 cents, "And you're seeing the best basketball in the country." The bleacher seats reached the sideline, making them pinching distance from players running by. The basket near the stage was suspended from the ceiling, while the other one hung on the wall near the Pennsylvania Street entrance. There was little room under the stage basket, which was close to the wall. No modern padding cushioned a player shoved into the stage.

To save money, teams dressed together in the basement. When ready, the Celtics charged past the spectators near the concessions. A drunken fan staggered toward Lapchick, yelling. The crowd's buzz increased as Celtics Green made its entrance onto the armory floor to begin warm-ups, followed by the blue-and-gold-trimmed Kautsky team.

Unlike today's arenas, there was no game clock or scoreboard. The score was posted at the far end of the gym by dropping numbers into a slot. Some old gyms used a chalkboard and a scorer who rewrote numbers as they were tallied. The official scorer at mid-court often doubled as timekeeper. It was his duty to fire a starter pistol at halftime and the game's end. The Kautskys' running game was often slowed down from the slippery spots on the wooden floor left by professional wrestling the night before. It bothered the owner enough that if conditions didn't improve, he threatened to play the remaining games at nearby Pennsy Gym.

While entertaining to the fans, Celtics warm-ups were also instructional and allowed future coaches to scratch notes in their pads. Part of the Celtics mystique was learning from the best. After fifteen minutes of pregame loosening up, the referees signaled team captains to half-court to set the rules. Lapchick's graceful strides and confident smile could intimidate opponents. After a lifetime of globe-trotting, he had earned the look. He looked and acted like a world champion.

The tall center and the Purdue All-American Wooden sized each other up like prizefighters in a ring. There was an intensity about Wooden, "The stern, single-mindedness of a preacher," Lapchick thought. Pros questioned the ability of college players, and the Celtics center had reservations about hotshots. Having played against Wooden, he saw him as a great prospect who scored bushels of points but gave them back on defense. The captains agreed to unlimited personal fouls, so fans could see the stars play, shook hands, and headed back to their teams. Lapchick paid attention to handshakes. Personality was conveyed through them. Game psychology was in full bloom.

Lapchick strutted an erect, military walk to the center jump—a much smaller circle than that of today—one that squeezed centers together. The official's vertical toss caught "Stretch" Murphy off guard, and Lapchick's quickness and extra-long reach guided the ball to Dehnert, whose perfectly timed, over-the-head flip led the streaking Banks for an easy layup.

Fireworks ignited a minute into the game. A loose ball brought the Kautsky enforcer, Clarence "Big" Christopher, crashing into Nat Hickey, burying an elbow into the Celtic's midsection while all 240 pounds landed on him. War erupted. Hickey, who had gotten the worse of it, came up swinging. The pair tangled, ignoring referee whistles and fan hoots. After a half-dozen well-intentioned but misguided punches, local police separated them with threats of arrest. Both players were ejected. The fans, loving it, rained abuse on Hickey with their shredded programs while "Big" Clarence received a hero's send-off as he headed to the dressing room. The game's tone was set, warning officials they were in for a long afternoon. Down to five men, the aging Celtics sorely missed Hickey. Physical play caused both teams to lose focus, but by halftime the Kautskys led, 20–12.

Schwomeyer delivered Cokes as the teams poured into the dressing room. "It was exciting seeing professional players, the ones you read about the next day. You kind of felt part of the game. I was surprised to see them smoke and joke around."

Lapchick led his squad aside to regroup. He reached inside a bag for his Lucky Strikes as drinks were passed around. Needy hands begged for a smoke. As they cooled down, each volunteered second-half strategy. They knew as pros that 8 points was a big lead, and it would take careful play to get back into the game and to try to make only one basket at a time.

On this Sunday the Kautskys were not to be denied. The second half was controlled more by the referee's whistle than team play. Calling thirty-eight personal fouls with twenty-four against the visitors, the Kautskys' lead was steady in spite of Celtics attempts to disrupt their tempo. But as the game was coming to a close, an incident occurred that Wooden never forgot.

As he took an outlet pass and raced up court, he suddenly lunged forward out of control and sprawled onto the floor. He turned to see big Joe Lapchick nearby and assumed that Joe had tripped him. "I went down hard, and I came up 'fightin' mad' and I went after him." Lapchick, realizing Wooden's mistake, tried to defuse the potential argument, but the fired-up Hoosier came after him, flailing away at the veteran center.

"But I couldn't get to Joe; his long arms held me by the shirt and I was swinging wildly but not getting anywhere," Wooden said. "I was mad momentarily." After several exhaustive efforts, he realized it was hopeless. "It finally got funny and we both laughed. We were good friends from that time on."

Lapchick believed tripping was the lowest form of sportsmanship. "Pros were geared to almost any indignity as far as rough play was concerned, but tripping was unforgivable." When word made the rounds that a player was tripping, "He was taken care of physically and eased out of the game." To this day no real basketball player trips an opponent.

Playing shorthanded and with little rest, the Celtics couldn't catch the Kautskys. "Stretch" Murphy earned his money that afternoon. He scored inside and controlled the center jumps. With five minutes left, the Kautskys' 3-point lead looked solid. By dribbling and passing and eluding attempts to tie him up, Wooden's ballhandling, plus all seven free throws he made down the stretch, helped ice the game. The gun sounded with fans enjoying the final score: Kautskys 37, Celtics 29. The players congratulated each other and headed to the dressing room. Frank Kautsky was ecstatic. As his players soaked up the victory with their Cokes, he pulled each one aside.

Professional athletes during the Depression thought they were blessed being paid to play a game they loved. "Frank always paid in cash; he didn't put your money in an envelope," Baird recalled. While the players dressed, he'd get out a roll of bills with a rubber band around it—what Baird called the head of lettuce—and handed it to the players. Baird made $25 a game, but he remembered a great game against Cleveland. "I scored 33 points, and I got $50 that night, the most I ever got." No one even looked at what he paid. "We'd just put it in our pockets. If he was particularly pleased, or if you had a good ball game, sometimes he gave you a little extra." With bags packed, the Celtics said their farewells and exited to their next adventure. Kautsky, happy with the performance, added $75 to their $250 guarantee.

Indiana basketball was different from what was played in the East with cities like Fort Wayne, Evansville, and Indianapolis generating some of the best energy in the sport. There was electricity present, a quality that made Hoosier basketball memorable.

"Basketball," Dr. Naismith, the game's founder, insisted shortly before his death, "really had its origin in Indiana, which remains today the center of the sport." Made famous in Indiana, Midwestern fast-paced play changed the game. Its quick, high scoring overshadowed its defensive limits. What the founder saw above all in Indiana basketball was its enthusiasm.

Since basketball had a Northeastern origin, New Yorkers in particular believed it was their city game. Its trademark of crisp ballhandling, gluelike defense, and percentage shooting blossomed in urban neighborhood playgrounds and local settlement houses. City kids learned that smart passing forced defensive errors. "Give and go" basketball became New York's style.

Indiana's basketball was most clearly observed in its scholastic play. That's where "Hoosier Hysteria" blossomed. There was something about the almost fanatical enthusiasm that rural folk brought to its local games. It was special and representative of what America was about. It was passionate basketball at its best.

If Norman Rockwell had painted in the Midwest rather than New England, he would have had a landscape filled with subjects that represented the rugged individualism that made up America's tradition—rural life, with its simple blessings that nature freely offered. Basketball was a bonus that enriched lives that took pride in their local hamlets' play.

Hoosiers attended games, but when they were unable to, they listened to them on the radio or read the extensive newspaper coverage.

Why such hysteria in Indiana? What made it different from other midwestern states? Basketball was played in winter when little else was going on. It was a game played between harvests and planting seasons. Local towns were too small to field football teams and too poor to buy equipment; basketball was less expensive. A nailed-up hoop with a makeshift ball allowed a youngster to play.

Civic pride had a hand in Hoosier basketball, too. Its popularity was also helped by statewide newspaper and radio coverage. High schools received front-page attention, helping to immortalize players like Bob Plump. "The whole state was behind the sport, and that really got the attention of the players and the community," recalls the Milan, Indiana, legend. Rural bragging rights depended on how well a town fared in the tournament.

Nationally known for sinking the winning basket for miniature Milan High and upsetting big school favorite Muncie High in the 1954 state championship final, and immortalized by the film, *Hoosiers*, Plump is a prototype of Indiana basketball. Many of today's coaches and corporate institutions interested in motivation use the film. Plump went on to a respectable cager career at Butler University and is now a successful businessman in Indianapolis. The former hero knew that the possibility of an underdog knocking off a favorite was the basis of Hoosier enthusiasm. It was the element that made folks howl for more and build athletic facilities that matched their fanaticism more than their means.

"There were no pro teams, no other state tournaments except track," Plump said. It was the only game in town. "The banner in our Milan High School gym reads: '1954 State Champions.'" It did not bother to identify sport or gender. There was only one state tournament in Indiana. Until recently it pitted all schools in one large effort. "It created a lot of excitement."

By the 1930s, college and professional basketball made inroads into Hoosier hearts. During the height of the Depression, sixteen thousand fans packed Butler Fieldhouse for barnstorming professionals like the Celtics and the Rens. The Celtics toured throughout Indiana.

Indiana was by no means a wealthy state; however, when it came to building large gymnasiums, it led the nation. A recent report that the state has more gyms with a seating capacity of more than 4,800—more than the other forty-nine states combined—demonstrates Hoosier passion for basketball. Indiana has fourteen of America's fifteen largest high school gyms, with New Castle the largest seating 9,325. There was something American about "hoop-crazy Hoosier land." It's what made the state stand out, a reason for the little rural towns to swell their chests with pride.

O

The Original Celtics, like the New York Yankees and Notre Dame, were special to sports fans. In 1959, in its first year, the Basketball Hall of Fame in Springfield inducted the Celtics team, while later Lapchick, Holman, Beckman, and Dehnert were honored individually. In its early days basketball needed missionary zeal. The Celtics provided it when they traveled the small towns of America spreading Dr. Naismith's gospel.

When Walter Brown, the owner of Boston's pro franchise, picked a name in 1946, he chose a winner. According to Holman, Brown had purchased the rights to the Celtics name from Jim Furey. In an era when team names disappear with turnstile speed, "Celtics" has stood for a winning tradition, and it was the natural progression from the old barnstormers to what would eventually be the most celebrated NBA franchise. But in spite of the Celtics' cherished reputation, not all of the former players were ready for retirement. With the exception of Holman and Lapchick, most of the Celtics struggled after their playing days. Barry, Banks, Hickey, and Carl Husta were athletes who made few preparations for the future. Holman had landed in college coaching. It was Lapchick's turn to decide on his future.

O

Joe Lapchick looked out the rain-splashed kitchen window of his Yonkers flat, blowing smoke from a half-spent cigarette. He noticed for the first time the clothesline that dangled in the spring wind, tossing Donny and Barbara's clothing around as if they were rag dolls. The shaky rope was a metaphor of what the future had in store for him—walking a tightrope as they did in vaudeville shows. He felt uncertain and afraid to think too much into the future.

Thirty-five was a critical age in most men's lives, a point of no return, and Joe Lapchick was no exception. His body was worn down and a wife and two children looked to him for food and clothing. His limited education barred doors that Holman, as a college graduate, easily entered. The Celtics did provide an education of sorts, one that taught him about life. Lapchick had developed a toughness that would serve his future. Everything about the team revolved around manliness, just like military training or an initiation into a college fraternity. He had also paid attention to sportswriters when he took on team managerial responsibilities, and he learned how to deal with them. As a pro he recognized that quality play resulted from team harmony and studying teammates. The Celtics—uncoached and yet in many ways the best coached—believed each player was a floor leader, that Celtics helped each other.

But of all the words and sentiments that stuck with him, pride was the one that supplied the energy that sparked a tired bunch after all-night drives in a storm to play before a handful of eager spectators. Every time they tied on their sneakers they believed they were world champions. Pride would accompany Joe Lapchick to his grave. He wanted to stay in basketball where he had made his name, the sport he loved and knew best.

What Lapchick didn't realize was that in the mid-1930s he had basketball knowledge and people skills few others possessed. He had more than twenty years of practical experience and was eager to succeed. But who would hire an aging ex-pro with a limited education?

Chapter 4

Call Me
Coach

Joe Lapchick limped to his locker after another game for the Kate Smith's Celtics and frantically reached for a Lucky Strike. The pain from his swollen knee caused the old warrior to yell out as he slammed his fist into the tinny locker door. Dutch Dehnert, his long-time teammate, looked up with understanding eyes as he began to undress. Lapchick, calmer now after taking the first deep drag on his cigarette, smiled and rubbed the knees that had carried him nearly thirty-six years.

Kate Smith was sponsoring the remnants of Lapchick's Celtics. Entertainers in the 1930s enjoyed being involved with athletic teams, and the nationally known singer, whose "God Bless America" hit was on every home's radio, was no exception. When her schedule allowed she liked sitting on the bench cheering for the team and wearing her shamrock-green-and-white jacket. As player-coach, Lapchick found it a delight dealing with the entertainer and her business manager, Ted Collins. But as wonderful as they were, his barnstorming days were numbered, and it was time to move on, but where?

Through the winter and early spring of 1936, Lapchick hobbled on throbbing knees to maintain a living. But as he traveled he learned he wasn't the only one with a problem. Father Charles Rebholz, the athletic chairman of St. John's University, needed a replacement for Buck Freeman, the brilliant "Wonder Five" coach, winner of 85 percent of his games and considered one of the country's best.

Father Rebholz asked athletic director Walter McLaughlin for help. McLaughlin had officiated in the disbanded American pro league and had observed Joe Lapchick. They didn't always see eye to eye, but Lapchick impressed him. When McLaughlin asked veteran officials Dave Walsh and Johnny Murray, they also endorsed Lapchick. After several interviews, Lapchick was offered the job.

With the position in his pocket, Lapchick questioned whether he could adjust to college players. He was used to rough, uneducated pros who drank after games. Now he was asked not only to coach, but also to head one of the better college programs. Undecided, he turned to former teammate and well-known CCNY coach Nat Holman for advice. "Take the job," Holman insisted. After discussing the offer with Bobbie, Lapchick was finally convinced.

In the summer of 1936, Joe Lapchick signed a $2,500 contract to coach basketball and baseball at the Brooklyn school. Through the 1950s it was common to be hired for two sports. In some ways Lapchick felt more comfortable with baseball than basketball. In the future, Lapchick would receive St. John's contracts with incentives paying 10 percent of the net receipts of postseason games, but for now he was happy to have a job.

O

The dark orange MacGregor laced leather basketball glanced off the head of tall, thin senior captain John Shanley as he turned near the basket to talk with teammate Gerry Bush. "When is he going to have us do something besides shooting?" Bush shrugged his shoulders. "He's a Celtic," the strong forward assured his teammate. "He knows the game."

Joe Lapchick had assembled the St. John's varsity that October afternoon for the first practice in dingy DeGray Gym on Lewis Avenue in Brooklyn. After an hour of informal shooting, and sensing that Lapchick was in a predicament, Shanley approached the new coach.

"What would you like us to do?" he asked. Lapchick was seated high in the bleachers by mid-court, a strategy he'd heard experienced coaches used. He stared at the captain. "I'm evaluating the talent," he answered calmly. "Continue to shoot."

Lapchick's fear made him react as if he had never been in a basketball gym before. Shanley returned to the squad and relayed the orders. "This was a lot different from playing for Buck," the captain said.

While college coaches traditionally taught drills and set plays, the Celtics worked themselves into shape by playing. Lapchick never experienced structured workouts, but learned from pros who acted as surrogate coaches, teaching one another, and by experimenting on his own. Pro ball was trial and error. Lapchick gradually realized how he learned to play.

Forty-five minutes later, Lapchick whistled the team to the sideline and nervously informed them that he was still evaluating their skills. Collecting his composure, he ordered ten laps around the gym and showers. "I'll see you tomorrow at 3:30 P.M. sharp." Lapchick shakily turned and walked away. It took two more days of shooting and uncertainty before scrimmaging began.

The new coach's problem was transmitting his experience to college men, who he felt saw his limited education peeking out from under his sweatshirt. He felt sensitive to their imagined polish. But much of Lapchick's uncertainties were imagined. "Most of us came from blue-collar backgrounds similar to Joe's," Shanley realized. "I was the first in my family to get out of grammar school."

The coach's uneasiness drove him to Father Rebholz. Thinking he would be let go, Lapchick was surprised by the priest's response. "Joe, we know you will do well. It's just a matter of time."

Out of fear and confusion, Lapchick turned to Clair Bee, the knowledgeable Long Island University coach. Bee, author of the well-known Chip Hilton children's sport books, came from Cleveland and from Slovak roots, like Lapchick. In fact, the sharp-featured, average-sized coach used to watch the Original Celtics play.

Bee was embarrassed for the former pro after he poured out his insecurities. "Why ask me about coaching? The Celtics were the best in their time," Bee reminded Lapchick. "Why couldn't you teach what you performed?" Lapchick's pride made him feel as if he had been slapped across the face. His friend was right. With renewed determination, Lapchick rolled up his sleeves and analyzed his task.

He had been with the best pros, and he now returned to Celtics play for inspiration and guidance. Lapchick reviewed how the team had executed the fundamentals of rebounding, ballhandling, and defense. How did they execute basics so well? Gradually, Lapchick realized the key to teaching was "a matter of steps." As he mapped it out, he learned there were basic steps for every skill. Slowly, he developed confidence by teaching himself. Eventually, Lapchick blended a pro's tricks of the trade and the ability to feel good basketball with a straightforward way of communicating.

He often discussed coaching with Bee, who asked what Lapchick's players called him. "They call me Joe," Lapchick answered. Bee shook his head. "That's no good." Bee recommended "Mister Lapchick" or "Coach." By the following season, Lapchick got the message to his team. Drawing a professional line between himself and his players helped maintain the team's respect.

Lapchick took his lumps the first year but salvaged a 12–7 season that included a thrilling double overtime win over St. Joseph's in Philadelphia. Coaching mistakes bothered him, from poor substitution to questionable end-of-game strategy, but he learned "on-the-job." He learned the importance of preseason conditioning by having his team run for two weeks.

That first year Lapchick also found out about superstitions, a lesson that welcomed him to the coaching fraternity. He invited Bobbie to his first Garden game. Lapchick had maneuvered his team to seven straight wins and now faced his old Celtics teammate Nat Holman, who coached CCNY. After a sluggish first-half effort, the new coach's undefeated Redmen were decisively defeated by the upbeat Beavers, 39–21. It took another thirty years before Bobbie got over her uneasiness and attended another game.

○

Joe Lapchick probably didn't see it coming, but college basketball was changing in front of his eyes. Until the mid-1930s, when he took over at St. John's, it had been a local or regional sport played on school campuses primarily in the East and the Midwest. One of the most dramatic changes occurred in December 1934, when Ned Irish's brainstorm to move college games from campus gyms to Madison Square Garden became a reality. The big arena venue revolutionized college basketball into a national sport and a financial success. Thousands of fans who would never have seen a college game were suddenly fighting for the hottest ticket in New York.

Much has been written of how Ned Irish "invented big-time basketball." As a sportswriter for the *World Telegram* in the early 1930s, he was assigned to cover a Manhattan College game, but an overflow crowd barred him from the gym. Mayor Jimmy Walker further piqued the young sportswriter's imagination by sponsoring several fund-raising college doubleheaders that drew big Garden crowds. Aware of the game's popularity and its promotional possibilities, Irish would take an unprofitable sport and make a quantum leap.

He approached Garden president General John Reed Kilpatrick with a proposal backed by Tim Mara, owner of football's Giants, that would run college basketball as a concession, guaranteeing the Garden $4,000 a night. Kilpatrick agreed and big-time basketball was born. Two days after Irish quit his newspaper job, the first college doubleheader was played in Madison Square Garden in December 1934 with more than sixteen thousand fans watching NYU defeat Notre Dame, 25–18, while St. John's bowed to Westminster, 37–33. It proved so successful that in one night Irish earned the equivalent of six months' pay as a sportswriter. He never doubted his instincts.

By 1946, the Garden booked twenty-nine doubleheaders, drawing more than a half million spectators while averaging near-capacity crowds of eighteen thousand. Irish recognized his power when booking colleges that wanted exposure. He paid them $500; they grumbled, but took it. "My terms, or back to your gyms." Irish was the boss. With its strong East Coast ties, basketball revolved around Madison Square Garden. Media coverage and Garden attendance made the late 1930s through the 1940s a peak period for the college game.

Things couldn't have been better for Joe Lapchick. He again accidentally found himself in the middle of another transitional period of basketball, which he owed to Ned Irish. "He was a tough man, but he took basketball out of the dance halls. He gave it the respectability it deserved. No one ever did more for the game." Irish's innovation, which started as a college attraction, would later include the new pro league.

Irish's Garden games blossomed when boxing slipped and arena owners were looking to fill dates. But basketball's national attention was also helped by its internal changes. A game that had moved its backboards away from the wall and got rid of the twelve-foot netting around its courts now improvised rule changes that encouraged a more popular, faster game. Youngsters around the country who played flat-footed and with two-hands, suddenly began shooting running one-handers.

During Lapchick's first season at St. John's, he watched an energetic but clever West Coast player electrify a large Garden crowd with one-hand shooting. On a cold night in December, Stanford's Hank Luisetti helped snap LIU's forty-three-game winning streak and challenge its national power. The curly haired, 6'3", 175-pound forward's 15 points and innovative offensive play had everyone talking. Luisetti—who is recognized as basketball's first modern player—was considered twenty years ahead of his time. His one-hander baffled New Yorkers, as well as the Blackbirds, who had seen little of the shot. But the West Coast star represented more than revolutionary shooting. Coached by Naismith disciple John Bunn, the San Franciscan added the behind-the-back dribble, quick-hand steals off exceptional defense, and floating drives to the basket where he looked both ways, then fired up a spectacular shot. Luisetti's performance in the media capital demonstrated the game's future.

In 1936, the NCAA's rules committee created a "three-second" area within the free throw lanes that limited the offensive player's time near the basket. By 1937, the "three second" rule and the end of the archaic center jump after a basket helped energize and increase game scoring from the '30s to the '50s. With added speed—and taller players—physical play and personal fouls increased, causing the rules committee in March 1944 to raise personal fouls from four to five. Chicago, Boston, Philadelphia, and Buffalo imitated New York by building large arenas, while university facilities like Butler Fieldhouse in Indiana and Rupp Arena in Kentucky also helped spread the passion for sports.

Lapchick's coaching career mirrored the game's growth in 1939 by earning St. John's its first of seven National Invitation Tournament invitations over the next nine years. Sportswriters added to Lapchick's reputation by immortalizing his Celtics days, making him a well-known figure. Lapchick was becoming a celebrity in the biggest sports market in America. But he was going to discover there was a shadowy side to the glitter of big-time college basketball.

○

Irregularities in football, a game that galvanized college sports during the first half of the twentieth century, are well documented and caused the leading universities to create in 1906 the National Collegiate Athletic Association. But as college basketball blossomed by the end of the 1930s, universities began to view it as another way to increase enrollment and alumni funding. As a result, schools stepped up recruiting, which often stretched their ethical standards. While the NCAA tried to "regulate and supervise college athletics nationally," colleges saw themselves as lords of the realm and did not allow the NCAA to dictate to them. If schools strayed too far, the others quietly blacklisted the offenders by refusing to schedule them. This, however, did not stop an ostracized school from competing and gaining recognition.

Lacking the power, the NCAA appealed to universities to police themselves. The "self-help" system worked with schools that placed sports in its proper perspective, but failed with "win at all costs" programs. Many university heads, more interested in being "winners" than ethical "losers," rejected rules that could bar them from publicized tournaments. When the NCAA attempted to establish a "sanity code" in 1948 with specific academic and recruiting guidelines, even the more legitimate schools refused to comply, fearing the NCAA lacked enforcement power.

Though easy to condemn, the problems of big-time basketball have to be judged in their times. Many top athletic programs in the past looked on fractured academic and recruiting standards as acceptable behavior—until caught. While college sports battled rule violations, the more serious problem of sports gambling sprang up.

One-time Connecticut prep school math teacher Charles K. McNeil was credited in the early 1940s with devising point-spread handicapping, which he called "wholesale odds." McNeil determined how many points the favorite should win by rather than wagering on whether an underdog could pull an upset. Under the new system, betting an underdog with the added points became a good bet and sparked gambling. For example, if an underdog was slated to lose by 8 points, that total would be added to its score. If a bet was made on the underdog and it lost by more than 8 points, the house won. When a favorite won by more than the indicated point spread, those who wagered on the favorite collected. The simple system mesmerized gamblers while guaranteeing bookmakers an edge because gamblers were forced to bet $11 to win $10.

The enthusiasm for basketball gambling turned out to be the seed of a sports scandal because it increased the risk of fixing games by point-shaving. Gamblers, too, learned they could easily bribe players to shave points, which created a sure bet. The intention was not to lose the game, but most fixes resulted in "dumped" games where the team lost.

Only after a disaster of major proportions in college sports came to light did university heads finally allow the NCAA to "put their houses in order." And it was not until the 1951 gambling scandal in basketball and the West Point football cribbing that universities began to encourage the NCAA to regulate and restore faith in college sports. The awareness of a gambling problem in collegiate basketball first began to turn into a nightmare in 1945, when five Brooklyn College players decided to turn the rumored tales of fixing games into a reality.

O

The nineteen-year-old basketball guard liked hanging by Pete's Parlor, the pool hall off Eastern Parkway in Brooklyn, listening to Brooklyn Dodgers ticker-tape scores when his team was on the road. The neighborhood kid enjoyed Dodgers announcer Red Barber's re-creation of the game and the underworld atmosphere. He became friendly with local gamblers, and one day he was introduced to Henry Rosen.

The basketball player was back from the service and played on a rejuvenated Brooklyn College team, which hoped to compete with local powers like LIU and St. John's. Coach Tubby Raskin was offered five Garden dates for the 1944–45 season. When Brooklyn defeated a better-than-average Western Kentucky early in December 1944, the sports world took notice. Henry Rosen, a thirty-year-old, medium-built gambler called "The Mustache," also became aware. The gambler had his hands in several illegal schemes but couldn't resist a "sure bet." He approached the college kid and asked if he would like to make some easy money. The 5'9" guard thought fast. "Sure, let's talk."

Harvey Stemmer, a local bookmaker with underworld connections, agreed to bankroll the fix, and Rosen offered each of the five starters $200 with a promise of $4,000 to be divided on completion of the fix. The game chosen was to take place in Boston Garden against Akron University on January 30, 1945.

The players thought they were doing what other local teams had done, but when it came time to deliver, some of them changed their minds, and it was left to the quick-thinking guard and teammate Buddy Barnett to tell Rosen. Unknown to them, the gambler was under police surveillance for selling stolen goods gathered from a ring of high school kids stealing from local department stores. When the authorities tapped Rosen's phone, they accidentally uncovered the basketball fix.

The two Brooklyn College players were arrested in Rosen's house, and later in the station house they admitted the scheme to the police. The five players were expelled from school but were not held because they cooperated with the investigation. The problem was how to charge Stemmer and Rosen.

The Black Sox baseball scandal of 1920 produced laws against bribing professional athletes, but in 1945 these laws did not regulate amateur events. The two fixers were eventually charged with "conspiracy to defraud a bettor on a contest" and served a year in jail. Laws were quickly drafted and passed for future offenders. Although no fix had taken place, the incident stirred a storm of public consciousness. The supposed pristine college game, the darling of sports fans that packed arenas around the country had been exposed. What had only been whispered about point-spread betting now gained credibility.

The word on New York streets, from neighborhood bookmakers to local sportswriters, was that college athletes had been fixing games. The attempted Brooklyn College fix, the first confirmed in modern history, foreshadowed the future. Although universities promised to scrutinize their teams, nothing changed. Brooklyn College sounded a warning, but no one took it seriously. With rumors of players fixing quietly circulated, gamblers looked for discontented athletes or those interested in fast money.

The mind-set in the 1940s was a kind of "no harm, no foul" attitude to point-shaving. Everyone talked point spreads, and like today, newspapers published the odds. Fixing games went on, no one seemed hurt, and bookmakers almost enjoyed detecting an occasional scam that forced a game "off the board," or refused bets on suspicious ones. Players realized there was little schools could do. In most cases, institutions and coaches were unaware of player deals with shady characters. Point-spread betting lent itself to game tampering and just as naturally into the gambling scandal of the 1950s. The accused athletes learned from unethical colleges breaking recruiting rules, a rationale many fixers used to justify their actions. A player reasoned if universities made money, why not the athlete. It was a short step from a school's lack of ethics to point-shaving.

O

Lapchick's first year coaching was filled with valuable lessons. Bee's advice made sense and helped him develop a better grip on his team. He found himself in a competitive fishbowl, where a coach's worth was measured by victories. But he was ready for the challenge. In spite of the pressure to win and surrounded by a sea of ethical violations, Lapchick tried steering his players clear of gamblers. By nature he was a moral man, and his principles would be challenged throughout his career.

While Lapchick was gaining coaching experience and college basketball was expanding, the metropolitan sportswriters proposed a national postseason tournament. The concept of a national champion fueled endless discussions among sports enthusiasts. By selecting who they believed were the best teams in the country, a single champion would be crowned. The idea quickly became a reality.

In 1938, the Metropolitan Writers Association started the National Invitation Tournament and initially selected six outstanding teams to decide the nation's best. Irving Marsh, the association's president, and his fellow New York writers believed the interest in the college game would make the NIT a natural. It proved an instant hit with Temple, its first champion, trouncing Colorado, 60–38.

With the success of the NIT, the NCAA the next year tried its hand at a regionally balanced eight-team tournament. No one mistook its effort for the celebrity of the NIT. The Garden tournament caused every college to hold its breath in anticipation of a bid.

Chapter 5

The Double
Crown

By the end of the 1938–39 season, Lap-
chick's Redmen compiled a 17–2 record and earned a bid to the National
Invitation Tournament. The tournament was loaded with quality teams.
LIU, Loyola of Chicago, and New Mexico A & M were undefeated, while
Bradley and St. John's had only two losses. Roanoke College also entered
on a twenty-game win streak. The tournament offered Lapchick his first
opportunity to compete in a national setting. The season had been a
strange one, with two losses sandwiched between lengthy win streaks.

Set-shooting guard Ralph Dolgoff and floor leader Dutch Garfinkel
led St. John's. Dutch was another in a long line of Thomas Jefferson High
School players who excelled at St. John's.

But the late season performance of senior Bill Lloyd was the ingredient that made the Redmen a dangerous tournament team. Lloyd was
proof of the strange bounces in sports. In preparing for a mid-season Garden game with DePaul, Lapchick used Lloyd, a 6'3", second-string forward, in practice to simulate the opponent's low-post play. Despite foot
problems, Lloyd's pivot hook shot caught fire, and he blossomed into an
effective scorer for the second half of the season.

As St. John's prepared for its opener against Roanoke, Lapchick decided to ride his instincts by starting both Lloyd and 6'5" George Palmer.
It turned out to be the right move. Lloyd set an NIT record, scoring 31

points, a total he never reached before, and propelled the Redmen to a lopsided 71–47 victory.

St. John's reached the semifinals against Midwestern power Loyola of Chicago, led by 6'9" Mike Novak, a giant who could score, block shots, and rebound with the country's best. The game seesawed with neither team pulling away. Novak, who was allowed to station himself in front of the basket, blocked nine shots. Tall players like Novak could legally change a game by interfering with shots on its way down, intimidating a shooter into rushing. Today's "goaltending" awards the shooter 2 points, but at that time, interfering with a shot "on their way down" was allowed until the 1944–45 season. In spite of late-game heroics by Garfinkel, Novak's defensive advantage decided the game for Loyola in overtime, 51–46.

St. John's loss proved helpful to LIU's coach, Clair Bee. Bee, who played Loyola in the final, visualized a solution: force Novak to play LIU's best shooters on opposite sides of the basket, and by moving the ball quickly, LIU would get open shots that Novak couldn't recover to block. The strategy, along with LIU's collapsing defense, helped the Blackbirds win the NIT and remain undefeated. The victory is noted by the fact that forty-seven years after basketball was invented, its creator, Dr. James Naismith, stood at center court to present the NIT championship trophy. Lloyd walked away with MVP honors, having scored 50 points in the tournament. It was a fine start for Lapchick, who would be back many times.

In the early 1940s, St. John's played ten to eleven Garden games a year, regularly meeting ranked teams like Colorado, Oklahoma, Kentucky, and Tennessee, along with traditional metropolitan powers, and usually ending up with the NIT's best. Lapchick avoided no one. Slowly, he molded winning squads. But to get to the top he needed the help of two of New York's finest players. Harry Boykoff, 6'9" center, and his 5'7" Thomas Jefferson playmaking teammate Hy Gotkin suddenly decided to attend St. John's instead of LIU. Gotkin had dreamed of playing for St. John's from the time he watched his cousin Java Gotkin play for Buck Freeman. Hy's fondest memory was of an old pair of game sneakers three sizes too large that Java gave to him. Convinced of their magic, the spunky youngster stuffed paper in the toes to make the dream come true.

As Gotkin and Boykoff's reputations grew, Adolph Rupp of Kentucky wrote offering them "full scholarships" and "alumni benefits." Leroy "Cowboy" Edwards was a Kentucky All-America center who left after his sophomore year to join the newly formed National Basketball

League in his hometown of Indianapolis. The rumor was Rupp couldn't pay him enough to stay. Gotkin didn't like what Rupp represented. He had also heard whispered stories that the Kentucky coach was a harsh disciplinarian who squeezed the fun from the game. Lexington, Kentucky, didn't appeal to the New Yorkers. On the other hand, St. John's was the Yankees of college basketball, the team coached by the well-known former Celtic, Joe Lapchick.

Clair Bee made every effort to recruit Gotkin and Boykoff for LIU. He got them summer jobs at a local beach club he directed that paid $35 a week, a comparable salary at the time for the head of a family. But after working two summers for Bee, and with graduation approaching, Boykoff became apprehensive over what his scholarship entailed. LIU assistant "Pic" Picarello told Boykoff the scholarship included room, books, tuition, and "whatever you want." Boykoff was uncomfortable with "under-the-table" dealings. He had heard that Bee's success was through underhanded practices. After a successful two years at Rider College, Bee transformed LIU into a national power, and from 1932 through 1951 he amassed a 370–80 record, an amazing .822 winning percentage.

Confused over LIU's open-ended scholarship, Gotkin and Boykoff contacted St. John's. "Have you spoken to Coach Bee about this?" Lapchick asked. The two players told him they had discussed their concerns with LIU, which only reinforced their desire to attend St. John's. Athletic director Walter McLaughlin later informed them that he would check their story and get back to them.

In September 1940, Gotkin and Boykoff received scholarships that met their family needs and enrolled in St. John's. Boykoff still carries scars from a letter accusing him of betraying the coach. Bee, a skilled writer, compared the big center to Judas Iscariot, claiming he "collected shekels" like the wayward apostle by taking the summer job. The coach's bitter metaphor demonstrated the high stakes when recruiting in the 1940s.

O

"Fuzzy Levane is a coach's dream," Joe Lapchick responded to a sportswriter's question about what made his future pro guard and NBA coach such an asset. "He plays defense and ballhandles with the best," Lapchick said, "and makes his teammates better." The glowing evaluation fit the 6'2" curly haired Neapolitan dynamo.

Lapchick assembled a promising team for 1942–43, and after an outstanding 18–2 season, St. John's again qualified for the NIT. The team was built on toughness and experience and was inspired by Andrew "Fuzzy" Levane, a senior guard with "winner" written all over him. Fuzzy came up with game-winning plays that earned the respect of both his teammates and the New York press. Slim, 6'3" forward Larry Baxter, along with sophomores Boykoff and Gotkin, complemented Levane. As the tournament's second seed, St. John's drew highly touted Rice as its first opponent.

With one minute left in the game and with the score tied at 49, Levane signaled with a raised left index finger that the team would hold the ball for a final shot. Unable to get the ball inside to Boykoff with fifteen seconds left, Levane passed to Gotkin on the right baseline and crashed the boards. With the clock ticking down, Gotkin winged up a twenty-foot set shot that caromed off the left side of the rim where Levane scrambled for the loose ball. He again spotted Gotkin and flipped it to him under the basket for the game-winning layup as the buzzer sounded. "Rice argued that I got the shot away after the buzzer," Gotkin recalled, but the score stood. Unknown to St. John's, Rice was going to be their toughest opponent.

The Fordham Rams, a team they easily defeated earlier, 63–47, was next for the Redmen. Form followed and St. John's again ran away from the Rams, winning by more than 20 points, 69–43. The semifinal victory resulted from a well-balanced offense and inspired defense led by Levane, who helped seal the win by holding Fordham's high scorer Bob Mullens to two field goals. The victory placed St. John's in the final against a tough Toledo team. But Lapchick had more than Toledo to worry about. Near the end of the Fordham game, Levane tried to save a loose ball going out of bounds under the basket and went crashing into the seats, injuring a thigh muscle. Lapchick blamed himself for not removing his star from a game long decided.

In preparation for the championship game with Toledo, the newspapers were filled with as much concern with Levane's injury as the Ohio team's personnel. Dutch Garfinkel, former St. John's playmaker, warned that Toledo should be taken seriously. He had seen their 6'3" black forward Davage Minor play in the Midwest and rated the freshman the best college player he had ever seen. The Monday NIT final found Levane assigned to guard the heralded Toledo freshman. After a seesaw first half,

Toledo came busting out in the second half and knotted the score at 22. But that was the Midwesterners' final run as St. John's rolled to a lopsided 48–27 NIT championship. The team's defense, headed by Levane who held Minor scoreless, along with the scoring of Boykoff, Baxter, Gotkin, and Al Moschetti, overpowered Toledo.

Boykoff had the soft touch of a surgeon. His perimeter and low-post scoring was unstoppable, and with his rebounding, he was a unanimous MVP choice. The gold watches were distributed to the victorious Red- men, and then Fuzzy Levane was called back and presented the Haggerty Award, symbolic of New York's best player. Lapchick had guided his team to the NIT championship and was sitting on top of the basketball world.

Before Lapchick could appreciate his team's victory, St. John's was asked to represent the NIT in the first Red Cross game against Wyoming, the NCAA champions, in Madison Square Garden. For the first time, the game would determine the national champion. Wyoming's more physical 6'7" center Milo Komenich easily balanced the thinner 6'9" Boykoff, while Levane's guard play offset the high scoring, jump shooting speed of Kenny Sailors. But 6'5" Wyoming forward Jim Weir would make his presence felt.

Wyoming would spurt ahead while the Redmen found ways of tying the score. With little more than two minutes left and St. John's trailing 46–39, the Redmen made their final run. An outside shot by Moschetti, fol- lowed by a Levane steal, which drew Komenich's fourth and final foul, elec- trified the Garden crowd and drew hysterical approval from the St. John's bench and its fans, who remained standing for the rest of the game. Both viewed the departure of the Wyoming center as the game's turning point.

After Levane's second free throw popped out, Boykoff quickly jammed it back into the basket. With twenty-six seconds left and down 2 points, Gotkin made a miraculous save of a ball going out of bounds at half-court and flipped it over his head in the direction of the St. John's basket. Levane caught up to it and passed to Moschetti for the tying bas- ket. The Garden rocked with approval as the game ended in a tie and both teams prepared for overtime.

Wyoming's Jim Weir scored quickly to give the Cowboys a lead. Up 2 points, Wyoming nursed the ball to a 5-point victory. The 52–47 final score masked how close the game was. Lapchick later complimented Wyoming. "They were just too good for us, had too many weapons." But he added, "Those kids of mine did fight, and I was never prouder of them than I was tonight." This was not a loss Lapchick agonized over. He knew both teams were champions.

After the tournament, Columbia Pictures filmed ten minutes of the team, which was narrated by the popular sports announcer Bill Stern. *The Kings of Basketball* demonstrated St. John's winning style of play, showcasing its ballhandling as well as Boykoff's polished size. Lapchick directed his players through hook shots, five-man weaves, and underhand free throws, all standards for the period. A perfectly executed between-the-legs dribble by forward Moschetti seemed out of place for the times. "After the filming, Coach called us together," Gotkin recalled, "and divided his fee equally." Every player received $20. Boykoff was appreciative. "Coach knew we could use the money."

Lapchick was enjoying coaching, realizing college kids weren't the monsters he had anticipated. He and his players had grown from his experience. Progress was measured in ways other than wins and losses. Besides learning to coach, he sharpened social skills and learned to communicate more effectively. His interviews with the press were smoother, more thought out, and usually included something quotable. As Lapchick counted his blessings, he looked for new ways to improve.

It was not long after the NIT victory was packed away that the new season was on the coach's mind. World War II had decimated most teams, and St. John's was no exception. Most of Lapchick's experienced players would be gone before the season started. As Lapchick walked his Yonkers neighborhood that spring, he wondered what kind of a team he would field. That season would further test his coaching skills.

O

On a brisk, sunny November afternoon in 1943, World War II took a backseat to Coach Joe Lapchick's preseason luncheon. St. John's underclassmen assembled in the back room of Larry's, a popular Brooklyn restaurant. Because many athletes were drafted into the service, freshmen were sanctioned to play. President Roosevelt thought it would be good for morale to play major league baseball and for as many colleges as possible to field teams. St. John's canceled all sports except basketball. "It was like keeping the flame," Jack Griffen, team manager and future sports editor for United Press International believed.

Missing were the leaders from last year's NIT champions: Boykoff and Baxter were in the service and Levane had graduated. It left the coach with a nervous stomach. Everything pointed toward rebuilding unless Lapchick "rallied his troops." As the room reverberated with talk and laughter, the tall coach was amazed at how young the players looked. He realized how great an effort was needed to produce a successful team.

Besides the freshmen, the team included athletes with physical ailments that denied them military service. Bill Kotsores had a heart condition, but it never stopped the sophomore from giving his best. Also in the crowd was an asthmatic and a diabetic. And Ivy Summer's poor vision forced him to wear taped-on glasses with lenses as thick as bottle bottoms. He would become famous for flapping glasses and hustle. And yet, as he chatted with wartime athletic director Father Joseph Browne, Lapchick sensed a hunger in the young faces.

Dick McGuire, the cherublike seventeen-year-old Rockaway Beach playmaker, didn't say much but had recently gained attention. McGuire was 6'0" and 170 pounds of controlled energy. Sparks from his play on a basketball court could light up a London blackout. New York basketball would have to dig deep to come up with a playmaker who approached his skills. He was a star ready to blossom. By February, however, the future Knicks' first-round pick would also be called into the military, but not before Redmen fans got a taste of his special talent. Other St. John's players would follow McGuire, moving around to military bases faster than property on a Monopoly board. But on that November afternoon, while McGuire and his teammates sat patiently, they were unaware of the changes military obligations would cause even for freshmen.

With several steady taps of his teaspoon against a half-filled water glass, Lapchick got everyone's attention. "Every sports fan in the country is watching you," Lapchick reminded his novice audience as he narrowed his eyes to scrutinize their reaction. "You are defending NIT champions," the coach proudly emphasized, raising his voice slightly, saying it slowly while lingering on the words "NIT champions," wanting them to sink in. "But they don't realize you're not the fellows who played last year." Lapchick never bothered explaining who "they" were; he wanted the team to fill in its own answer, from "the media" to "neighborhood friends," whatever motivated them. The coach wanted to inspire, to rally around a cause for hard work while reminding them of the pride he, as well as they, carried inside. "They only know your jerseys say 'St. John's,' and expect you to be winners."

The coach continued to weave a web for his inexperienced audience as he closely gauged them. How could they know what it took to win last year? Most of them were kids playing high school games before a handful of students and friends. How would they react to a packed house of eighteen thousand at Madison Square Garden?

"Sitting among you," Lapchick emphasized, "is a teammate who was in your shoes last season." Lapchick pointed to Hy Gotkin, a smiling wisp of a leader. "Hy was a sophomore who helped win that championship," the coach paused, "and is ready to show the way again." The young men turned to look at Gotkin and offered a delayed but enthusiastic applause, as he smiled again while launching a military salute.

Lapchick finished with the focus of his talk. "Together we are going to try to live up to their expectations. Together we can do it." The young players, feeling more enthused by the coach's talk, clapped hands, slapped the table, and whistled enthusiastically. Lapchick needed a committed team to produce a season they all could be proud of, one they could share with friends and family.

The coach said his piece and sat down, energized for the new season. By the end of the talk, Kotsores and Summer felt more comfortable defending a national championship. It seemed simple, and besides, their coach looked confident, as if he knew what to expect. As they passed rolls and tore into their meatless wartime breaded codfish, Lapchick wondered how they would fare. If guts and effort produced success, they should do all right and might even reach the NIT. "I wanted to give them hope," Lapchick whispered to the priest. "We all need a lift." At the start of the 1943–44 season, Lapchick's hopes were modest.

○

Ivy Summer didn't know what the letter was about. The envelope's seal read "St. John's University's athletic department" and was dated June 25, 1943. He tore it open and read—in what appeared to be a matter-of-fact tone—that he was practically being ordered to report for a "final interview." Since he had never visited St. John's or had any initial talks, he was confused. Summer, who had played successfully for Brooklyn's James Madison High School, realized as he read on that he was being "offered an athletic scholarship to play for Coach Joe Lapchick." Ivy had never met the famous St. John's coach but had heard good things about him and was intrigued and flattered by the offer. Lapchick had played against Summer's high school coach Jamie Moskowitz in the 1920s. "He's a good man," Moskowitz stressed, when they discussed the offer. Summer had planned to join the service, but the attraction of a free college education and to play a major college schedule in Madison Square Garden for Joe Lapchick put a hold on any military plans. "I decided to enroll in St. John's."

Summer was unaware that he was to replace All-America center Harry Boykoff with all of his 6'6", 190 pounds of inexperience. Since the war years allowed freshmen to play, he earned a starting position with floor leaders Gotkin and McGuire. But by the middle of the season, McGuire, the team's star guard, was also drafted, and with McGuire gone, according to Summer, "We had no chance" to win any tournament. But before championships could be dreamed of, Summer had an unforgettable experience with his coach.

A few weeks into the season, Summer was invited to a bachelor party at the Casa Madrid, a Spanish restaurant in New York City. After heavy celebration, the lean center, in no condition to make his way home, found himself in the early morning crawling on the sidewalk on hands and knees. Then, out of nowhere, a car pulled up and a head popped out of a rolled-down window. "That's no way to make the big leagues," a familiar face and voice reminded the inebriated player. It took Summer several seconds after the car drove away to register that the voice belonged to his coach. As a former barnstormer, Lapchick had seen his share of drunken athletes. He also knew the bespectacled freshman had to be taught a lesson.

Shortly after the incident, St. John's played Cathedral College at home in DeGray Gym, and Lapchick saw his opportunity. When the starting lineups were announced, Summer, who had started every game, found himself on the bench. For much of the game, the score was close. Every time the coach roamed down the bench past him, he thought he would play. But it never happened. With a few minutes left, and the game decided, Summer, by now totally frustrated, left the bench and headed to the locker room. After Lapchick congratulated his opponent, he was stopped as he made his way to the locker room. "Joe, what are you going to say to Summer?" sportswriter Garry Schumacher of the *New York Journal* wanted to know. "What do you mean, Garry?" asked Lapchick.

The writer informed his friend of Summer's quick exit. The coach rarely showed anger, but now he was close to it. If anything challenges a coach's authority, it's a player acting out his unhappiness in a disrespectful display in front of his team and a gym filled with spectators. After showering and dressing, Summer passed the tall double row of lockers, when suddenly, out of nowhere, two long, strong arms, acting like a cherry picker, yanked the startled freshman off his feet and pinned him to the rattling lockers.

"Don't ever embarrass me again, mister," Lapchick angrily warned, "if you hope to play for me." To punctuate his point, the coach shook him again. "Never do anything like that again." Then he loosened his grip, allowing the wide-eyed player to make a hard landing onto the locker-room floor. Nothing was mentioned about Summer's "night on the town," or sudden exit, but the lesson stayed fresh in his mind. Years later a mature Summer fully understood Lapchick's reprimand. He learned that his coach wanted respect, and did more than make substitutions to win games. "He cared deeply for us."

O

"We could have blown the whole season," Lapchick moaned to Father Browne, his full-time father-confessor, as the train rumbled along to Philadelphia. The coach was still shaken after a close call the previous week with a team he thought would not be challenging. "Who knew Brooklyn Army Base was going to show up with a trunk full of All-Americans?" the padre agreed, as he tried consoling the disturbed coach. Lapchick's Redmen, expected to be mediocre at best, had put together an 11–2 record, with losses only to Kentucky and a loaded wartime West Point team. Realizing that every game counted if there was any chance for the NIT tournament, Lapchick wanted the upcoming Canisius game to be well scouted. But, without an assistant, he was forced to make the trip to Buffalo himself.

To fill schedules during wartime, games were played with military bases. Since Lapchick's reports claimed Brooklyn's Army Base should have been an easy game—a "blow" as he described it—he asked Father Browne to coach while he scouted. Because of a sudden change in military assignments, a new, more experienced Brooklyn Base team showed up at DeGray Gym, headed by Rice All-American Lee Craddock and future Knick Sonny Hertzberg. It was a surprise that almost derailed St. John's NIT hopes. Fortunately, the priest's prayers were answered when Summer scored 9 points for the overtime victory.

The team was on its way to play St. Joseph's at Convention Hall in Philadelphia. As the rhythmic motion of the train began to soothe his worries, Lapchick turned his thoughts to the players' casual attitude toward their college education. He had never underestimated its value, even if his players did. Many were missing classes or simply were not serious students. Lapchick never forgot his limited education and couldn't understand anyone taking one for granted. Realizing his responsibility to the young team, he decided on a strategy. "I'm going to shock this bunch," he told the priest, "lay it on the line to show them what they're missing." To Lapchick an education was more important than the St. Joseph's game.

As the team dressed, Lapchick made his way through the low-ceilinged locker room, trying to avoid hitting his head on its steam pipes. He placed a foot on the worn brown bench and launched one of the strangest pregame talks. "You probably know that I played for what some people say was the greatest team of all time, the Original Celtics." At the mention of the Celtics, Lapchick had their attention, and he got right into his carefully prepared lesson.

"I'll tell you what it earned us. Except for Nat Holman and myself, it got us nothing lasting because we played for nickels and dimes." Of all the Celtics, only Holman and Lapchick shaped successful lives after their playing days. Knowing the odds of succeeding without an education, Lapchick plugged on. "You are a lot more fortunate than we were," he insisted. "Your ability to play has earned you a college education, which, if you're smart enough, will take care of you the rest of your life."

"But some of you are throwing it away," Lapchick warned as he wagged an index finger around the room. "You think you're pretty good players, but let me tell you that you haven't proved anything in life yet." If it wasn't such an emotional talk, it deserved to be applauded. As he ended, the team sensed his frustration. After a long silence, Father Browne led the team in prayer. Without planning it, Lapchick had motivated his team into a stunning victory that acted as a springboard into the NIT.

Summer remembers the St. Joseph's talk as if it was given yesterday. "We had recently lost a few games, but he only talked about getting an education," Summer said. "Lapchick's talk put everything in perspective." It wasn't the game that night that mattered to him, but it was graduating with a degree. Summer retained the message and made sure he left school with his diploma.

Basketball was more to Lapchick than wins and losses. To him it involved dealing with humanity and not moving players like plastic pieces on a chessboard. The key to coaching was reaching young men, and if victory wasn't to be, best effort was just as important. Summer continued to play well enough to help St. John's overcome its loss of players like Boykoff, Baxter, and McGuire to the military. With a 15–4 record, and as defending champions, St. John's received the eighth and last bid to the 1944 NIT, a memorable one for the team, but especially for Summer.

O

"We could do well in this tournament," Lapchick complained to sportswriters, "if we only had a center." That was a strategy he used to relax his opponents. But the coach was also indirectly challenging his young center by stating to the press that Summer was too young and inexperienced to compete against some of the nation's best big men. Success in the tournament boiled down to the bespectacled freshman shutting down Bowling Green's 7'0" Don Otten, Kentucky's burly 6'8" Jim Brannum, and DePaul's 6'10" George Mikan. After the Redmen got past Bowling Green in the first round by 4 points, they were matched with Kentucky, a powerhouse team that had beaten them handily in December. When questioned about the rematch, Lapchick praised his opponents but welcomed another chance to play them.

The Redmen trailed Adolph Rupp's once-defeated Kentucky Wildcats before the year's largest Garden crowd, but inspired by loud cheering, the team reached down for a little extra. The game had been tied eight times when Kentucky's Jack Tingle collided with blond-headed Wade Duym with 1:47 left to play. The St. John's freshman got off the floor dazed, but he refused to come out of the game and sank the second of two free throws to give the Redmen a 1-point lead, 47–46.

With fifty seconds on the clock, the Wildcats missed a hurried shot but were in position to rebound the miscue when fate interfered. Referee Pat Kennedy, trying to get out of the way, obstructed the Kentucky players as the ball slid out of bounds and was awarded to St. John's. As the Redmen attempted to freeze the ball with a 1-point lead, Ray Wertis spotted utility forward Don Wehr open under the basket for a layup and game clinching 3-pointer. The official's interference had inadvertently given St. John's the eventual victory.

As the Wildcats left the floor, Jack Tingle and Wilbur Schu brushed against Kennedy and heaped insults upon him. But even Kentucky had to accept the 48–45 final score. With Bowling Green and nationally ranked Kentucky out of the way, St. John's focused on DePaul and its All-American George Mikan. Lapchick again moaned about Mikan's advantage over Summer, hoping some magic would prevail.

Lapchick's coaching instincts were at work preparing for the final round of the NIT. Knowing DePaul was a heavy favorite and anxious to probe his players' desire to win, he decided to test them. "The NIT champion plays the winner of the NCAA Tournament in the Red Cross benefit game," he told his team, "and I wondered how many of you would be available to help out around the Garden," for the game, he implied. It was the Garden's practice to hire college athletes to help on game nights, but it only took seconds for Lapchick's ploy to sink in.

"What do you mean work, Coach?" Hy Gotkin, who was determined to get there, answered. "We're going to be playing that night!" Although the experts didn't think it was possible, the Hollywood script called for St. John's to stop DePaul's All-American and win the game. Realizing that Coach Ray Meyer anticipated a slow down, Lapchick decided to run with the fast-breaking Blue Devils.

As the team prepared for DePaul, Lapchick took Summer aside and gave him a tip. "Joe Burns is officiating the game," Lapchick instructed, "and he likes making the big call." Summer looked confused and asked, "What's that?" Lapchick smiled. "Mr. Burns comes from the school of dramatics; he feels he's part of the night's entertainment and wants some of the game's spotlight," Lapchick explained. "You got the picture, Ivy?" Summer, a bright student, nodded.

Lapchick instructed his freshman to stand directly behind Mikan and hold his ground. Since the huge center used his elbows to dig into an opponent's chest when pivoting in the low post, Lapchick reasoned the smaller, slighter Summer would fly back like the scarecrow from *The Wizard of Oz* and draw fouls. Burns's theatrics would take care of the rest.

When the centers lined up, Summer, all 190 pounds of nervousness with vertical strips of white adhesive tape holding his eyeglasses in place, stuttered, "Gggood gggame, Mr. Mikan," as Burns flipped up the opening tap, which Mikan easily controlled. As Lapchick predicted, Mikan bulled into Summer on more than one occasion in the first half, and Burns, as if on cue, made the big call, racing to the opposite end of the court, flapping his whistle and his arms as if he were alerting the National Guard of an invasion. The game was close at halftime with St. John's holding a slim 26–24 edge. The second half seesawed after DePaul took an early lead, 29–28. Five minutes into the second half, Mikan again muscled into Summer, committed his fourth and final foul and forcing him out of the game, thus ending DePaul's chances to win. The loss of their All-American proved too much to overcome. For Lapchick, the dream sequence never seemed to end.

"I was under a doctor's care and taking medicine designed to quiet me down," Lapchick recalled. "But when Mikan fouled out," he remembered, "I suddenly realized we were going to win. It was too much." At that point, the coach passed out on the bench.

Lapchick sheepishly referred to the incident as the day he made coaching history when his Redmen put away one of the best teams in the country while he lost consciousness on the bench for more than eight minutes. He did not fall down or look like he was suffering a heart attack but just slumped in his seat, as if he were enjoying a midday nap. Several minutes expired before anyone noticed him. Father Browne alerted the team physician who rushed to the bench to revive him.

When the doctor reached into his bag and broke a smelling salt pellet under Lapchick's nose, the coach kicked his legs forward and slowly began to shake his head, acting as if he didn't want to be awakened from a peaceful dream of his Redmen winning the NIT. "The next thing I knew was that we had a 12-point lead with less than five minutes left."

Gotkin, concerned about his coach, had circled the bench, trying to get a reading on his health. "Are you all right, Coach?" he yelled out as he dribbled, "are you all right?" After the final horn trumpeted the upset, Lapchick realized the strategy had worked. Still groggy, he accepted the winner's trophies and watches, hugged Bill Kotsores, who was the tournament's MVP, and tried smiling for photographers. It was a triumph in perseverance all around. Later he joked with the sportswriters about how many coaches win a national title while out cold during its critical stretch. Lapchick was heard moaning afterwards how he, "set coaching back fifty years." While he was "making history," his Redmen set an unmatched record with back-to-back NIT championships in 1943 and 1944.

When Lapchick was rehired at St. John's in 1956, he reminisced in an interview about the 1944 NIT. Although underdogs, "I apparently convinced the boys in the dressing room it was possible," Lapchick confided. "I certainly didn't convince myself."

During an interview the next day, he was still euphoric. "It's a wonderful day," he said as he watched the heavy downpour of March weather. To the victorious coach, "The sun is shining brightly and everything's wonderful," he insisted. Lapchick kissed his wife, Bobbie, patted Bingo, his smooth-haired terrier, and climbed into his blue Oldsmobile to head to St. John's to answer the barrage of congratulatory phone calls that flooded its switchboard. Nothing could dampen his mood.

Lapchick's Redmen had a further honor bestowed on them. As repeat NIT winners, they again had the honor of playing in the Red Cross Game for the national title. St. John's would meet Utah, the NCAA champs, in the Garden. As college basketball's popularity increased, fan interest gravitated toward a natural climax to decide a true national champion between the winners of each tournament.

There was nothing more important in basketball to Joe Lapchick than talking about the tournament. He had a way of making the NIT sound as if a player had inherited a large sum of money or had a date with a GI pinup or a Miss America. The word was something special in his lexicon. The NIT, with its assortment of top teams playing in the nation's highly visible Madison Square Garden, was where Lapchick would establish his coaching reputation.

By the 1970s, the NCAA's domination of college basketball had produced "March Madness" and helped solidify its power over college sports. Today's sixty-four-team tournament is recognized as the best and most lucrative, while the NIT ranks a distant second. But no tournament touched the NIT in the 1940s, when the Garden rocked to capacity. It was only matched in importance by New York's baseball rivalry among the Yankees, Dodgers, and Giants. College play by LIU, St. John's, and CCNY could evoke neighborhood battles similar to those caused by fanatics who swore the Yanks' DiMaggio was better than the Giants' Mel Ott, and that both were superior to all the lovable Bums of Brooklyn.

Unlike the year before, both St. John's and Utah were surprise winners and drank from Cinderella's slipper. Utah had been knocked out of the first round of the NIT by Kentucky, but when Arkansas dropped out of the NCAA, the team was asked to fill in. Led by freshman forward Arnie Ferrin, Utah defeated St. John's. The reward for the Redmen was the satisfaction that the Red Cross added $41,000 to its war chest. Although disappointed, Lapchick was proud of his team and gained experience battling for national titles. He was where he had always wanted to be. He was now talked about as one of the country's best coaches.

Lapchick's 1944 NIT champions took a special place in his memories. They were a team of underclassmen who by the middle of the season molded into winners with Hy Gotkin leading the way. Sophomore Bill Kotsores matured enough by March to be voted the NIT's MVP. Even with the loss of Dick McGuire, Lapchick's Redmen persevered. The war years had generated a certain magic. "There is no doubt," Tommy Holmes of the *Brooklyn Eagle* insisted, "this tournament stamped the old Celtic a master of his profession." Joe Lapchick stood a little taller in the spotlight of much-deserved praise.

After the season, Gotkin received a letter he kept all these years. Apologizing for not attending his wedding, Lapchick used the opportunity to tell the floor leader what he thought of him. Lapchick described several former players as "leaders of men with more than a bit of character." Fuzzy Levane, Dutch Garfinkel, the deceased Frank Haggerty, and Larry Baxter were outstanding leaders who were a credit to the school. Lapchick placed them in his "inner circle," players who seemed to read his mind. "But today," he wrote, "I nominate you to captain all the players who ever played for me," he wrote, an exceptional honor bestowed on the humble floor leader. He never forgot Gotkin, who proved to be a loyal supporter and later helped with scouting and recruiting. There was little Gotkin wouldn't do for him. Their bond lasted a lifetime. How often does a coach tell one of his players, "You're the best."

O

More had come out of the postseason play than initially met the eye. College basketball, unlike baseball, needed major rule changes. The game's deficiencies generated enough heated discussion to recommend them. With the support of the National Association of Basketball Coaches, the National Rules Committee went into action. In spring 1944, the most important change was the goaltending rule, which awarded 2 points to the offensive team if a defensive player interfered with a shot on goal "on its downward flight." The rule attempted to neutralize the advantage tall players had standing in front of the basket. With players like Otten, Mikan, and Oklahoma's 7'0" Bob Kurland, attention was drawn to basketball players' size.

With the change, shooting percentages increased along with a player's confidence around the basket.

The St. John's-DePaul NIT also caused the rules committee to increase personal fouls from four to five before a player was disqualified. Mikan, fouling out early in the game, brought attention to the fact that players were bigger, stronger, and more likely to commit more fouls. Basketball, unlike football or baseball, could remove a player for rule infractions. The new rule hoped to keep better players in the game longer.

Joe Lapchick's career mirrored basketball's national growth. When he started at St. John's in 1936, he joined its popularity, solidly fixing himself on basketball's map. As the well-publicized coach of St. John's, with a historical link to the game's inception, Lapchick became identified with the most respected figures in the game. As his career dramatically grew during the war years, he realized he was not only competing with the best teams in the nation, but also with a host of outstanding New York schools. New York overshadowed America's other basketball hotbeds, like Indiana, Kentucky, and Ohio, by producing great players and outstanding teams. Schools like CCNY with Nat Holman, Clair Bee at LIU, Howard Cann and his Purple Violets of NYU, as well as Manhattan, Fordham, and even Brooklyn College, were vying for New York's bragging rights.

A successful coach at a pivotal New York school, Lapchick was swept up by the game's glamorous momentum as well as its media exposure. The national attention he experienced coaching in Madison Square Garden provided a showcase for his many marketable qualities that Garden basketball impresario Ned Irish admired. Lapchick's NIT success and close relationship with the sports press guaranteed his next employer positive media exposure.

At forty-four, he was a successful coach with a likable personality— an attractive combination. He was also a humble man who couldn't help wondering what was next. Lapchick was becoming the obvious choice to lead Irish's postwar expansion into professional basketball, a dream that needed New York's validation. After the war, the rumors that Lapchick would return to the professional ranks gained momentum. He seemed a perfect fit, but what did Ned Irish think? It was a pleasant way to occupy Lapchick's insomnia.

Chapter 6

108th Street, Rockaway Beach

Basketball has always been something special to the kids of New York's bustling streets. Two decades ago, it fed the dreams of the Irish athletes on famous playgrounds, such as the one on 108th Street in Rockaway, Queens. Those playgrounds produced Bob Cousy and Dick McGuire and other superb playmakers.

—Pete Axthelm,
The City Game, 1970

I played and coached in the NBA for fifteen years, earning a total of $150,000. The game was bigger than the buck. We would go anyplace to play. We never feared hurting our bodies. We played for the fun of the game. During the summers we'd go to Rockaway Beach and play 108th Street.

—Carl Braun, Knicks,
1950s NBA all-star

○

Sunday was the day. And the 108th Street Park in Rockaway Beach, Queens, was the place where New York's finest three-on-three summer playground basketball was played below the rim but above the eyebrows. The netless rim, with its faded battleship-gray, tinny backboard attached to a pole, attracted some of the game's biggest stars. Its black asphalt half-court was nothing special, measuring fifty by thirty-five and bordered by weathered white paint, and a four-foot screen fence by the swings and monkey bars. All the games were played on the first basket past the entrance with any orange-looking rubber ball that happened to be around.

It was the 1950s, with kids dreaming of the chance to go against some of Joe Lapchick's Knicks. They fantasized about playing in Madison Square Garden and swishing a game-winning shot like Vince Boryla did with his two-hand bomb or snaking up a soft teetering Carl Braun fall-away jump shot. These dreams filled a tiny beach park with kids lined up to show their stuff.

Joe Lapchick's love of and dedication to basketball were contagious. Carl Braun was a Knick who caught it, going wherever there was competition. On any Sunday, NBA pros, polished collegians, and hungry high school kids like me butted heads in three-on-three play for bragging rights.

During my St. Francis Prep days in the early 1950s, I hitched rides to the beach with other hoop dreamers. To play, I called "next," and waited like in a bakery. When my number came up, I played. On different Sundays, most of Lapchick's Knicks showed up, from Braun to Dick and Al McGuire, Connie Simmons, Ray Lumpp, and Ernie Vandeweghe. The park would occasionally find NBA greats like Dolph Schayes, Tommy Heinsohn, and LIU All-American Sherman White. These were the marquee names, the ones we saw on WPIX or heard announcer Marty Glickman rave about on the radio.

During the summer season, college and high school hotshots tried "holding court" against "the names." It was the wannabes way of force-feeding fame by outdrawing the gunfighters. It was different then. Pros played with little fear of injury or bruised reputations. There was no need to pay to see them. Anyone could reach out to touch Boston Celtic Bob Cousy or the Knicks' Ernie Vandeweghe. They weren't deities worrying about big agent deals or jumping teams; just guys having summer fun. And they were my heroes.

By the early 1950s, the New York Knickerbockers and their legendary coach were in their prime. Lapchick was molding a young team of primarily New York players into serious contenders for the NBA crown. Most of them were comfortable playing New York basketball, which Lapchick played and taught throughout his career. Rockaway Beach's 108th Street Park was an early example of what made the game popular and effective in New York. The community, in its own way, influenced the way Lapchick's teams would play in the 1950s.

Unknowingly, what attracted my neighborhood friends and me to the park was classic New York basketball, possibly the most sophisticated style of play in the city.

Joe Lapchick and other pioneer basketball legends had been teaching it for years. When he taught his Knicks to patiently "Let the ball do the work" and to move without the ball, they were two basics of the game that grew out of the clockless era that made New York different from the Midwesterner's run and shoot. The 108th Street Park indoctrinated disciples of its tradition, helping to make New York's game famous.

Ray Lumpp, former New York University player and Knicks regular, remembers the park's sound play. "You stuck to the basics—weave, pick and roll, give and go, look for the open man, no crosscourt passes. When you get a rebound, don't bring the ball down or they'll swipe it away. Above all, move without the ball." Added to this was the aggressive defense that was necessary to survive at the beach. This was New York basketball at its best.

There was a passion that developed in Rockaway basketball that made it exciting. It was as if 108th Street was a filling station where New York–style players came to get their batteries charged and then returned to their communities all over the metropolitan area to spread how the game should be played. And the prince of play was Dick McGuire.

Dick McGuire was my hero. He seemed to embody the qualities of a champion and let his actions speak for him. He treated everyone the same; if a new player showed up in the park, an unspoken bond was created.

Shy and self-effacing, he didn't waste time talking, but when he did, it had a rough, gravelly timbre to it, almost like a low bark from a dog. Those around him noticed Dick either didn't know or had forgotten people's names and would make them up. When I went to the beach with neighborhood friend and future St. John's teammate Butch Dellecave, he became "Cal" while I was "Al," because he mistook my name for "Al Fieri."

Future St. John's great Bob Zawoluk came to the park while still at St. Francis Prep. He had grown to the point where his jeans were several inches up his leg and he looked like a hick. Dick started calling him "Zeke," and the name stuck.

Occasionally, Dick played left-handed to emphasize the importance of both hands in the game. I never forgot that lesson and taught it when I later coached. Dick was a Rockaway five-star matinee performer and became the park's best example of New York basketball.

Almost biblical in character, McGuire never boasted about "being the greatest" or listed his accomplishments with Joe Lapchick's Knicks or all the other places where he starred. When questioned why the passing game blossomed at 108th Street, he deflected his talent. "We weren't as good as the modern player who could hit the jump shot," he humbly answered. "We had to look for the open man."

McGuire's spectacular ballhandling got Joe Lapchick to repeat that Dick "created plays I couldn't diagram on a blackboard." Clips of McGuire's play have to be seen to be appreciated. His joy was distributing the ball and making teammates happy. Magic flowed from his quick hands and mind, and he had exceptional peripheral vision. "He was two plays ahead of everyone else," Rockaway favorite Buddy Ackerman remembered. Tricky Dick's kinetic energy blurred the ball instinctively from his hands to its intended receiver faster than the defense could react. "The thrill of playing against Dick," Ackerman recalled, "was not blocking his shots, but breaking up one of his passes."

One hot summer Sunday, after weeks of coming to the park and watching McGuire and the other talented players, I finally got my chance center stage. Dick and Al McGuire holding court needed a third player. "Hey Al," Dick mistakenly called me. "Do you want to play?"

Do I want to play! Me, a fifteen-year-old kid play with two NBA pros! I nonchalantly stuttered, "SSSure!" At 6'2", 190 pounds, I was bubbling with size and good intentions. As a high school sophomore, I told myself, I was at least physically in their league.

I tried acting as if I belonged and almost pulled it off. I scored on several needle-threaded bounce passes from Dick. He never yelled, but his muted message was clear, especially to a rookie. Dick taught by actions, a simple nod of his head or a side glance telegraphed when to cut to the basket. I quickly learned his telepathy and that he only passed to a cutting player.

While Dick stoically performed his magic, Al was more likely to ream you out for poor play. "Dumb play, kid," the younger, dark-haired McGuire said after I was picked off and let my man score an easy layup. I felt embarrassed, as if my grammar school teacher had scolded me. In spite of my limited contributions, the McGuires managed to run off six games before Knicks teammate Connie Simmons tapped in a loose ball and beat us. As my moment in the Rockaway sun came to an end, I drifted off to the water fountain by the entrance and walked into the cool beach-front breeze of oblivion until next Sunday.

Dick McGuire had no ego problems. Not noted for scoring, he later made a career "setting the table" for Knicks teammates. Knicks work-horse Harry Gallatin was "smart enough to keep his eyes on my brother," Al McGuire pointed out. "If you got open, he'd always get you the ball."

Gallatin never believed they were brothers. "Mrs. McGuire," he once asked, "are you sure no one left Al on your doorstep?" Although they loved basketball, the comparison between the two ended there. Dick was older, silent, and gifted. Al was less talented, impressed with Irish charm, and possessed the overachiever's energy. Seemingly unemotional, Dick was a perfect foil for Al, who argued and kicked air wearing (Lapchick's sponsored) Kinney's revolutionary red low-cut sneakers. Dick avoided what Al faced head on. Dick threw perfect but clumsily handled passes and would bark out, "My mistake, my mistake." When provoked, Al was more likely to swing fists, which broke noses and loosened teeth.

Ironically, Al is the McGuire most modern basketball lovers immediately know. Al worked his way into major college coaching and won the 1977 NCAA championship while at Marquette. He later gained greater fame as arguably the best college color television analyst in the business. When McGuire teamed with the well-known Billy Packer, they were difficult to beat.

O

Builder Robert Moses never would have believed his work shaped the history of New York basketball. "The 1939 World's Fair had a hand in it," according to Normie Ochs, a park pioneer whose family owned the delicatessen on 109th Street, one block from the McGuire family's bar, and a lifelong friend of the McGuires.

"The City had to build access roads to the fair; one was this road right along the boardwalk where the buses had to come, and at the end of that new road the city built a playground." Unwittingly, the city had built the new park that would become the incubator of New York's basketball talent.

Ochs and the McGuires benefited from another twist of fate. With the new park came Jerry Schlicter, a local elementary teacher who doubled as a basketball guru in the green fatigues of New York City's Parks Department. "Jerry was a basketball junkie who ran leagues and clinics," Ochs recollected. The parkie turned Rockaway kids away from baseball and football and onto basketball. They were hooked.

But the chemistry needed a final touch. It appeared in the form of a wispy, 6'0", 149-pound bolt of lightning named Bobby Wanzer. The young, future Rochester Royals NBA star and Hall of Famer mingled among city people attracted to Rockaway's ocean. "Wanzer was Schlicter's model of what he wanted us to be," Ochs remembered.

"Wanzer came to the park in a group," Al McGuire recalled, "and they all wore their Benjamin Franklin city championship jackets." That was the way it was. "You never showed up by yourself; it was always an entourage." Through Wanzer's appearances, word spread about the park like a hot Broadway ticket.

"My family had a bungalow," recalled Wanzer. Cottages were rented for the season, which lasted from Memorial to Labor Day, and usually went for $300 to $500. Rockaway originally attracted the city's working-class Irish, who looked to get to the shore to enjoy what Al McGuire described as "seashells and balloons."

"We rented one almost every year," Wanzer recalled, "and I started gravitating to 108th Street with fellows I grew up with. You were going to show your neighborhood was the best, but I always remember if you lost a game—go swimming. There was good competition and you had to play your best."

Wanzer and the McGuires' talent often allowed them to play longer. "If you were an outstanding player with a big reputation, you'd probably get asked to play again," Wanzer recalled.

After losing there were choices other than swimming. Some kicked the four-foot chain-link fence that separated the court from the swings in absolute disgust, while others drank at the water fountain. Smart kids learned to force matchsticks into the spout to get the water to shoot up.

Others climbed the playground's monkey bars for a better, cooler view of the action. The outdoor shower at Fitzgerald's Bar, fifty yards up 108th Street, attracted the college players. They drenched themselves before downing a few beers at the bar. The more energetic walked farther up 108th Street to the corner of Rockaway Beach Boulevard for a cold 10-cent Schaefer's at McGuire's. Life was simple, and after hard play, refreshing.

There were few bent rims in the 1950s. "Only through vandalism," Al McGuire remembered. Basketball in the past was played differently, with more finesse and below the rim. When Lapchick spoke at a function in the 1960s, he pointed out the lost art of ballhandling. "We shoot better, jump higher, but pass poorly," the old pro insisted. Lost was the fundamental play so reminiscent of Rockaway Beach. Many war veterans who played there knew the game and would have pleased Lapchick with their basic skills.

Rockaway Ball was different. There were no slam dunks, 360-degree spins, or 3-point shots; rather it was a chess match of intuitive smarts coupled with aggressive quickness for possession of the ball, and a feeling that this was the way the game should be played. If I played three-man ball today, I would pass and cut or screen away, something today's player would not instinctively do.

As a result of players like Wanzer, and then through the influence of Dick McGuire, the emphasis was on clever playmaking. What McGuire loved was having a teammate step toward him, then change direction and cut to the basket so he could "thread the needle" with a bounce pass that would be waiting for the cutter to cash in for 2 points.

To "play smart" was the character of the park. That meant if you had a hot shooter on your team, you set screens to launch his set shot. Today's 3-point bonus encourages outside shooting, but Rockaway players instinctively looked for the open man rolling off a pick. That would be the smart play and make the gallery murmur its approval.

While not every player was a leaper, most knew how to position themselves defensively to block out or deny a second shot or rebound. At Rockaway, smart play was expected; it was a calling card. It came with the territory. The highest accolade was that you "knew the game."

O

One Sunday I witnessed a remarkable piece of Rockaway lore that would get no ink in today's basketball coverage. A typical Rockaway game was in progress when I arrived with my Greenpoint, Brooklyn, group. Mickey Hannon, a former Seton Hall player who had his career cut short by injuries, was guarding a well-known 1950s Fordham guard named Buzzy Larkin.

Larkin was a smart, 6'1" city guard with brown curly hair, an average build, and slightly better-than-average speed but with excellent quickness. Hannon, out of John Adams High School in Howard Beach, Queens, had set a freshman scoring record of more than 600 points in the late 1940s at Seton Hall. At 6'3", 200 pounds, he was supposed to have all the skills of the period's super players. But then fate intervened, and in a freak accident while getting off a train, he slipped and severely damaged his knee. What looked like a promising career was added to the junk pile of what could have been.

But on this Sunday, the prematurely gray Hannon, armed with a constricting knee brace, showed the full house of gallery critics circling the court that while his college career may have ended, his instinctive skills were still present and intact.

Not once, but twice within a span of three minutes, Hannon, with all the quickness of a pickpocket, swiped the ball from Larkin. It came not off the dribble the way most of today's steals are recorded, but while he was guarding Larkin head up. He just plucked the ball out of the hands of one of the city's best handlers, making the experienced Fordham guard look foolish. Hannon proved he could still play, that he, too, knew the game. To a fifteen-year-old, it was circus magic never forgotten.

There was a tradition at 108th Street that was always respected. When players came from all over to play—from the city, New Jersey, with college and high school friends from out-of-town—no one interrupted the focus of the game. It would be as if a crucial free throw was being shot in the final of the NIT, and a ten-year-old kid dribbled to the other basket and started a game of HORSE.

Each neighborhood's blacktop had its own peculiarities, its own folklore. "There were only two baskets in the park," Al McGuire remembers, "but no one ever played at the far end." Ochs agreed. "You had to play at the one by the entrance gate." That one basket was center stage, like Carnegie Hall, and no one dared disturb it. "The remarkable thing about it," McGuire added, "no matter how many people there were waiting, they didn't play at the other basket, and I've seen it go to eleven or twelve winners games called. I don't know what it was, but the other basket was never used; never, never used."

The games had other unwritten laws everyone followed. "Always seven and out, seven baskets and out, that's what you played, and winners out," McGuire explained, which allowed a sharpshooter who got hot to run the table without opponents getting off a shot. Seven baskets won, but a team had to win by two baskets.

That meant if your team scored, it kept the ball until it missed a shot or turned it over. After a possession change, the ball had to be taken past the free throw line before a try to score and, after a score, the ball was put into play from under the basket. Today, in many park centers, the ball can be shot immediately after it is retrieved, creating more of a jumping game around the rim. That was not the case in Rockaway Beach.

The rules of 108th Street maintained order. Without referees, play ran amazingly smoothly. The Rockaway code encouraged an honor system, and all followed it. "You called your own fouls, sometimes on yourself," Lumpp recalled. "I had the habit," Rockaway regular Buddy Ackerman recalled, "of saying 'sorry' after committing a foul." The weekends at the park were "prime time," according to Al McGuire. "You knew here come the real gunfighters."

Ackerman was a local "gunslinger" who could run the table. He attended LIU on a scholarship in the early 1950s, where he teamed up with 6'11" center Ray Felix and lasted for a thirty-two-game "cup of coffee" with the Knicks. Ackerman was a 6'0", blond, curly-haired 175-pounder who became one of 108th Street's most effective players.

Buddy had a sneaky, quick one-hander that had "home court" written all over it. He knew every inch of the court, especially the backboard's dead spots for his bank shots, and he could probably shoot in the dark. The legendary Rockaway resident's soft one-hander often teetered on the rim, like a tire developing a flat, before flopping in. As a name at the beach, Buddy never worried about losing. He knew someone would always pick up his option.

"108th Street had its pecking order," McGuire insisted, which is so true in every playground. Sunday was the big day, the huge day, the day when the older guys would come. McGuire remembered all the excitement as a skinny ten-year-old. "So you would go to early mass at St. Camillus," the former Hall of Fame Marquette coach remembered, "go to eight or nine o'clock mass and go down to the 108th Street playground, get on a team, or get maybe fifth or sixth and wait for two of the better stars to come in and pick them on your team." This was the best way to stay on the court. If he was lucky, Al "stuck around" for three or four games.

"Then, as you got better when you'd go to high school," McGuire said with a smile on his face, "you'd go to a later mass, and when you'd come down to the park kids would run up and pick you." It was a cycle that pleased the budding St. John's Prep star and fed the confidence he constantly needed to compete.

"Finally, as you went to college and the pros, you went to the last mass—twelve fifteen—stayed in the back of church so you wouldn't get caught with the third collection," McGuire sheepishly admitted, "and then got your sneakers and kinda strutted down to the blacktop." As he entered the park, good high school players would rush over to ask Al to play.

"Then the years went by and now you're older. All of a sudden no one picks you," McGuire relates how it was for some old-timers who had passed their prime. "Now you have to make a decision: either give up basketball or go back to the eight o'clock mass!"

McGuire smiled with the tale he had told a thousand times but never tired of retelling. There was too much truth and nostalgia for him to ever let go of his roots, memories he frequently returned to in conversation and thought.

Unlike most other NBA teams, Lapchick's Knicks primarily came from New York with many working on their off-season skills in schoolyards and playgrounds like 108th Street. Dick McGuire and Ernie Vandeweghe, along with Carl Braun and Connie Simmons, had something in common besides being Long Island natives. Each of them loved the game enough to risk getting hurt to play as often as possible, to prepare for their pro season with Lapchick.

I'm sure the tall splinter of a coach never watched a three-man game at the beach but was happy it was there. It made his players competitive and ready to go in the fall. It was all part of the love affair he and the early New York pros had with the game, one that lasted a lifetime for them.

In the postwar era, 108th Street was the summertime playground in New York. To McGuire it was more. "It was really a happening, but you didn't realize it was a happening, you just thought it was the same all over. The park on 108th Street was before the parks in Bedford-Stuyvesant or

Harlem or Jamaica, Queens. Its blacktop may have been the original."
McGuire thought for a moment. "We didn't realize it then, but we were
laying the foundations of the modern NBA." Lapchick would have
agreed, especially after watching Dick McGuire and Bob Cousy play.

This was the world of the 1950s that Joe Lapchick and those who
enjoyed basketball found themselves in. The 108th Street park was the
summer-stock stage thousands of players used to audition, to measure
their talent while demonstrating their love of the game.

In the postwar period, Lapchick also found himself back in the professional game and, by the early 1950s, competing for the NBA's brass ring.
Many of the cast of characters who regularly made their way to the 108th
Street park were in some way connected to the tall coach either as players
or fans. It was an exciting time, one where Joe Lapchick, too, could compete as a coach against the best there was in professional basketball.

"108th Street was the mecca of basketball, like the 49th and 8th Avenue Madison Square Garden of its time," to Al McGuire. "You might
have played in Boston, Philly, or Chicago, but the trip was really to play
in the Garden. In some way, in a player's mind, that's what 108th Street
was, and if you couldn't play reasonably, you weren't going to get the
chance unless it was your ball."

Chapter 7
A Vote of Confidence

Joe Lapchick tapped his fingers on the end table in Ned Irish's outer office as he waited to meet with the basketball guru of Madison Square Garden. The cushioned, tan leather chair made it hard for him to sit erect, but he tried not wrinkling his suit jacket as he flipped through the *New York Times* he borrowed from the receptionist's desk.

The headlines on the March sports page discussed West Virginia's elimination of St. John's from the 1946 National Invitation Tournament the night before. The coach was disappointed with the loss, but after cooling down Irish buttonholed him in the Garden runway and suggested they meet.

"You can go in now, Coach," the conservative-looking secretary said, awaking him from his daydreaming.

"Hello, Joe," Irish greeted in his most positive tone as they shook hands. After talk of the loss, Irish got to the point of their meeting. "Coach, I'm sure you've heard of the new professional league that is starting up." Of course, Lapchick knew of the rumors and was interested in finding out more. "Yes, I have, Mr. Irish," was the coach's simple reply.

"I will head the New York team, and I want you to coach it," the executive stated.

Lapchick tried to harness his excitement. This was a chance to return to the pros, something he knew he wanted. "I'm flattered, Mr. Irish," the old pro finally got out without stumbling. Irish looked carefully at

Lapchick to gauge his true interest. The New York franchise would be the league's most coveted coaching position. It would have financial backing, the best facility, and the largest metropolitan fan base. It was a dream come true for Joe Lapchick.

Irish wanted Lapchick in charge. The general manager had the right to expect a winner with Lapchick's professional and college success. After he emphasized Lapchick's authority and promised that he would be the highest-paid coach in professional basketball, Lapchick accepted the offer. "Together we'll make New York the best franchise," he concluded as he reached out to shake his new boss's hand. With the new job tucked in his pocket, Joe Lapchick floated out of the Garden, looking for a telephone booth to call Bobbie with the exciting news. The kid from the Hollow, the "Big Polack," as his sportswriter friends liked to write, was now the coaching king of New York.

Before Lapchick took the Knicks job, he met with Father Rebholz at St. John's. He owed much to the priest, and he wanted to complete the coming season before joining the Knicks. Irish had agreed. By the end of World War II, soldier-athletes were returning to civilian life, and Lapchick was anxious to get to unfinished business before he turned his attention to the pros. With playmaker Dick McGuire and 6'9" All-America center Harry Boykoff returning to school, he dreamed of another national championship, but it was not to be. Although St. John's would finish 16–7, it was beaten in the first round of the 1947 NIT by North Carolina State, 61–55, and Lapchick was disappointed that the Boykoff-led team didn't do better. But in spite of his disappointment, Joe Lapchick was excited.

In May 1946 in a letter to Joe Barreras, a former St. John's player, he tells of the formation of "a professional league" that was "going to be a honey." He had heard more than talk of the new basketball league kicking off, one backed by a group of hockey arena owners. What really thrilled him was that Ned Irish, the head of Madison Square Garden, had secretly tapped him to coach the New York franchise in the new Basketball Association of America. The formal announcement would come later.

O

In 1946, the *New York Times* headlined America's increased interest in sports. The nation was told, "SPORTS POPULARITY HIT ALL-

TIME PEAK." Having the means to do so, Americans joined the culture of entertainment. A nation that had experienced Spartan denial broke loose from the Depression and a world war. While baseball and college basketball were popular, hockey was gaining traction, and professional football formed a second competing league. Boxing's appeal filled local club halls and forced metropolitan arenas to promote additional matches. With sports booming, arenas looked to fill open dates, and the possibility of pro basketball was discussed.

Large numbers of veterans who had played competitive basketball in the service were now attending colleges. The media was about to explode with radio broadcasts of home and away games, and the advent of TV would eventually provide publicity and the financial means to expand sports markets. The enormous interest in college basketball caused hockey arena owners to huddle over starting a nationwide professional league to help pay bills and allow fans to watch former college favorites play. Boston's Walter Brown and Al Sutphin of Cleveland, hockey arena managers, and the *New York Journal's* sports editor, Max Kase, sparked rumors of a new league that ignited curiosity. Arthur Wirtz, head of Chicago Stadium, seemed to have the ear of Midwestern owners and quickly drew other hockey moguls into the mix. With other major cities getting involved, New York's Ned Irish and Madison Square Garden took notice.

In June 1946 in New York's Commodore Hotel, a new eleven-team professional league, called the Basketball Association of America, the forerunner of the NBA, was formed. Irish was voted New York's crown-jewel franchise, with its much needed media power to energize the new league. No facility could match the Garden's magic; no franchise could touch its glamour. With New York, the new league's chances of survival improved, and Irish knew that.

A popular 1940s magazine accurately described Ned Irish as "Basketball's Big Wheel." His control of the college and eventually professional game in the biggest and most prestigious market in the country placed Irish on top of basketball's world. His power exceeded other franchise heads. But there was much that never reached the surface with this upwardly mobile executive.

Ned Irish, with tortoiseshell rimmed glasses resting on his forehead, always seemed agitated. A balding head, reminiscent of a monk in a friary, topped his 5'10" medium-build body, but that could not confuse him for a gentle soul. A smile was not something the general manager liked to sport often in public. He picked his friends carefully, and trust and self-esteem were issues he wrestled with his whole life. He was an Ivy Leaguer from the not-so-exclusive wilds of Glens Falls, New York. Gold cuff links sparkled from his wrists, while a bright fob from a vest pocket watch designated his Penn fraternity. A well-tailored blue suit framed his trademark light-blue dress shirt with a white collar. He was the best example of an elitist—or the invention of one.

As the nation's largest metropolis, New York served as both the media and publishing capital. The sports coverage of college teams by ten metropolitan newspapers stimulated interest. More than a half-million fans annually packed Madison Square Garden to watch college basketball, and the continued postwar attention caused Irish to focus on pro basketball. Although his primary concern was the college game, he felt he could best protect his interest by controlling New York's pro team.

Once the franchise was awarded, its name was democratically selected. "We all placed slips of paper into a hat," Irish's assistant Fred Podesta recalled. Irish, Lester Scott of the publicity department, and several Garden executives each made several choices, but the majority favored Knickerbockers, while Knicks worked well for fans and the media.

Knickerbocker conjured up a rich seventeenth-century Dutch New York tradition that went back to its original settlers. Father Knickerbocker was a generic name used by writers like Washington Irving in the early 1800s to describe a typical New Yorker. For their colors, the new Knicks selected orange and blue, the popular colors of the 1939 New York World's Fair and those of the future New York Mets.

All of the new franchises, with the exception of the Washington Capitols, had direct ties with professional hockey. New York, Boston, Detroit, and Chicago had National Hockey League teams. The Knicks started with sixty scheduled games for the 1946–47 season with only a few played in Madison Square Garden. Because pro basketball carried less weight, it was forced to play around established attractions such as the circus, college basketball, and boxing. Even the Ice Capades evicted the new Knicks. Irish tried renting local college gyms, but in the end he settled for the 69th Regiment Armory. Since the Knicks were forced to play in the armory, Irish refurbished its seating, locker rooms, and lighting and replaced the floor. While Garden tickets sold from $1 for general admission to $5 for cushioned loge seats, armory prices ranged from $1 to $3.50.

Besides good intentions and large arenas, some magnetic force was needed to generate the BAA owners' dream. The most unlikely solution appeared in the diminutive form of Yale attorney Maurice Podoloff, the league's first commissioner. Although slightly taller than five feet and not athletic, he nevertheless had experience with professional hockey franchises. But his strength was showing owners how to survive on a shoestring.

With his business sense and tactful ways, the Ivy League attorney manipulated owners by acting like a shipwrecked captain on a lifeboat with limited rations. Only with utmost frugality would they survive. Under his direction, players took a backseat, and their requests tabled while Podoloff and the owners huddled to solve financial issues. Besides money issues, the new league had to contend with a shortage of talent. The better players were stocked in the Midwest.

In 1937 the National Basketball League had surfaced in the Midwest loaded with experienced talent. The league's upbeat style spotlighted Bobby McDermott, George Mikan, and Bobby Davies. But the NBL's problem was it lacked big city markets and financial backing to become more than a regional attraction. With the exception of Indianapolis's Butler Fieldhouse, most NBL facilities were high school gyms or armories with seating capacity for only three to four thousand.

Frank Kautsky, the successful Indianapolis grocer, was a typical NBL owner. His Kautsky AC, which resembled more a semipro team, hired ex-college players with full-time jobs who played mostly on weekends and were paid cash. Other franchises represented Oshkosh, Sheboygan, and Hammond, cities most Americans couldn't find on a map. In spite of its quality play, the NBL couldn't shake its small town image, but despite its problems the league survived into the postwar era.

Crucial help came to the BAA from Boston's Walter Brown and Eddie Gottlieb of the Philadelphia Warriors, along with the credibility of Joe Lapchick. With his reputation as a pioneer Celtics player and successful and congenial college coach, Lapchick was a natural choice for the new league and New York. When he promised sportswriters that the new league would succeed, they believed him. It was the assurance Podoloff and Ned Irish desperately needed.

The Knicks interim coach was Neil Cohalan, the former Manhattan College mentor, who worked closely with Lapchick to make sure the Knicks were prepared. Lapchick accompanied the Knicks to their first training camp in the Catskill Mountains, watched most of the Knicks home games, and scouted rival clubs. Thrilled that the team made the playoffs, he traveled with the team to Cleveland for the first round of games. But while there, the old pro's loyalty to his players intervened to make sure Harry Boykoff would be settled in his professional career.

O

"Hello," Joe Lapchick answered as he rushed, annoyed and dripping wet, from the shower to answer the early morning phone call in his Cleveland hotel room. The Knicks had made the first Basketball Association of America playoff, and Lapchick wanted to see his team play the Cleveland Rebels. But because of the early hour, and since it was April 1, 1947, he thought it might be a prank.

"Hi, Mr. Lapchick. It's Julie Rivlin, coach of the new Toledo team," the anxious voice responded. The Toledo Jeeps was a recent entry into the competitive National Basketball League. "How can I help you, Coach?" Lapchick got to the point. "We're interested in your big guy, Harry Boykoff, and would like to discuss his future."

Boykoff had played his last game at St. John's, with both coach and player making plans for careers in professional basketball. Lapchick was signed with the Knicks, while the big center, who was getting married, was still undecided where to play.

"Why don't we meet in your hotel for breakfast, in say about an hour, at 9:00 A.M., and talk," Rivlin suggested. Lapchick agreed. Boykoff had been everyone's All-American as a sophomore when he led St. John's to a national championship with a stunning performance in the 1943 NIT. He walked away with MVP honors and the respect of the basketball world. But in spite of his height, Boykoff joined the army for the next two years. After the war, it was obvious something was missing. Heavier, slower, and less-focused, Boykoff showed only glimpses of his former self. But this did not stop Lapchick from helping him sign a pro contract.

But on one night in March against St. Francis, just prior to the NIT, the big center made everyone take notice. Boykoff felt everything was right in warm-ups and seemed his old self as he poured in 54 points, setting the St. John's as well as the Madison Square Garden record for most points in a college game. Boykoff was still considered one of the game's best big men.

"Jerry Bush and LIU's Jackie Goldsmith will be part of our club," Rivlin told Lapchick over scrambled eggs and coffee. Bush had been outstanding at St. John's while Goldsmith was considered one of the game's best two-hand set shooters. As Lapchick listened, he became more interested in the Toledo Jeeps.

"Where does Harry fit into your plans?" Lapchick asked as he lit a Chesterfield cigarette. The Toledo coach scratched his head and thought for a moment. "He would be the hub of our offense, the guy we would count on for inside scoring and rebounding." Lapchick liked the sound of the commitment. He knew Boykoff's limitations but also understood the risk new pro franchises faced in the 1940s. Pro basketball was struggling to survive, especially in small NBL Midwestern markets. Rivlin, however, convinced Lapchick he wanted the big man and could persuade the owners to meet "reasonable requests."

"Well, I don't think my requests are exactly reasonable by today's standards," Lapchick insisted. Then, using his index finger to point down to the checkered tablecloth, he said, "but they will have to be met if Harry is ever going to wear a Jeep uniform." He allowed his words to settle before speaking again and then outlined what it would take to sign the big center.

"Boykoff's money has to be guaranteed," Lapchick began. He often told barnstorming tales of local promoters who occasionally skipped town after a game, leaving a keg of beer in the locker room instead of their fee. To avoid this, Lapchick demanded Toledo owners place Boykoff's entire salary "which would have to be at least $10,000," with a reliable local bank before he would sign a contract.

Lapchick wanted Boykoff with a solid NBL team, and the Toledo Jeeps would do fine. He had played in the city near the end of his Celtics days and liked the town and the people. If Boykoff were sitting in the restaurant with them, he would insist on the same demands that protected his future, only the coach could say it better. "Kegs of beer don't go too far paying bills," he said smiling. Rivlin did some quick math with a pencil on the red-checkered tablecloth, froze for a moment, then answered, "I think we can do it." The old Celtic smiled again as he extended his large hand. "You've got a deal."

Boykoff not only had his salary protected, but also was hired as an accountant in the owner's firm. Boykoff, who later would do supporting acting roles in Hollywood, referred to his old coach as a *mensch*, the highest honor bestowed on a man in Jewish culture.

○

One of the problems of the new BAA league in 1946 was forming competitive teams within a $30,000 salary cap. Salaries averaged from $3,000 to $6,500, with most players making closer to $4,000. Since it was difficult to evaluate talent, most was done by educated guesses. And since players were frequently signed by "word of mouth" or tryouts, there was a "revolving door" quality to BAA rosters that resembled pick-up teams. Newspapers announced the signing of a new player who never appeared. By the first year's end, twenty-two players wore the Knicks' orange-and-blue woolen uniforms. Most teams had similar experiences. The league's uncertainty also applied to coaches. Former Celtic Dutch Dehnert was fired in Cleveland after a dozen games, while the Providence Steamrollers also had several coaches the first year.

While the NBL was stocked with seasoned, rough-hewn players, Irish and Boston Celtics' Walter Brown sought players from popular colleges. Irish reasoned fans would respond to former local college stars. He felt the college game was fresher, spirited, and more up-tempo than the old pro leagues that had the smell of beer halls. The New York fan in particular was familiar with the Garden's college game, and with proper packaging, Irish believed the BAA could emulate its success by distancing itself from the professional's rowdy reputation. The Knicks' general manager estimated that the ten thousand annual local graduates could help the new league's attendance.

Since the Garden hosted the nation's top colleges, Irish tried to sign what he believed were the best players. Quality local players Sonny Hertzberg, Ozzie Schectman, and Leo Gottlieb were added to his team. Much of the better talent, however, came from returning veterans who had played service ball. The Knicks' boss also preferred players with social standing. Princeton's Bud Palmer and Butch Van Breda Kolff, Colgate's Ernie Vandeweghe and Carl Braun, and Notre Dame's Vince Boryla, who played in the 1948 Olympics, were examples.

But not everyone rushed to play in the BAA. Many players questioned the low salaries, mediocre play, and few guaranteed contracts. The standard "make good" contract only paid a player after he made the team. Mike "Monk" McCarron led the Toronto Huskies in scoring the first year, but the Seton Hall graduate quit because pro teams couldn't meet his modest salary demands. Consequently, the early BAA trailed the established NBL's talent, with local colleges bragging about their superiority over the Knicks after scrimmaging them.

Some college stars favored the financial security offered by amateur industrial teams. Bob Kurland, the 7'0", Oklahoma State All-American, surprised many of the pro teams when he signed an American Amateur Union contract with the Phillips Sixty-Six Oilers, an Oklahoma-based petroleum company. Other collegians followed Kurland's example. And yet, when St. John's Fuzzy Levane joined with the NBL's Rochester Royals for the better than average rate of $5,000 for five months' work, it was ten times his father's $25 weekly salary.

The BAA tried to avoid competitive bidding for talent by holding its first player draft in 1947. To help local attendance, the BAA also introduced "territorial picks," which permitted teams to pick outstanding local players. Dick Holub, the 6'7" center from LIU, was the Knicks' first territorial pick, and in 1949, it selected St. John's Dick McGuire. In 1955, Philadelphia's Eddie Gottlieb convinced Podoloff that Wilt Chamberlain, who played for Overbrook High in Philadelphia and later for distant Kansas, fell under the Warriors' territorial rights.

As teams stocked their rosters, some faced problems with their arenas, which were old and in need of repair, or faced a variety of other indignities. While BAA cities attracted fans, funding was not available to update arenas, and Podoloff preached patience. Boston Garden and Chicago Stadium matched Garden seating, but needed work, and cow palaces like the Baltimore Coliseum had to be replaced. However, despite a lack of luxury features, the old arenas' character and war stories made them memorable.

None of the original franchises had arenas like Madison Square Garden, but if the circus, ice show, or Globetrotters came to town, the Knicks and other teams were evicted to local high school gyms or to dimly lit armories. Irish didn't make it any easier for the Knicks when the team played smaller market franchises. The Knicks' general manager despised upstate Syracuse and Rochester and described Sheboygan, Wisconsin, and Moline, Illinois, as "great towns for dairy and meat packing," that didn't belong on his Garden marquee. His snobbery created lifelong resentments and caused many fierce brawls in Syracuse and Rochester. Fans energized their team to defeat the nasty New Yorkers whose boss thought little of them or their city. Syracuse's War Memorial Arena fans also demonstrated their disdain by shaking the basket during playoff games and flicking lit cigarettes at passing players.

Another sore spot was playing over ice. Since most arenas housed hockey teams, wooden floors were laid directly over ice without any insulation. The Garden also regularly booked ice shows headlined by movie star Sonja Henie. Players often flew off the edge of the court onto ice, making the early Knicks' woolen uniforms practical. Wearing skimpy shorts and lacking sweat pants caused shivering players to curl up on the bench. Once Bud Palmer took a pass and went barreling toward the basket. His momentum carried him off the floor crashing into the show's stage.

Until the mid-1950s, the Knicks played many games in the 69th Armory. The smaller armory was especially disappointing when the Ringling Brothers Circus cut into Garden playoff dates, making them feel second-rate. Even though Irish improved the seating and locker rooms, the new floor was laid over cement making it as hard on legs as Astroturf, and brutal when a player crashed to the floor. In spite of the armory improvements, the Knicks preferred getting taped and dressed in the Garden and taking a chartered bus to the game.

But there were other reminders of the BAA's inferior status. When it was formed, the *New York Times* never bothered telling its readers, and didn't even cover the league's first all-star game in Boston in 1951. A sports fan would have to flip to the last sports page to find the game scores, and then only after baseball, hockey, boxing, and the Westminster Dog Show.

O

Ozzie Schectman remembers scoring the BAA's first basket that Friday in November 1946 against the Toronto Huskies in Canada. "It was a simple give and go," he recalls. Knickerbocker guard Leo Gottlieb received Schectman's pass, flicked a quick return as his teammate changed direction and cut to the basket to complete a patented New York–style play. The field goal made history of sorts.

Neil Cohalan accidentally achieved the honor of coaching in the first BAA game because the Toronto Maple Leafs, who traditionally played hockey on Saturday nights, forced the Huskies to play the first league game the day before everyone else. To attract fans, the Huskies offered a free pass to anyone taller than its 6'8" center George Nostrand. The league no longer played with laced balls but new ones with better spin and more balance and accuracy. However, the two-hand set shot still kept the game flat-footed. The jump shot was peeking over the horizon with players like Joe Fulks and Kenny Sailors, but the game still drew few fans.

An unexpected aid to the new league was the electronic buzz of radio. Marty Glickman, a young, energetic former all-around athlete fresh from the service, convinced WHN radio head Bert Lee that the public was ripe for basketball broadcasts. Reluctant at first, Lee finally agreed. Radio became a reality for Knicks fans when Ned Irish met with Lee and Glickman at Toots Shor's restaurant shortly after the war. Irish, who knew little of the medium, asked what the broadcast would cost. When Lee said there was no charge, and that the Knicks would be paid $250 a game, Irish agreed.

WHN's Glickman delivered vivid play-by-play coverage, home and away. His voice rang with clarity and understanding, a sound that became as familiar around the house as that of the late President Franklin Roosevelt. Youngsters could listen to the Knicks playing in Fort Wayne, Indiana, and keep score while rooting for their heroes. Radio was the "free introductory offer," which attracted imaginative fans in 1946 to the new league's color.

Glickman quickly developed a strong following, making him and Nedicks' fast-food restaurants part of the culture. Looking for more pop for its money, sponsors urged Glickman to come up with a catchy phrase that would help sell their food. The energetic announcer coined, "Good, like Nedicks'" when a goal was scored, much to the sponsor's delight. The brand name became part of the announcer's signature expression. When Glickman was shooting around in practice one day with Carl Braun, the Knicks sharpshooter labeled a successful shot that touched only net a "swish." Glickman quickly added it to his lexicon.

Radio was not greeted from every quarter with rave reviews. The print media demonstrated resentment for the newcomer. Some sportswriters, who lived and died with deadlines, perceived "the radio press" as postgame poachers who pushed microphones in front of athletes and were in their way. Since the print press previously had a monopoly, animosities developed.

With time sportswriters realized radio not only reported results faster than their morning accounts, but they also sensed radio was looking over their shoulder, second-guessing them, forcing sportswriters to be more accurate. The press gradually developed a more personal style that delved into the "whys" of a story. The public came to expect postgame locker-room reactions with quotes and insights from athletes that delineated more than the game's facts and figures.

Glickman was the first to describe basketball in terms fans could follow. He painted a vivid picture of the ball being passed to the "50th Street end" or "up the right side of the court," toward the "8th Avenue basket." Radio audiences liked seeing what they heard. In January 1951, WPIX finally allowed television audiences to see games. There had been limited televising before, but eventually announcers Bob Wolff and Bud Palmer "colored" the game with analysis. Wolff, "The TV Voice of the Knicks," offered a clear style that became a permanent part of Garden sports coverage. Palmer was one of the first to provide an athlete's insights in the broadcasting booth. But Palmer would be remembered for another contribution to the game.

○

In 1946, during a Knicks scrimmage Bud Palmer hit the brakes, jumped straight up, soaring over defender Tommy Byrnes, and swished an unusual two-hand, eighteen-foot shot. Before his feet touched down, Coach Cohalan was all over him for unleashing his secret weapon. "What a crazy, dumb shot," he shouted as he yanked Palmer from the floor.

Today, it's difficult to imagine basketball played without jump shots, but that's what play was like in the 1940s. From its inception, basketball was flat-footed and physical, with a knockdown style of defense and a code of conduct the profession swore by. The game prided itself, especially in the East, on pinpoint passing and long-range, two-hand set shooting. Pivot play relied on soft, ambidextrous hook shots that were almost impossible to block. To a pioneer pro, having a shot blocked was the ultimate embarrassment, and it compared only to someone dunking in your face. The "behind the back" dribble, popularized by Rochester Royals great Bobby Davies, was also frowned upon. Players judged both insults and reacted accordingly. Old NBA pro Alex Hannum thought dunking "showed a guy up," and it was treated with a retaliatory response similar to a baseball batter being hit by a pitch.

Rebounding was primarily a below-the-rim effort with 85 percent of them snared that way. Getting position and tipping the ball were two prerequisites of strong rebounding. Position involved taking a spot where a missed shot was likely to carom off the rim. The wise rebounder leaned on or "positioned" himself next to an opponent, with hands held high to block him from recovering a loose ball.

Adjusting to change in sports is challenging, but forward-looking visionaries accept new imaginative ideas. In the 1930s, some players started shooting one-hand, and word spread to kids around the country. Shooting after they left their feet made it harder to block. The shot was different, new, and exciting.

With time, word filtered through the pros of a new shot that some "rebels" were heaving up, something called a "jump shot." Everyone shot it differently. Two- or one-hand, behind the head or in front of the face, leaning forward, falling backward, off the dribble, only when stationary, as a player started his jump or at its peak or on the way down—it made no difference. For some time the jump shot, like many other newfangled ideas—new drugs or the horseless carriage, for example—was discouraged in professional circles.

Palmer's story was similar to that of other pros. He played effectively for Princeton in the early 1940s and flew planes for the navy during the war. After the war, while waiting for a business deal to materialize, he saw the new Knicks play in the Garden. Realizing he had played against many of them in the service, he felt he could compete. The next day he asked Ned Irish for a tryout. Irish, liking his Princeton credentials but knowing little of his talent, called Joe Lapchick. "Sign him," Lapchick urged his future boss, explaining that St. John's had nearly lost to Princeton. "Palmer played well," Lapchick recalled. Irish signed him. It did not take him long to blossom as the Knicks' best player.

Early BAA pros like Joe Fulks, Kenny Sailors, Belus Smawley, and Palmer worked to convince their coaches the jump shot had a future. Palmer used all his persuasion on Cohalan, in spite of the fact that most Easterners perceived the jump shot as a poor percentage shot. Palmer demonstrated that the traditional ground-level game, which could more easily smother a shooter, played into the hands of the defense. With the jump shot, the advantage shifted to the shooter, who often forced the defender to react—usually a split-second too late. The shooter now had time to release an uncontested airborne shot with no hands waving in his face. With practice and time, Palmer convinced Cohalan and Knicks fans of the shot's value.

Palmer's jump shooting helped him lead the Knicks with 9.5 points per game and a .307 field goal percentage. What Palmer couldn't foresee was how the jump shot and the twenty-four-second clock would revolutionize the game, and how the 1950s would see the shot become its most innovative offensive weapon.

O

On the last day of March 1947, at the Metropolitan Basketball Writers Association's final luncheon at Toots Shor's, Ned Irish officially announced that Joe Lapchick, approaching his forty-seventh birthday, had agreed to coach the New York Knickerbockers. Irish picked the best possible coach when he inked Lapchick to a guaranteed three-year contract. He met Lapchick's salary demands that made him, according to media releases, the highest-paid coach in professional basketball.

Lapchick's contract also insisted no Knicks player be paid more than him, believing pros could be more easily disciplined when management demonstrated the coach's value. The agreement called for Lapchick to select scouts and to have a say in player personnel. Lapchick was one of the country's most respected coaches, posting a 181–53 record at St. John's, with a .773 winning percentage. His Redmen were regular NIT participants and the only school to win the postseason tournament back-to-back. Lapchick was comfortable in the Garden, where the metropolitan press helped his reputation. He seemed to have been around the game from its inception, and, in a way, he was. He identified with professional basketball and felt it was where he belonged, fitting better with old-time owners like Walter Brown and Eddie Gottlieb than with academics.

Playing for money was how he started as a fifteen-year-old in Yonkers, and he knew in his heart the new pro league was right for him. Like Babe Ruth or Jack Dempsey, the former Celtics giant was an instantly recognized sports figure. He was as big a name and as popular a personality as basketball had produced. His size alone demanded attention and forced people to look up. Entering the pro world again, he was more mature and better prepared with the social graces needed to succeed.

Former Knicks forward Lee Knorek came to recognize Lapchick's social improvement. As an Ohio teenager in the 1930s, Lapchick and the visiting Celtics captivated him. After they met, "Tall Joe" became his role model. When Knorek later played for him in 1947, he told his new bride that his coach was a fine man who had "rough edges." After meeting the coach, she marveled at his polish and poise, wondering what her husband was talking about.

While Lapchick was now positioned to tackle the most important coaching challenge of his life, Podoloff admitted the first year had gone well but quietly added that the new league lost more than $500,000. Joe Lapchick, who represented basketball credibility, willingly threw his support behind the new league.

Irish was well aware of the positive, regular guy reputation Lapchick carried. A man of his word, drenched in respectability and character, Lapchick offered qualities needed to promote the new league. He was unique: a gentleman and a true ambassador of the game who would help through his positive press coverage. Lapchick understood that placing the league in its best light helped all the teams. Unlike Boston's Red Auerbach, Lapchick praised league stars like George Mikan and Bob Cousy, even if they didn't wear the Knicks orange and blue. He seemed to envision the game's future; one he loved and hoped to achieve.

O

On the first of October 1947, eighteen Knicks hopefuls assembled at New York's Bear Mountain Inn, a short distance from West Point, to begin two weeks of basic training. Being a lifelong Yonkers resident, Lapchick was familiar with the inn. The picturesque training facility with vivid sunsets splashed with multicolored autumn leaves provided crisp, elevated air as well as a rugged surrounding for the team's conditioning.

The Bear Mountain facility was part of the Palisades Park Commission, which included a ten-thousand-acre parcel of land donated to the state commission by the aristocratic Harriman family. Its athletic facilities included a well-lit makeshift outdoor basketball court set up on the side of the skating rink that served as the battleground for a handful of men. The Knicks were not the only team to use Bear Mountain. The New York football Giants and Brooklyn Dodgers, and even Frank Leahy's Notre Dame footballers prepared there for one of their classic wartime games against the army's invincibles, Glenn Davis and "Doc" Blanchard. In April 1945, it was where the Dodgers gave tryouts to two black players, Terris McDuffie and Dave "Showboat" Thomas, when they were thinking about breaking baseball's color line.

The Knicks training camp conditions were primitive by today's standards. The workouts were on an asphalt outdoor court bordered by painted white lines with a pair of handmade wooden backboards and three-by-four-foot pads mounted across the mid-section of each of the backboard's wooden supports. On one side there was a lake and a set of wooden bleachers for spectators. To simulate game conditions, Lapchick hired league referees to officiate "skin and shirt" scrimmages, where one team removed their shirts to separate the units. The outdoor lights provided an option to practice at night, allowing Lapchick two daily sessions with a four-hour break in between.

There were only five returning Knicks in camp from the first season, and the league shrank from eleven to seven teams. Podoloff invited the Baltimore Bullets, a regional power from the American Basketball League, along with its shabby Baltimore Coliseum to complete an eight-team, forty-eight-game BAA league.

War veterans Dick Holub, the LIU 6'7" rebounder, and Lee Knorek from Detroit University gave Lapchick some quality board strength. Missing was a true big man. The Knicks also signed Carl Braun, a thin, 6'5", twenty-year-old Colgate freshman, who along with Palmer provided much-needed scoring punch. But Braun's ability didn't mean the rookie could coast through practice. Lapchick seemed intent on getting the best out of his talented guard. His manly approach still allowed him to light into a player who screwed up. Braun remembered that on occasion his coach would get on him.

"Lapchick could be critical but you didn't feel hurt," Braun recalled. His criticism was always positive, never personal. Working from experience and confidence, Lapchick never lost touch with reality. He didn't have time to correct every error and refused to beat on someone who was about to be dropped. Instead, he focused on those he felt had potential. He tried to bring out talent by reaching inside a player. Responsibility was what the coach sought, but once he reprimanded a player, it was forgotten. Lapchick had his players moaning from daily morning runs around the lake. Rookies and veterans alike thought his conditioning was an eye-opener. "It was a large lake, and it took a strong effort to complete," rookie Holub recalled.

As a well-traveled coach, Lapchick expected the team's attention. But there were days when he wasn't satisfied. One afternoon, after a particularly listless practice, he ordered the team to "run the mountain" again.

The winding trails up Seven Lakes Drive were approximately seven miles. As the unhappy campers tackled their punishment, Knorek convinced rookie Ray Kuka, a struggling 6'3" forward from Notre Dame, to take a shortcut with him. "Lapchick will never know," Knorek assured the edgy Kuka. Since only trainer Jim Nevins was topside timing their endurance run, they decided their deception could work. As they cut through the woods, the two came upon a brown picket, four-foot fence, which they easily scaled. What happened next, Knorek still remembers vividly.

Two uniformed Chinese Nationalist soldiers pointed loaded rifles, freezing them in their tracks. The foreigners, speaking only Chinese, didn't disguise their angered order to stop. Luckily, an English-speaking official intervened. He explained that they had stumbled upon Madame Chiang Kai-shek's lodge, and the two had better leave.

In October 1947, during a critical time, China's Madame Chiang Kai-shek, the wife of its military and political head, was a guest of the United States. President Truman supported her husband's Nationalist regime, which was eventually run out of China by Mao's Communist army. Knorek and Kuka had accidentally entangled themselves with international politics. Both Knicks streaked back to the inn in record time to confess their sins to an understanding Lapchick. They never did get to the top of the mountain.

O

As the popular coach of the Knicks, the most powerful franchise in the BAA, Joe Lapchick received opportunities to endorse products. After the war, footwear companies began to see potential with celebrity endorsements. Most basketball players in the 1940s wore either Converse's popular Chuck Taylor All-Stars or Spalding Double S sneakers. Since Kinney wanted to compete in the sneaker market, Lapchick was asked to increase his involvement with the company, which he had endorsed since his Celtics days. Black or white canvas high-cuts were the basic sneakers. Players spent little time worrying about them. Seldom in the past did an entire team wear the same sneakers, although some did. Many players laced up and made a final, stylish wraparound before knotting them at the back of their ankles.

Lapchick first endorsed Kinney's footwear near the end of his 1930s barnstorming days when he received an offer he almost refused. Cliff

Anderson, a former pro rival who had played for Nat Holman at CCNY, asked the Celtics during the Depression to endorse Kinney's sneakers for $100. Reluctantly, Lapchick accepted the offer for the team.

Although Lapchick would maintain a lifelong relationship with Kinney, Chuck Taylor preceded Kinney in sneaker endorsements. His All-Stars were identified in 1923 by the ankle patch with his signature on it. Taylor was not a coach but an old basketball barnstormer who walked into Converse's Chicago office and never left. His dedicated efforts made Converse world famous and the standard for basketball players into the 1960s.

Through the 1940s, Kinney marketed the "Joe Lapchick" black high-cuts, which sold for $3.75 and made Lapchick one of the first basketball celebrities to endorse a sneaker. Like the Chuck Taylor sneakers, Lapchick's flowery signature appeared on the ankle patch. He also helped sales by putting together a pamphlet on basketball fundamentals that was distributed with each purchase.

Kinney tried to compete with the leaders by promoting the Lapchick sneaker and later getting the Knicks to endorse their royal blue sneakers. Although high-cuts dominated the field, by the early 1950s low-cuts appeared when Al McGuire of the Knicks popularized them. He had worn red low-cuts at St. John's, which Kinney special-ordered for him. As a high school track runner, McGuire regularly taped his ankles, making it difficult to pull high-cuts over his socks. He became the first NBA player to wear them and later lamented not patenting the concept with his coach when they became popular in the 1950s and 1960s during the Cousy-Russell Celtics era. In the 1960s, Boston Celtics players like Sam Jones, Tommy Heinsohn, and John Havlicek all wore low-cuts. They appeared to make players faster as if a Mercury-like element was woven into the fabric. However, Lapchick had more serious issues to handle as the Knicks coach than the sale of sneakers. What he never anticipated was that the changes he made to improve the team would cause resentment. There were many around the Knicks that interpreted Lapchick's cutting of Jewish players as tinged with discrimination.

○

From the beginning, Lapchick reshaped the Knicks' style of play. Gone from the original team were Ralph Kaplowitz, Nat Militzok, and Hank

Rosenstein followed by Leo Gottlieb and Sonny Hertzberg. They were all local players who represented a sophisticated style of New York basketball; one he felt couldn't deliver the aggressive punch he needed.

Lapchick preferred players like Ray Kuka, 6'3" and 215 pounds, Tommy Byrnes, 6'3" and 175 pounds, and Lee Knorek, 6'7" and 215 pounds—aggressive types who were not the most talented but offered a physical presence. He was later drawn to unpolished players like Al McGuire, whose spontaneous combustion would spark teams. But the single trait he most admired was aggressiveness, which made dirt-eating athletes dive for loose balls and bang against opponents while fighting for rebounds. Lapchick also believed a pro had to shoot well from the outside to prevent the defense from sagging onto the pivot man and clogging the middle. He looked for speed, good hands, and competitive spirit. Lapchick envisioned that a top pro "makes the play" by passing to a closely guarded teammate cutting to the basket.

Lapchick, however, disagreed with many of Irish's selections that were often based upon a player's New York popularity. After spending a lifetime with hard-nosed pros, Lapchick also believed that aggressive defense was most important and could be taught quicker than shooting, which required greater innate talent. The coach responded by offering Knicks uniforms to players who filled his physical mold.

It was a quality Lapchick sensed from his Celtics days and had to do with size but more to do with what a player did with his athletic gifts. It centered more on what the old Celtics saw as mental toughness, and slighter players like Tommy Byrnes, and future scrappers like Al McGuire and Ernie Vandeweghe all swam in it.

The times offered no scouting services, few statistics, or videotape to help, and Lapchick was forced to rely on contacts in the field coupled with an instinctive ability to recognize talent.

One of the earliest examples of Irish's failure to understand Lapchick's needs involved the signing of 5'7", 150-pound Wat Misaka. Irish was enthralled with Utah's upset victory over national power Kentucky in the 1947 NIT final. The tiny guard shut down the Wildcats' All-American Ralph Beard, one of the game's finest. Irish saw Misaka as a crowd-pleaser and flew to Salt Lake City to sign him to a $3,000 contract. But what Irish didn't understand was that Misaka's collegiate success couldn't buy him a seat on Lapchick's bench. When he arrived in the fall for the Knicks' training camp, Misaka assumed he had made the team. Lapchick quickly realized he lacked the physical size and strength to compete with pros, and after the third game, he told Misaka the bad news.

Irish later told Misaka that he felt differently but admitted he could not contradict the new coach's decision. Irish, however, did something rare in sports by paying Misaka his entire year's salary. Misaka was only one of Irish's well-intentioned personnel errors. Today Misaka best serves as trivia, being the NBA's first Japanese-American.

After Lapchick cleaned house, Irish was not the only one to question his judgment. One of the departing players interpreted Lapchick's choices as anti-Semitic, because most of those who were dismissed were Jewish. With New York's large Jewish population and its strong interest in basketball, it was a serious charge. Carl Braun, a member of the team in 1947, saw the changes as strictly a coaching decision. Lapchick had clearly defined his preference for physical play, which was necessary for effective defense. No corroboration of the allegation ever surfaced, and the rumors disappeared. The irony was that most of Lapchick's closest acquaintances, like Lester Scott, publicity man of the Garden, and sportswriters Ike Gellis and Lennie Koppett, as well as the Kutshers, the resort owners, were all Jewish.

While the issue died, the leadership of the BAA and the NBL began to realize each had what the other needed to succeed. Gradually, the idea of a merger caught the attention of the professional basketball world.

Chapter 8

The New
NBA

Maurice Podoloff was no fool. He understood even though the 1947–48 season drew more fans, the Basketball Association of America needed the National Basketball League's best teams to succeed. He also knew that Fred Zollner, the owner of the Fort Wayne Pistons, was a wealthy industrialist who loved his team and had the financial means to keep the league afloat. With this in mind, he quietly flew out to Fort Wayne to visit with the Piston's general manager, Carl Bennett, and suggested that the top NBL franchises join the BAA. The Minneapolis Lakers, Fort Wayne Pistons, Rochester Royals, and Indianapolis Kautskys, with their enthusiastic fan base and talent, joined the league for the 1948–49 season. Stars Bobby Davies, Jim Pollard, and Arnie Risen were now part of the BAA, making it the best professional basketball league in America.

By the start of the 1949–50 season, Podoloff "absorbed" the remaining NBL teams, forming a seventeen-team National Basketball Association. The commissioner never called it a merger, which would have placed the older league on an equal footing with the new NBA, a fact he was unwilling to admit. But what the new league needed besides large arenas and great players was a positive hero, a savior, someone to energize it. Someone like George Mikan.

○

Maybe if George Mikan, the tall, serious-minded young man, had entered the priesthood as planned, Ned Irish and the other NBA moguls would not have struggled to win championships. But without the prolific center, their dream of a national league would have faded like earlier efforts.

Mikan decided against the priesthood and made basketball history instead. He was the name, the poster player, and the glue that held the early NBA together. Big George blossomed from an awkward Chicago youth into a 6'10", 245-pound, DePaul All-American destined to lead the Minneapolis Lakers to the league's first dynasty. The NBA's first superstar was the standard of excellence, someone to gauge stardom and inspire opponents.

When the Lakers visited New York, the Garden marquee often read: "George Mikan vs. The Knicks." Although Mikan never flew through the air or had acrobatic finishes to his shots, he possessed the brute strength opposing fans loved to hate. Huge, bespectacled, and with clutch ability, Mikan was noted for grinding granitelike elbows into an opponent's chest. He was compared to Goliath, Paul Bunyan, and every hated comic-strip monster who ever walked the earth, the ones Superman and Captain Marvel battled. He was the tension that got fans rooting for the home team and the meal ticket that fed struggling franchises.

From 1948, when the Lakers jumped to the new league, until 1954, Mikan was by far pro basketball's most dominant player, and he helped his team win five of six championships. During that stretch, Mikan led the league in scoring, field goal percentage, and rebounding. While the Lakers scored in the seventies, George averaged 25 points and 13.5 rebounds a game. By the mid-1950s, with the excitement of the twenty-four-second clock, Big George vacated his crown for Boston Celtics rookie Bill Russell and Wilt Chamberlain to fight over.

When basketball aficionados talk of the "keyhole" big men grazed, they are describing what changed because of Mikan. In the 1940s, the narrow six-foot area between the two free throw lanes, when added to the semicircle area above the foul line, formed an imaginative keyhole. This battleground allowed low-post players to double-park three feet from the hoop. An adept, ambidextrous low-post threat like Mikan could pivot across the keyhole lane, extend his arms, and practically drop a hook shot into the basket.

It is difficult for modern fans to understand Mikan's powerful court presence. Films reveal a large, slow-moving, Hummer-like force who lacked the agility of today's superstars. However, by the 1951 season, at the insistence of Ned Irish, the NBA widened the foul lane from six to twelve feet to force Big George away from his low-post happy zone. Few rule changes were ever so clearly directed at one player.

There was something about Mikan's work ethic that was admirable. It was apparent that he had labored to master basketball. As a young athlete, he faced rejection when he was cut as a high school freshman. Father Burns, his coach at Joliet Catholic High School, said his glasses were the reason. Though challenging his confidence, this rejection didn't stop his passion. After Mikan arrived at DePaul, he improved under Coach Ray Meyer from "a work in progress" to an All-American. Lapchick praised the Laker as the game's best, the "Babe Ruth of Basketball." The media agreed. Mikan would be voted basketball's best big man of the first half-century, while Lapchick would have many opportunities to respect his title. George Mikan, like his elbows, left a deep impression.

О

While Mikan's work ethic inspired the Lakers, the NBA was fortunate to have attracted coaches like Boston's Red Auerbach, John Kundla of the Lakers, and Joe Lapchick, all of whom took pride in what it took to get the most out of their players.

What made Joe Lapchick's teams play hard? Players claimed they would go through brick walls for him. Why? Because none of them ever confused Lapchick with a textbook strategist or a proponent of trick defenses. Lapchick believed it was a simpler game. His motivation stemmed from pride, an invisible vapor that seemed to intoxicate his teams, driving them to their capacity. Lapchick was all about pride, whether talking about his Celtic days or inspiring a player to hustle. While instilling extra effort, his paternal sincerity made it difficult for players to shortchange him or face their coach after a loss.

Lapchick also talked about respect, saying it had to be earned and that it didn't come by accident. He put energy into gaining it. Once earned, it created a debt, one that most of his teams honored. "As a player you didn't want to let him down, to fail him," Fuzzy Levane explained. "You wanted to please him," like a son wanting good grades for his father.

Lapchick's style proved comfortable for him and his players. It called for fitting a flexible freelance offense to the team's talent while stressing defense. Lacking a dominant center, he successfully built teams around speed, defense, and precision passing, while recognizing the advantage of fast-breaking for easy baskets.

His freelance pro style used few set plays but encouraged responsibility. Since pros then understood fundamentals, he let them play. The game demanded instant reaction, decisions no coach could orchestrate style from the bench. The freedom required confidence that generated from Lapchick. Although young, the Knicks were mature enough to handle it.

O

The Knicks' running game required conditioning to compensate for limited size. The team got by with average-size forwards like Harry Gallatin and Sweetwater Clifton, but the Knicks had trouble consistently battling taller, more physical teams like the Lakers and the Rochester Royals. "You can't score unless you have the ball," Lapchick preached about the value of rebounding.

Fast-breaking in a forty-eight-minute game required a deep bench. Lapchick theorized the game wasn't won in the first quarter, which he considered least important. Most teams sparred at the beginning, putting few points on the board, and he believed at times he could get by with less-talented but scrappy players. His system often called for starting two or three "kick-start" players and then inserting fresh regulars in the second quarter. The eight-man rotation allowed regulars to rest while wisely building confidence for the bench. His first-quarter strategy grew from challenging regulars to scrimmage the day after games. If the second team outplayed them, the hustlers started the next game. This aggressive strategy made practice more meaningful and also strengthened the team.

Like most coaches, he believed that it was the players on the floor at the end of a game who were the most important. Lapchick loved Ernie Vandeweghe's style of play, but because of the young intern's medical obligations, he couldn't make it to Garden games until well into the first quarter. Consequently, Vandeweghe may not have started many Knicks games but filled Lapchick's needs by being well-rested to play the end of games when it was all on the line.

Lapchick liked unselfish players, calling them coaches on the floor. Decision-making, he believed, broadened responsibility. Since there was no money for assistant coaches to rub ideas off of in the pros until the late 1950s, Lapchick made "assistants" of his Knicks and at times appointed them to coach games. When he was hospitalized from exhaustion in Indianapolis, Lee Knorek helped out. After subbing too early and blowing an eighteen-point lead—a familiar rookie coaching error—he sheepishly visited Lapchick with the bad news. "Did you learn anything about coaching?" Lapchick asked. Knorek nodded.

Lapchick occasionally left the team prior to the playoffs to scout the NCAA tournament and had Butch Van Breda Kolff or Ray Kuka coach. Kuka directed eight games by the end of the 1948–49 season. The former Notre Dame forward had suffered a back injury that prematurely ended his season. Lapchick, seeing the advantage, asked Irish to keep Kuka on as an assistant.

Lapchick again demonstrated faith in his players' judgment by distributing ballots for them to pick the starting lineup for one of the early playoffs. He welcomed their insights, knowing it made them feel more involved. In the heat of battle, a player might see the game differently than the coach. Lapchick allowed his teams latitude to participate in game strategy. Prior to the twenty-four-second clock, when teams fouled for possession, Vince Boryla enjoyed pointing out which opponent should be fouled at the end of the game.

After the 1948–49 season, the Providence Steamrollers disbanded, and their key players were to be dispersed among the remaining teams. The Knicks needed outside shooting, and Kenny Sailors and Ernie Calverley, two outstanding shooters, were available. "Should we go after them?" Lapchick asked the team. After they agreed, Lapchick then asked, "Who should I let go?" Suddenly the team grew silent. While Lapchick solicited their opinion, something the modern front office reserves for general managers and scouts, he revealed the difficult decisions coaches are forced to make.

Like most pro coaches, Lapchick relied on a few set plays. He particularly liked one triggered by calling out a city, like Rochester or Syracuse. Most quick-scoring plays involve blind-side screens, which pick off, or block, a defender while catching his teammates off guard. Since zone defenses were prohibited, it was difficult to defend. The set play fit so well into the flow of an offense that opponents rarely detected it.

Lapchick never liked team rules that narrowed his effectiveness, but he did encourage proper behavior. He didn't believe in stringent rules "painting himself into a corner." Because Lapchick treated pros responsibly, he rarely dictated morals, leaving such decisions to player judgment. In general, the team was expected to make the right choices, ones that didn't hurt the organization.

However, if a player used vulgar language, he often was asked if he spoke that way in front of his wife. And when on the road, Lapchick and trainer Don Friedrichs invited many Knicks to join them at Sunday mass. The team enforced its own curfews, whether players were indulging in postgame carousing or a quiet beer. There was a time the Knicks medical advisor, Dr. Vincent Nardiello, recommended that each player receive $2.50 for a few postgame "medicinal beers" to replace bodily fluids. A common scene at halftime was Lapchick lighting up an Old Gold or Camel, with Dick McGuire, Ray Lumpp, and Connie Simmons mimicking their coach.

Missed practices, however, bothered the coach, and if not addressed, he believed team discipline could break down. During his first Knicks season, a reserve player missed a morning workout. When the guilty party sidled up to him to offer an excuse, Lapchick, who was watching a team layup drill, turned and gave him only half his attention. "I didn't even know you missed practice," he said. The player now really had something to worry about. He never missed another one. And yet, there was subtle motivation in Lapchick's coaching. His job was to create harmony in a relaxed atmosphere, and this encouraged players to give their best.

Lapchick had a rule. If winded, a player pointed to his chest, signaling to be removed from the game. The truth was, Lapchick didn't want anyone asking out of a game. His Celtics training rejected this reaction to fatigue as a lack of toughness. He liked the competitor who persevered, endured pain, and fought through injury, fulfilling Lapchick's traditional perception of the mentally tough's character. Those who signaled found themselves lingering on the bench longer than necessary. The lesson was clear to the attentive player.

There was also a certain gentle predictability to Lapchick's style. He wouldn't run up scores, didn't tolerate blowhards, and always perceived himself to be an ordinary guy trying his best. He lost in cards, drank with sportswriters and sports friends, but never started a press conference with the word "I" or spotlighted his achievements. He often used his ethnicity as a sign of humility. Although a Czech, sportswriters characterized him as a Big Pole because it made better copy for their stories, and he even described himself to friends in letters as, "A Big Polack," never bothering to correct the error.

Lapchick knew the value of having game officials in his corner. Although he treated them with respect, he never forgot that a referee's random error could cost championships. And yet, he listed game officials among his friends. Included with the guest list for his retirement banquet were Pat Kennedy, Stan Stutz, and Sid Borgia, NBA officials with whom Lapchick had lived and died.

Pro sports are part of America's culture of entertainment. Joe Lapchick never lost sight of the fact that the referees were a significant part of the show. Lapchick reacted differently to questionable calls by pro officials than he did in a college game. While he respected officials, at times he questioned their fuzzy rule interpretations. Occasionally, officials and Lapchick were drawn into the entertainment by subconsciously trying to please home teams. It was understood in the past, and to a degree today, that officials favored the home team if for no other reason than it was a popular position.

Home court advantage prior to television also had a bearing on the coach's demeanor. When his sense of fairness was violated, Lapchick sent visual messages to fans. While dragging on a cigarette by the bench in a hunched position, Lapchick might immediately spring up like a jackknife after a questionable call and walk stiff-legged to the far-end watercooler. If a call was critical, he might kick the watercooler soundly for emphasis. He also had perfected coin tricks. One had him reaching into his pocket and flipping a handful of change across the playing floor in the direction of the whistle-tooter. Officials did not immediately recognize the significance of the act.

One Christmas day in the Garden, Sid Borgia entered the dressing room during halftime. "What do you think Lapchick means?" a plain-clothes cop asked the official about the coin flipping. Borgia shrugged his shoulders. "Do you remember the organ-grinder who traveled the neighborhoods with the monkey on his shoulder who would pick up coins thrown to him in the streets?" the cop asked. This reference to the monkey with poor eyesight started to boil Borgia's blood. The veteran official began to see Lapchick's coin act had a disparaging twist to it. He stormed back to the Garden floor and presented Lapchick with an ultimatum.

"The next time you flip coins onto the floor, Joe, when they hit the hardwood, you're out of the game!" From then on, Lapchick saved his coin-tossing for less-schooled officials.

For special occasions, when he was steaming, Lapchick had mastered bouncing a silver dollar on the hardwood and catching it, implying that only a bribe could produce such a poor call. His performance usually produced scattered applause from tuned-in local fans. The last staged theatrical complaint found the tall, thin coach placing hands on hips and glaring at the whistling culprit as smoke steamed from his ears. None of these gyrations ever caused a single call to be changed, but they did soothe the pain while often entertaining the selected onlookers who caught his tricks. They were all in their own way trying to help the pro league survive. Better days were coming, and the NBA would give much enjoyment to millions of sports fans. Lapchick was going to do everything he could to make his Knicks the best.

Chapter 9

Knicks
Chemistry

A modern NBA team boards a plane, stays in a hotel near the arena, has a pregame "shoot-around," eats a quick meal, plays a game, and immediately returns home. Little time is available for any close association because today's pros don't even room together. On the other hand, Lapchick helped build team chemistry through the many travel trips to games.

Coaches and players viewed the long train trips early pro teams made as a positive form of male team bonding, an activity that created the camaraderie that most winning teams possessed. Roommates on the road enjoyed friendships and good-natured clowning. The tongue-in-cheek inferences from Bud Palmer in a 1947 letter to Knicks roommate Lee Knorek are characteristic of the period.

"What is this I hear about you getting married?" Implied was the unconscious concern that the good times, the college pranks associated with athletic teams, might be ending and that Knorek's impending marriage was the cause. Team bonding represented a player's youth, a time when he could act as a boy. Both Knorek and Palmer's pro careers ended in two years, but the good memories remained with them.

Palmer signed his letter to Knorek "El Tigro," an obvious reference to his Princeton days. Most athletes liked nicknames, names that highlighted their strengths, ethnicity, or some physical or personal characteristic. The names, too, helped form a common bond. When Van Breda Kolff was called "Butch," Harry Gallatin "The Horse," or Clifton "Sweets," affection and pride were implied.

Lapchick was better than most pro coaches at creating a college atmosphere, a spirit that encouraged chemistry and grew through daily contact. "We are a team," he bragged to the press after the Knicks ran off twelve of fourteen games early in December 1948. He felt he coached "guys who like, understand, and help each other." He later referred to them as "boys" with a "group spirit"; one he felt created a winning attitude.

To create harmony, Lapchick tried recognizing player needs. He allowed Van Breda Kolff to occasionally miss practice to attended classes at NYU to complete his bachelor's degree. Ernie Vandeweghe's medical school demands initially restricted him to home and a few weekend road games. Although Vandeweghe didn't make all the practices, he worked to stay in shape. Lapchick understood. Once Dick Holub's fiancée phoned him before a game in Boston. Shortly after he hung up, Holub received a call from his coach. "Is anything wrong?" he inquired, ready to help if needed.

Much of the early Knicks' camaraderie emanated from their travel on long, tedious pre-air trips. "Coach liked road games because we got closer as a team," Knicks forward Vandeweghe remembered. "Teams did a lot of traveling on trains, which gave us time to come together." While a train rumbled into the night, Lapchick and the sportswriters played cards and exchanged stories, with the team doing much of the same. Travel allowed time to relax, have a few laughs, and see each other in a more casual setting.

In the early 1950s after a Saturday night game in Rochester, the team rushed to the train station to board the Twentieth Century Limited to Chicago for a Sunday evening game in Fort Wayne, Indiana. Although everyone complained about the Pullman accommodations, the taller players in particular had to live with cramped berths. Sportswriter friends repeated descriptions of Lapchick's long legs curled into sleeping berths as well as being pretzeled into the backseats of cabs, forcing his legs to rattle under his chin.

At five o'clock in the morning, the team was ordered off the train in Waterloo, Indiana, an unscheduled stop not to be confused with the metropolis in Waterloo, Iowa. This postage stamp of a village listed its population as twelve hundred, and it was in the middle of nowhere.

Lugging large game bags, the players, trailed by their coach, trainer Don Friedrichs, a few hardy sportswriters, and announcer Marty Glickman, headed toward the curlicued smokestacks of the tiny community. After an unending walk in the frigid morning, they arrived at a combined general store, restaurant, and amusement center called The Green Parrot.

Team captain Carl Braun, a former minor league pitcher, was elected to hurl stones at the second-story window. "Oh, the Knickerbockers," a sleepy-eyed woman groaned, and she let them in. After breakfast, the group waited fifteen minutes for a caravan of cars to transport them the final twenty-eight miles to downtown Fort Wayne. By 9:00 A.M. all were in their hotel ready to sleep until the 4:00 P.M. pregame meal. NBA teams made this trip several times each year.

There is an interesting postscript to The Green Parrot episode. After the *New York Post* beat writer Lennie Koppett wrote about the travel adventures of the early NBA, he heard that Podoloff was steaming mad. "He made The Green Parrot," the commissioner sputtered, "appear to be a house of ill-repute."

In time, improvements in transportation reached the NBA. Eventually the Knicks flew to distant games on their own chartered plane, the Father Knickerbocker, which the press corps later labeled "Sput-Knick" in honor of Russian space accomplishments. Despite the rigors of early travel, Lapchick insisted the team appear properly dressed. This meant shirt, tie, and jacket for meals, in addition to topcoat and hat for flights or train rides. Once Palmer showed up wearing a turtleneck under his jacket and Lapchick raised his voice, sending the Princetonian to his room to change.

The Knicks were a first-class franchise. The players received fresh supplies for each game, and the franchise was the first to travel with Don Friedrichs, a full-time trainer. When players were traded they noted the difference. The Baltimore Bullets had horrible locker rooms with the home team having the only shower. When 6'7" Knicks forward Lee Knorek was traded to Baltimore in 1950, he complained about being spoiled by the Knicks. He retired after one game.

Joe Lapchick had learned what it would take to be champions in the new NBA. With Ned Irish, he tried to add as many of the necessary ingredients as possible. New York and Madison Square Garden were ready for the team's best effort.

○

By 1949, after two seasons of adjustment, Lapchick developed his best nucleus of players. From the original patchwork of slow-footed, local players that Lapchick inherited in 1947, he built a more aggressive, defense-minded team that reached the NBA finals three successive years from 1950 through 1953. Slowly Lapchick wove "desire to win" into a balanced squad of young newcomers who could rebound, ballhandle, and play defense, the essentials of a quality team.

"We were like a plate of minestrone soup," said Vince Boryla, describing how Lapchick compensated for the team's lack of size. It was stocked with better-than-average-size players who, though a few steps from stardom, filled valuable roles and were dedicated to a team concept. The Knicks had balance and flexibility, which Lapchick played like a trump card. On a given night, any of the first eight could lead the team.

Eastern style of play relied on good ball movement, while action guards like Dick McGuire, Braun, and Vandeweghe created flow. They delivered the ball into the low post to Boryla, Clifton, and Gallatin or "threaded the needle" with pinpoint bounce passes to players cutting to the basket. The guards set the table as well as the tone in Lapchick's free-flowing game. New York basketball required setting screens and moving without the ball, which was part of the freelance "give and go" style that made it famous. When its movement stalled, the Knicks outside shooting picked up the slack. Braun, Boryla, Connie Simmons, Max Zaslofsky, and, when necessary, McGuire, delivered two-hand set shots.

The first key to the future was 6'5" scoring guard Carl Braun, who the Knicks signed in 1947. Braun was a durable player in spite of his thin, 170-pound frame. In his rookie season, he led the Knicks in scoring, setting the young league's single-game record with 47 points against the Providence Steamrollers. Lapchick was aware of the lean, black-haired, silky-smooth shooter's talent, having scrimmaged his wartime Ft. Schuyler team where he and St. John's Harry Boykoff each scored 50 points. Braun had also signed another $4,000 contract to pitch for the New York Yankees. While trying to decide his future, a sore arm settled the issue. The Long Islander would go on to become one of the best all-around players in the league and one of the finest shooters in the history of the NBA, one who wanted the ball at the end of a close game—something many name pros don't relish.

Irish grabbed 6'6" Harry Gallatin from a small college in Missouri after his sophomore year. Gallatin proved a durable, positive addition.

With the late arrival of Gallatin in 1948, the Knicks added a rugged re-bounder with a stoic attitude toward hard work. "Harry the Horse" was unique. Setting endurance records by never missing any of his 610 games, Gallatin was one of the league's best position rebounders despite a limited vertical leap. The future Hall of Famer once led the NBA with nearly eleven hundred rebounds, averaging more than fifteen a game.

Gallatin knew his way around the boards well enough to become a dangerous "garbage man," scoring easy hoops that eluded the less gifted. It was difficult not to like the easygoing forward who found a warm sup-porter in Lapchick. "I came here in November of 1948, a farm boy in the big city," Gallatin said. "Right away Joe took pains to help me adjust. He gave me more time than any rookie had the right to expect." Gallatin more than repaid his coach.

By 1949, The Knicks had signed three key players—Dick McGuire, Ernie Vandeweghe, and Vince Boryla—who became vital parts of the Knicks' future. McGuire was a coach's dream and New York's 1949 terri-torial pick. He signed for $6,500 and was given a bonus of a new 1949 cream-colored Chevrolet convertible, which became the envy of his Rockaway Beach community. McGuire, who later was voted to the Hall of Fame, delighted fans with his ballhandling wizardry. Unselfish and team-oriented, he loved nothing better than being the deliveryman to a teammate's score. If a running mate cut to the basket, the ball was wait-ing on his doorstep, and as teammate Ernie Vandeweghe said, it was "in a spot where you could catch and shoot it." The Rockaway Beach ace made it look easy. He rarely looked to shoot, almost to the point of hurt-ing the team.

McGuire, however, was the lubricant that kept the Knicks' engine humming. His unlimited kinetic energy went almost unnoticed because he played effortlessly. McGuire's nightmare was a sportswriter praising him, preferring to let actions speak for him. He was most comfortable on the court where no one disturbed him. A better word than humble would have to be invented to describe McGuire. He was the game's best pure passer.

Led by McGuire, the Knicks peaked in the early 1950s, reaching three consecutive NBA finals by running opponents into submission and playing smart, fundamental basketball. Lapchick allowed the team's strengths to nurture and grow a cohesive unit. He enjoyed telling sports-writers about Dick McGuire's unselfish leadership and ballhandling cre-ativity rather than any of his own brainstorms.

Freelance play best demonstrated the spontaneous moves of Dick McGuire. McGuire typically took an outlet pass and raced downcourt with teammates filling the lanes. As he approached the free throw line, he looked one way but took advantage of his peripheral vision and made a bounce pass to Vandeweghe or Clifton for a spectacular finish. When the defense was set, McGuire often faked an outside shot and strolled down the three-second lane for an impossible last-second dish past an unsuspecting defender to a teammate.

Vandeweghe, the 6'3", 200-pound Colgate All-American, a college teammate of Braun's, was another Long Islander who unselfishly provided the drive winning teams demanded. Vandeweghe proved a valuable and versatile performer. The broad-smiling, crew-cut dynamo fitted basketball around medical school and learned to rush to airports or warm up in the Garden's runway after games started. "My medical career caused me to arrive late for home games. I was to warm up and notify Coach when I was ready." But when he told Lapchick he was ready, he delivered. There were times, however, when sitting on the bench, that he got anxious about a game. "I'd say, 'Coach, I got to play now,' and he would say, 'Go ahead, go in.'"

Vandeweghe's strength was intelligence coupled with an obvious energy. "Doc" was never afraid of body contact, and Lapchick wanted him on the floor when the game was on the line. He had the knack of filling in the team's cracks. He was a natural "sixth man" who generated the sparks that ignited wins, and Lapchick viewed him as the ideal, all-purpose player who came off the bench with intensity.

When the Knicks trailed late in games or found themselves flat, Lapchick inserted Vandeweghe and Al McGuire to deliver a shot of adrenaline. "Lapchick liked scramblers," McGuire admitted, "players who came in and created spark when things were flat." They could often stir things up by disrupting the opposition. "We called ourselves the No-Good Knicks," Vandeweghe recalled, when playing with the "shock troops." His defensive intensity, quick hands, and a sheer physical will to succeed, inspired wins. "I would come in with Al and we would challenge our opponents." Their defensive quickness and aggressive play made things happen. The coach loved their spirit.

Lapchick's nimble psychology could be seen in his dealings with Vandeweghe at the end of a Knicks playoff game with Boston in the early 1950s. Doc had just missed two free throws with a handful of seconds left, and the Knicks trailing by 1 point. Boston tried passing the ball up court, but Clifton stole it and called time-out. As the Knicks gathered around their coach, Lapchick realized the medical intern was disappointed with his missed shots. "We'll set up Ernie for the last shot," Lapchick ordered his troops.

Braun, the best pure shooter, frowned. "Coach, let me have the ball, and I'll win it." Braun, a high percentage free throw shooter, probably would get fouled. Lapchick, reading Braun's mind, gave Vandeweghe the boost he needed. "Any fool can make one out of three free throws," Lapchick explained to Braun and the team, as he patted Vandeweghe on the back and sent them out to play. Vandeweghe, with the confidence of his coach, took a pass from McGuire, drove baseline to the basket and was fouled. He went to the line and made both free throws for a 1-point victory.

When Braun entered the Korean War, Irish drew Max Zaslofsky's name out of a hat from the defunct Chicago Stags. Zaslofsky more than held his own as Braun's offensive replacement, scoring effectively, especially from the outside, and possessing the unteachable gift of shooting "touch."

A pair of effective free spirits rounded off the squad. Center Connie Simmons and 6'2" guard Al McGuire were both part of brother acts. Connie and John Simmons played the first BAA season for the Boston Celtics while Al joined Dick with the Knicks. Connie and Al were constantly involved in letting the good times roll.

In 1949, the Knicks traded with Baltimore for Connie Simmons, giving up Sid Tannenbaum. Simmons, a thin, 6'8" outside shooter, helped win games by creating mismatches and neutralizing the opponent's big men. He either pulled his man away from the basket by sinking open outside shots or by posting a smaller player under the basket. His speed, quickness, and shooting accuracy made up for his lack of consistent rebounding. Connie was a versatile addition.

Simmons had other attributes he didn't want on sports pages. One night after a Garden game, he joined Al McGuire for a few postgame beers. After both had words with a patron, McGuire claimed he got blind-sided by a punch. What followed was fuzzy, but Simmons had to escort McGuire to the local hospital to have a broken jaw wired. Irish's assistant, John Goldner, sheepishly told the newspapers McGuire had been in a car accident and would play with a mask, which he did.

While Al McGuire had limited skills and was nearly hidden in the shadow of his All-Pro brother, he nevertheless gave the Knicks a hefty blast for their money. But McGuire would have missed his chance with the Knicks if it weren't for a little Irish good fortune. "My brother was on the Knicks," Al related, "and I decided I wanted to play for them, too." When Al was drafted in 1951, he had made backup plans to join the police force if he didn't make the Knicks. "I was married and my son Allie was a few months old, and I felt I needed something to live on," McGuire admitted.

After a few days of practice in Bear Mountain, McGuire approached Lapchick about his future with the team. "That's hard to say at this time," Lapchick answered. After seeing that the coach would make no commitment, McGuire decided to join the police force. On the day police candidates were to be sworn in, he borrowed his brother's car and raced downtown to Centre Street in Manhattan.

As he entered the old gymnasium he saw all the "scrambled eggs," or what McGuire called the police brass with yellow rank markings on their hats, up front with the rookie cops who were ready to make a career commitment to law enforcement. As he took his place for the formal swearing in, he thought of all the security and benefits that went with the job. "Will all of you raise your right hand," the captain announced into the microphone, "and repeat after me." Al began to follow the rest of the clean-shaven novices when he suddenly jerked his hand back and sprinted from the gym. "That was the turning point in my life," McGuire admitted.

The dark-haired guard returned to the training camp ready for the challenge. McGuire had always been a fighter and somehow knew he would make the Knicks. Lapchick was surprised but happy to see him. He was fond of fighters like McGuire. He felt the rookie with the low-cut sneakers—his playing trademark—had that *something* that coaches look for, something McGuire delivered throughout his Knicks career.

McGuire's notoriety as a Knick centered on his clashes with head-liner Bob Cousy. He fell into a scheme to defuse the explosive Celtic. "I own Cousy," the flamboyant Irishman boasted. Although McGuire had some success, he often found himself on the bench after registering three quick fouls in the first quarter. Celtics owner Walter Brown was delighted. He loved the rivalry that helped fill Boston Garden every time the Knicks came to town.

Gallatin recalled an experience with Al McGuire in one of their out-of-town hotel stops. As Gallatin passed McGuire's room, he saw him propped up in bed, like a scene from a Hollywood film. "Hey, Farmer, come here," McGuire called out. Gallatin watched McGuire devouring a large breakfast from room service. "This," the flamboyant guard emphasized pointing to his tray with a slice of toast, "is how we do it in the Big City." Gallatin was impressed with the reserve player's cockiness.

But during McGuire's first year, the veteran pros had to teach him a lesson. "The rooks," as McGuire remembered, "had to lug bags when on the road." But part of hazing involved a clever routine regulars sprung on rookies.

"Vince Boryla was a bright guy," Al recalled, "who later made millions in real estate," while Harry Gallatin, "liked holding onto his money." One day the team arrived in Fort Wayne to play the Pistons and had to take cabs to the arena. McGuire didn't notice that both Boryla and Gallatin each instinctively headed for the back doors of the cab, but "The Horse," like a gentleman, held the door for McGuire to get in. McGuire found himself sandwiched between the two bruisers, who were casually discussing the game's matchups when the cab came to a halt. Both players suddenly bolted from the cab just as the driver turned around and said, "That'll be $3.85, please." McGuire never forgot the trick.

When no one was looking in 1949, Irish "stole" 6'5", 210-pound former Olympian Vince Boryla for his Knicks. Unpublicized player deals happened when the NBA was young. In spite of its bylaws, Podoloff would look the other way to allow shaky franchises to survive by breaking the rules. If a general manager needed a local college star who might help attendance, or if a team wanted to change its schedule, the president would allow it. Each team knew it had to compromise to stay afloat.

In 1952–53, when Philadelphia suffered one of the leagues' worst seasons, general manager Eddie Gottlieb drafted four local favorites: Ernie Beck was Penn's Ivy League scoring leader, Larry Hennessy led Villanova and the nation in scoring, and Norm Grekin and Fred Ihle played for LaSalle's NIT champs.

A chronic problem of the early league was its inability to accurately evaluate nationwide basketball talent. In the days before scouts, many teams relied on hearsay or phone calls made to coaches by former pros who might have seen a player. Also, owners often knew little of the players other teams wanted to draft. Rumors frequently influenced a club's judgment about a premium player's worth. A rival club in the old days could steal a quality player, while management, often guilty of poor evaluations, made major scouting blunders.

Boryla was an intelligent, solidly built athlete whose parted jet-black hair made him appear a business titan, like the one he later became. Irish complained to league owners that he was losing money and that without Boryla he would close down the franchise. Needing New York, Podoloff again allowed Irish to have his way. Although Irish signed Boryla, the Knicks had never drafted him. After more than fifty years of office relocations, NBA records of how Boryla was acquired, along with accurate minutes of the governors' meetings, were never preserved. Only some of Podoloff's memos survive in the Hall of Fame archives, along with the memories of a few living general managers.

With one year of eligibility at the University of Denver, he had been contacted by the Buffalo Bisons of the NBL, a team that would move west in 1947 and become the Tri-Cities Blackhawks. Although he refused the offer, it got Boryla thinking. Needing a few credits for a degree, he found the thought of skipping his last year to play professional basketball appealing.

When Irish received word Boryla might be interested in signing, he flew to Denver with an unprecedented offer for the twenty-one-year-old prize. Boryla received a three-year, guaranteed contract of $49,500, which amounted to a salary and bonus of $16,500 a year. The contract made him the highest-paid Knick, one of the NBA's highest-paid players, and the only Knick who was secretly paid more than Coach Lapchick.

While Al McGuire was happy with his limited contribution, the easygoing Simmons occasionally became dejected sitting out Garden games. One day during a practice, Lapchick saw Simmons launching two-hand shots at the basket from the bench. "What's going on?" Lapchick asked. "I guess it's the only way I'm going to score," the slender center shot back. The coach got the message. Despite minor differences of opinion, the Knicks were ready to test the NBA waters.

O

On November 28, 1950, the Knicks played the Syracuse Nationals in the feature game of an NBA doubleheader in Madison Square Garden. While thoughts of past struggles with their upstate rivals buzzed through the locker room, each player dressed to his favorite pregame ritual.

"Where's the chewing gum?" burly Vince Boryla barked at one of the ball boys as he entered the Knicks dressing room. Players loved biting into gum that kept their mouths from drying up, while for others it relieved pregame tension. He walked over to his favorite corner, placed his overcoat on a clothes hanger, and slipped it onto one of the hooks screwed into the wall. The corner became his locker. The benches built into the wall served as seats. No one seemed to mind the inconvenience. As the team dressed, trainer Jim Nevins gathered their valuables and secured them until after the game. The locker room had a relaxed atmosphere. The young athletes demonstrated none of the tension associated with pregame locker rooms.

As the trainer's teenage assistant breezed past with towels for the bench, he was reprimanded for whistling. "Not in the dressing room," Nevins reminded. Superstitions were as rampant in pro sports as in the theater or gambling. Even grown, intelligent men were suckered into rabbit-foot lucky charms. Fixed routines in their game preparation were strictly followed. Players fought over uniform numbers or who would be last out of the dressing room, taped fingers a certain way, or ate a lucky pregame meal. Some wore the same clothes through a win streak or if they were shooting exceptionally well. Others never varied their pregame meals—as if carrots or broccoli added to the menu could cause a loss. Gallatin wore the same socks after a good game hoping for more magic, while Lapchick wouldn't change a "winning" suit and necktie. Reserve forward George Kaftan stuck his gum on the locker-room wall as the team left for warm-ups. Vandeweghe liked doing his own taping. Since his high school days on Long Island, Vandeweghe also practiced the ritual of making the last shot at the end of warm-ups. He waited until the other players started toward the bench, and then he pivoted, drove to the basket, and released a final layup. Teammates, realizing his fetish, unconsciously tried to break his routine, but Ernie would manage to sneak back for the last shot. Dick McGuire possessed the habit of making a blurred sign of the cross before free throws. It resembled his rapid-fire assault on the English language and the high-octane way he played.

While the team dressed, publicist Lester Scott rushed into the room with his ticker-tape mimicry of the first game. "Celtics up 4, six minutes left," he reported. Ray Lumpp looked up and registered the score but was more interested in a new set of shoelaces from the ball boy. In the corner of the room, Connie Simmons pounded a ball off the carpeted floor as the ball boys distributed pregame equipment and itineraries for the road trip that evening. Lapchick entered some time after the players, wearing a dapper brown suit and clutching a favorite Old Gold. He began preparing for the game by pacing and worrying.

In another corner, Tony Lavelli and George Kaftan talked music as they dressed. Lavelli, an accomplished accordionist, collaborated with Kaftan on tunes, and they actually published several of them. They knew each other from their playing days in New England.

Sportswriters, seeking tidbits for the next day's story, led the parade of traffic into the locker room. They were free to circulate until a half-hour before game time. Since they were rushed by deadlines, the time was a lifesaver. Radio announcer Marty Glickman learned that Boryla's nickname came from playing for "Moose" Krause at Notre Dame. As Glickman hummed around the room, he discovered Vandeweghe was an excellent soccer player, while Clifton and Gallatin were minor league baseball players. "I pitched for Decatur, Illinois, and was 7–9 that one year," he pulled from Gallatin, the naturally quiet rebounder.

Bill Stern ran his new television sports show from the room next to the locker room. Players were rushed on the air to be interviewed. Once, when Stern was delayed by a snowstorm, Boryla and Al McGuire ran the show to rave reviews.

One visitor wasn't a celebrity yet. A future baseball superstar from Lafayette High School in Brooklyn was in the gym when a touring group of Knicks arrived. During the Knicks clinic, three students challenged the pros. "One of the kids dunked the ball during the game," Gallatin recalled. He was just slightly taller than six feet, with long angular arms. Impressed, Gallatin invited the future Los Angeles Dodgers' Hall of Fame pitcher, Sandy Koufax, to the locker room.

Middleweight boxing champ Ray Robinson, who was friendly with the Knicks' new player "Sweets" Clifton, came knocking at the dressing room door. Clifton, who had done some boxing, enjoyed feigning jabs and uppercuts with the sport's royalty. Harry Belafonte, another visitor, didn't know basketball well but loved its theatrical excitement. The team teased the singer about taking warm-ups with them. He would later be on Broadway in a musical revue with Vandeweghe's future wife, Colleen Hutchins, the former Miss America and sister of Mel Hutchins, who played with the Fort Wayne Pistons.

Clifton double-knotted his royal-blue high-cut Kinney sneakers as the last seconds of the first game ticked off and called to Simmons to flip him a ball. Simmons whizzed a high fastball, which Clifton snared one-handed, enveloping it in his huge hand. Clifton also liked squirreling away globs of illegal Stickum, which helped him dazzle crowds with one-handed catches during warm-ups. When the adhesive transferred from hands to ball, however, it made shooters like Max Zaslofsky angry.

When the locker room quieted down and the players were ready to battle their opponent, Joe Lapchick matter-of-factly started his informal pregame talk. "Sweetwater, you got Ratkovicz," he informed Clifton as he warned the team, "to help out if they go into a low double post." George Ratkovicz was a physical, 6'7", 225-pound former NBL force who spent his apprenticeship honing his skills and his elbows battling Mikan and other big men. Ratkovicz was having a career year and, along with Dolph Schayes, had to be stopped.

Joe Lapchick treated pros differently than college players, believing as men they should be responsible for their actions. An NBA schedule was the equivalent of more than two college seasons. There were no daily pep talks in the Knicks dressing room. Lapchick made sure the team knew who was starting and had their assignments. As professionals, they were expected to light their own fire, to motivate themselves, just as he had done in his Celtics days. "You're pros. Act like pros. I'm not going to give a pep talk before every game," Lapchick reminded his Knicks. He also made few bed checks. They were men—married men in most cases. Desire to stay in the league, he believed, was the greatest motivation. Professionals, like good stage actors, had to rise to the occasion.

As game time got closer, the Knicks privately gathered their thoughts. Syracuse brought out the worst in them, causing games to get nasty. Irish's harsh words about the unsophisticated upstate franchise helped kindle bad blood. Losing Schayes after drafting him was another cause for Irish's attitude. Syracuse's aggressive 5'11" player-coach Al Cervi egged on the feud. When rookie Dick McGuire drove to the basket, Cervi tried roughing him up. The Knicks playmaker claimed his athletic rights by whacking the fiery coach with his elbow to make room for himself.

The man with the cigar shouted over the locker-room noise, "76–74, Philadelphia, twelve seconds left." Two minutes later, it was game time. Led by guard Ray Lumpp, the Knicks jogged out of the runway onto the Garden floor. As they appeared, organist Gladys Gooding, the only person who played for the Brooklyn Dodgers and the Knicks, struck up "East Side, West Side," while announcer John Condon shouted over the din, "Welcome, folks, to the wonderful world of Madison Square Garden!"

O

By the early 1950s, the NBA was still struggling for major league status, and according to commissioner Maurice Podoloff, it needed an attention-getting attraction to "spark fan interest" and grab media attention. Attendance had not shattered any records, and by the early 1950s, the NBA trailed other professional sports. Publicity director Haskell Cohen thought baseball's all-star game was a magical event. The best players in the NBA had never appeared on the same floor. College basketball recently lost some of its luster with the point-shaving scandal, and fans were available to switch their allegiance to a league with integrity. Cohen discussed the idea with Podoloff and Celtics' owner Walter Brown. "I like it," Brown said, "and I'll host it in my place, no charge." The first NBA all-star game was played in the Boston Garden on March 2, 1951, three weeks prior to the playoffs.

Announcers Marty Glickman and Fort Wayne's Hillyard Gates, two of the best, worked the game on network radio. They met in the Copley Plaza Hotel, along with the historic roster of players and coaches. The two best-known pro coaches were chosen to represent their divisions. Joe Lapchick was excited about the game. His East team would face Laker coach John Kundla's West squad. Dick McGuire, Vince Boryla, and Harry Gallatin represented the Knicks. Each was having a banner year. McGuire would finish with four hundred assists, second only by a handful to Andy Phillip. Boryla's 15 points per game led the Knicks scoring, and Gallatin had gathered eight hundred rebounds, third in the league to Mikan and Dolph Schayes.

The game drew slightly more than the ten thousand fans needed to break even. Since the players had games sandwiched around the all-star date, they were expected to pay their own transportation. For their troubles, each received a $25 government bond, and later, a television set from a gracious sponsor. Only after several years did the league get around to presenting the game's MVP trophy to Boston's Easy Ed Macauley. There were just too many more important concerns for the young NBA.

Lapchick's East team quickly outran the taller but slower West. This was the era before the twenty-four-second clock, when teams could take their time nursing the ball up the floor. But seeing the huge front line from the Minneapolis Lakers, along with 6'10" Larry Faust of Fort Wayne, Lapchick knew his team had to run to make it a game.

With the clever ballhandling of Cousy and McGuire, it was like the 108th Street games they played growing up in Queens, New York. The final score was 112–94, with the East on top. Dolph Schayes, another

New Yorker, believed the freelance style suited the East squad, which knew the city game. "We ran them silly," Schayes enjoyed reminiscing. Joe Lapchick had fun, too. He saw his Knicks perform well, and the crowd enjoyed the pro game. Coaching the first all-star game to a victory went down easy with his first whiskey sour after the game. But now he had to get back to coaching the Knicks.

○

The 1951–52 season involved a three-way battle in the Eastern Division between the Knicks, Syracuse, and Boston. At the end of the season, the Knicks found themselves in third place and opened the playoffs in Boston by losing 105–94. In a best of three, the Knicks had to win the next two to stay alive, and they did just that.

After a hard-fought 101–97 win in the 69th Armory, the Knicks returned to Boston for a spectacular finish. Trailing by 9 points, the team rallied to force a double-overtime victory on a free throw by Vandeweghe, with two seconds on the clock, 88–87. The Knicks were led offensively by Max Zaslofsky and Connie Simmons. The victory jettisoned the Knicks into the best-of-five Eastern Division Final against their physical friends from upstate, the Syracuse Nationals.

Because the Knicks had finished third, the series opened in the War Memorial Auditorium in Syracuse before a rambunctious sellout crowd that never forgot Ned Irish's earlier remarks. Down 16 points and in enemy territory, the Knicks, led again by Simmons and Zaslofsky and strong play down the stretch by Vandeweghe and Clifton, were able to hold onto a 2-point lead, 87–85, as Wally Osterkorn of the Nationals launched an eighteen footer at the buzzer that missed. Later with the series tied at 1–1, the Knicks battled the Nationals in the 69th Armory for a 99–92 win highlighted by a five-minute brawl, which was encouraged by the bad blood between the teams, that drew more than one hundred spectators into the "festivities." The sellout crowd was also entertained by several spontaneous brawls that erupted between Syracuse's Dolph Schayes and Harry Gallatin and later George Kaftan. The Knicks then coasted to a 100–93 final win over the Nationals that demonstrated the balanced scoring that made the Knicks a dangerous team.

After two heroic playoff series, the Knicks were catapulted into the final with the Minneapolis Lakers, the perennial champs. New York—a young but competitive and finely tuned machine—had battled to the NBA final for the second year in a row. On April 12, 1952, however, during the first game of the best-of-seven series, the team experienced one of the most controversial calls in its history.

It began with one minute and fifty-one seconds left in the first quarter, with the Knicks trailing 19–13, when Al McGuire drove to the basket and was fouled by the Lakers' Pep Saul as he shot what appeared to be a successful layup. Officials Sid Borgia and Stan Stutz whistled simultaneously, but former Knicks guard Stutz deferred to the senior official. Borgia's closed fist indicated a foul on Saul. Since neither official tracked the shot, no field goal was signaled. As Borgia indicated "two shots," McGuire asked about the 2 points for the basket. Borgia emphatically said, "no basket." The large Laker crowd of more than ten thousand fans buzzed, realizing the officials had missed the score.

At that point, all hell broke loose. McGuire started jumping up and down while Lapchick seemed to be doing cartwheels on the sidelines. Borgia, seeing how agitated the Knicks had become, consulted his partner. "Stan, did that ball go in?" Stutz answered, "Naw, naw, it didn't," loud and clear. Years later in an interview Borgia admitted he might have ruled differently if Stutz had said he wasn't sure. Lapchick appealed to Podoloff and referee-in-chief Pat Kennedy, who were in attendance, to intervene. They refused to overrule the officials, and the call stood. The pugnacious Borgia awarded McGuire two free throws. He converted one.

The Knicks came out of the dispute with 1 point instead of 2 or possibly 3, which could have decided the game. Behind by 5 points near the end of the game, the Knicks fought back to cause three ties in the last four minutes and sent the game into overtime with a Connie Simmons tip-in near the buzzer.

With the game ending in a tie, the teams played a five-minute overtime with the Lakers winning 83–79. In the end, the loss was the difference, because the Lakers won the championship series, 4–3. The obvious oversight led to a rule change: when in doubt, officials were to consult the scorer. The Knicks never forgot the call. Ned Irish didn't, either. Lapchick's Knicks would never win a championship and never get that close again. Some believed it was an omen for Lapchick. Irish, the leader of New York basketball, the largest market in the league, wanted a championship. This drive to win eventually caused Irish to turn against his coach. Problems with Irish would snowball for Lapchick over the next few years.

One area of agreement between owner and coach, however, had been the decision to bring Sweetwater Clifton on board. Although in most games he was still the only black on the floor, he maintained a level of play that made fans forget his less-intense Globetrotter days. Clifton was an important component of Lapchick's equation for success. Clifton's defense when teamed with Gallatin's rebounding forged a winning combination. Sweets, one of the first black NBA players, accomplished yeoman tasks while never sounding a negative word. He may have been the most talented Knick, and when he came to play, he often proved it. But there was a mystery about the first black to play for the team.

Joe Lapchick cupping basketball. He helped win two pro championships playing for the Cleveland Rosenblums in the 1928–1929, and 1929–1930 seasons after the Celtics had been disbanded. The ball was called a pumpkin because of its size.

Classic Joe Lapchick pose as the young, up and coming center for the Original Celtics in the mid-1920s. Notice the boxerlike sneakers and reinforced knee pads he wore.

The well-dressed Original Celtics, "on the road," visiting with President Calvin Coolidge, on the White House lawn in February 1925. They are described as, "World's Basketball Champions," an honor they accepted with pride. Joe Lapchick is the one in the rear with the bowtie.

Babe Ruth (left), Jack Goldy (middle), and a young Joe Lapchick (right) in 1920. Lapchick played for the New York Whirlwinds at the time.

Power packed Original Celtics lineup in the 1920s. Left to right—Johnny
Beckman, Nat Holman, Pete Barry, Dutch Dehnert, Chris Leonard, and Joe
Lapchick. Beckman, Holman, and Lapchick were among the highest paid pros
of the era, each earning more than $10,000 a season.

The 1942–1943 St. John's NIT champs. Joe Lapchick (holding the winners' wristwatches). To
the left of the coach is sophomore Harry Boykoff, the 6'8" tournament MVP. To the right of
Lapchick is Haggerty Award winner, Fuzzy Levane. Hy Gotkin (12) was one of Lapchick's all
time favorite players.

Joe Lapchick's 1953–1954 New York Knickerbocker team that finished first in the NBA's Eastern Division. Nat "Sweetwater" Clifton (#8) was one of three blacks to integrate the NBA in 1950.

Author Gus Alfieri, 6'2" guard, played for Joe Lapchick from 1956 to 1959.

Joe Lapchick (left) *diagramming a play at Flushing Armory for his new assistant Lou Carnesecca* (middle) *and freshman coach Jack Kaiser* (right) *for the start of the 1958–1959 season.*

Joe Lapchick's 1958–1959 St. John's team, winners of the Holiday Festival and the 1959 National Invitation Tournament. Alan Seiden (33) and Tony Jackson (directly behind Seiden) both made All-American teams. Gus Alfieri sits in the middle of the second row.

Joe Lapchick, right, with son, Rich Lapchick, reading a scrapbook from the 1958–1959 championship season in their house in Yonkers, New York. Photo of elder son, Joe, football player from West Point appears over the fireplace. Dr. Richard Lapchick is nationally known in the field of sports social issues. PHOTO COURTESY OF ROUTEL STUDIO.

Joe Lapchick poses after being selected in 1962 for "Coach of the Year" honors by the New York sportswriters.

Joe Lapchick facing the media after his St. John's team's dramatic seventeen point, come-from-behind victory over the Cazzie Russell–led Michigan team, number one in the country, in the final of the Holiday Festival in Madison Square Garden on January 2, 1965.

Always nattily dressed, Joe Lapchick, right, *greets his good friend Clair Bee,* left, *in Madison Square Garden. Bee, famous coach of LIU, was also the author of the Chip Hilton children sports books.* PHOTO COURTESY OF UNITED PRESS INTERNATIONAL PHOTO.

Joe Lapchick (left) *relaxing before a St. John's game at Madison Square Garden, sitting on the bench with an unidentified coach.*
© MAJOR LEAGUE GRAPHICS.

Joe Lapchick waves good-bye in Madison Square Garden in March 1965 after his St. John's team defeated Villanova to win his fourth National Invitation Tournament. It was Lapchick's last coached game, and he went out a winner.
PHOTO COURTESY OF LIFE MAGAZINE.

Chapter 10
The Effigy
of a Coach

Richie Lapchick was five years old and had started school, but he still enjoyed playing in his room before dinner. He was particularly fascinated with his metallic toy soldiers, setting up military formations on his three windowsills. As he fantasized about war games, he heard loud voices in front of his brown-shingled, Yonkers home and peered through the window curtains. In the late afternoon darkness, he could see strangers milling around a long figure that was tied to the lower limb of a large oak tree in front of his home. The way it dangled from the tree, like a dead body, frightened him. Years later, Richie still remembered the horror of it all. "I didn't know what was going on, but I sensed danger."

"Mommy, look what's outside," Richie screamed as he ran down the stairs. His mother looked up from sorting dishes in the kitchen and ran to whisk Richie away from the window. "What's the matter, Richie?" she asked, rushing to him.

As she narrowed her eyes to adjust to the darkness, she saw what appeared to be a crude figure dressed in a basketball uniform and dangling from a limb of the tree. Its face was blackened, and the word "KNICKER-BOCKERS," written in blood-red paint on its chest, only added to the drama. Along with the unmistakable caricature of her husband were a half-dozen picketers waving signs and shouting racial epithets. The angry crowd was upset by the New York Knickerbockers' recent addition of Nat "Sweet-water" Clifton, one of the first NBA black players, and had come to Joe Lapchick's home to vent their hatred. Ned Irish, the Knicks' general manager, wanted Clifton. The team lacked that "little extra" to clinch a championship, and Clifton's 6'6" stature and 230 pounds of physical play and rebounding strength could help deliver it.

The public demonstration happened only once, but Lapchick never forgot the mock hanging. His first reaction was a mixture of anger and bewilderment. Who would believe in the 1950s that a New York professional coach was being harassed by a bunch of senseless racists? He realized local Yonkers residents, perhaps even neighbors, were involved, but he took no legal action and never called the police.

Lapchick received other threats shortly after Clifton joined the Knicks in the fall of 1950. He paced his attic retreat after late-night telephone calls labeled him a "nigger-lover." As in most communities, change brought friction. Several years before the incident, black religious leader Father Devine had bought a house diagonally across from the Lapchicks. While Devine rarely lived in Yonkers, his integrated Peace Mission commune bothered the solidly white, middle-class community, and rumors still circulate that a cross-burning occurred at the Devine house. Yonkers's smoldering resentment flared up when their neighbor made headlines integrating the NBA. Lapchick, who worried about winning a championship for Ned Irish, now added local hatred to his list of concerns.

O

Joe Lapchick's relevancy to the game was further enhanced by the role he played in the introduction of blacks to professional basketball. In May 1950, Lapchick guided Sweetwater Clifton, the first announced African-American to sign an NBA contract, into the Knicks and opened the way for future minorities to change basketball forever. When Lapchick's career is measured, his effort with integration is one of his finest accomplishments. Though Lapchick helped pioneer integration and welcomed Clifton to the Knicks, he realized the hot seat he occupied because New York was the media focus of the NBA, and not everyone cheered the racial changes. Both the coach and his player were targets in a battle with an invisible enemy who hid his bigoted feelings about race. Lapchick was also concerned about whether integration would upset the delicate balance of team chemistry.

Hotel accommodations in segregated cities like Baltimore and Fort Wayne, as well as fan reaction, could create turmoil that might affect Knicks play. But Clifton's easygoing manner meant he cooperated with Lapchick rather than challenged him, and he would be the least of the coach's problems.

O

Former Harlem Globetrotter Nathaniel "Sweetwater" Clifton was the most popular of the three African-Americans, including Boston's Chuck Cooper and the Washington Capitols' Earl Lloyd, who simultaneously integrated the NBA in 1950. Billed as 6'8" in Madison Square Garden programs, Clifton actually measured 6'6". But that wasn't the only misleading folklore spun about him.

Clifton lived in Chicago but was born in the Deep South of Little Rock, Arkansas, with roots that taught him to smile through white man's treachery. Some newspaper accounts said he played for Xavier University, while others rumored he never attended college. Although Nat Clifton was affectionately known as "Sweetwater" or "Sweets," his real name was Clifton Nathaniel, an unusual twist that seemed to set the tone for New York's first black Knickerbocker. When sportswriters later asked why he changed his name, the only answer Clifton gave was it fit better in box scores. There was a simplicity to this large man with the huge hands, and a personality that tried never to offend.

Part of Clifton's popularity stemmed from his colorful nickname. Sportswriters wrote how he loved soda pop and drank buckets of it. Sweets went along with their inventions. "I got the name when I was a kid," Clifton once said, "because all I ever wanted to drink was soda pop. You know, sweet water." The truth was "Sweetwater" originated during Clifton's childhood in England, Arkansas. His grandmother used snuff, and he imitated her by putting cocoa between his cheek and gum and then sucked in water to create a similar experience. Clifton also had a taste for alcohol and the nightlife, and the good times that went with them. However, when important games were on the line against taller opponents like George Mikan and Vern Mikkelsen of the Lakers, Clifton played with the passion of a winner.

Clifton's powerful body was topped with a large, long head and squared-off jaw. His hands were glued to extra long, loose arms and were made for palming and whirling a basketball to entertain and to catch a thrown ball with a single hand as if it were a baseball. He had the brute force of John Steinbeck's Lenny from *Of Mice and Men*, that if agitated had to be harnessed. Under the quiet facade fermented an explosive power capable of crushing an opponent's thoughts of bothering any Knicks teammate.

Like many athletes, Clifton improved his ballhandling skills with Stickum, a clear, unnoticeable adhesive used to grip better. Technically it was illegal, but Knicks ball boy Kurt Block kept it in a small paper cup on the bench. Clifton used more than Stickum when playing. Fanatical about personal hygiene, Sweets loved showering two or three times a day, laundering his own uniforms, and covering himself before games with a fragrant lotion, as well as French toilet water. He also liked lubricating his body, believing it protected his skin. Since he had trained with professional fighters, he knew it prevented skin abrasions, deadly for a boxer's face.

Listed at twenty-eight, and reputed by the Knicks press guide to have played in college before the war, Clifton seemed older. Teammates liked to speculate about his age. Vandeweghe nicknamed him "Methuselah," while Braun thought he had covered up his age. Before he joined the Knicks, Clifton played first base in the Cleveland Indians organization, while under contract with Abe Saperstein's Harlem Globetrotters. Many writers compared him to the Indians' colorful fastball pitcher Leroy "Satchel" Paige, who also entered a white man's sport considerably older than his recorded age.

Clifton's professional baseball career sprang from a recommendation by Saperstein to Cleveland Indians owner Bill Veeck. Saperstein, who doubled as a promoter of black baseball, told Veeck Clifton never played baseball but had major league potential. Baseball had recently crossed the color line, and Veeck, who tried to buy the Philadelphia Phillies in 1943 to introduce blacks to the major leagues, was interested. In 1948, the Indians' flamboyant owner assigned Clifton to his Dayton farm team, where Clifton led the league in homers, doubles, and total bases and hit .348. Moved to the Indians Double-A team in Wilkes-Barre, Pennsylvania, Clifton again powered the league in homers, RBIs, and total bases, with a batting average of more than .300. When Saperstein realized he might lose Clifton to baseball, he sent him on a Globetrotter tour during the summer of 1949 with instructions for him not to play baseball.

Saperstein, who owned the Globetrotters from their inception in 1927, is credited with providing blacks with an opportunity to play when other pro leagues refused them. He also initiated the American Basketball League's 3-point shot in 1962. The 3-point shot, standard today in scholastic, college, and NBA play, has changed much of the game's offensive strategy. On the other hand, Saperstein presents another page in the history of exploited black athletes. The diminutive son of a Chicago tailor, whose father stitched the first Globetrotter red, white, and blue uniforms, measured 5'3". However, he brazenly promoted himself as the "The Jewish Abe Lincoln," while cashing in on a virtual monopoly of black talent. Besides the New York Rens, Saperstein's Chicago-based Globetrotters were the only other successful black team prior to NBA integration.

Taking full advantage of his power, Saperstein demonstrated little compassion for his players. He paid low salaries for long, demanding game schedules. Dribbling wizard Marquis Haynes remembered, "He thought nothing of cutting corners in Globetrotter accommodations, forcing three or even four players to sleep across a bed."

Once in the midst of a salary dispute with Haynes, Saperstein insisted, "Blacks don't need as much money as the white man." Every Globetrotter knew white women and Cadillacs were rebellious symbols to his boss, and thus were out of bounds. His patronizing ways left a lasting negative impression on those who played for him. Saperstein enjoyed the power he had in the black player market. Athletes like Clifton, with little bargaining leverage, had no place to go. The Globetrotters owner held the trump cards and acted strictly for monetary reasons. When the NBA owners began to talk about integration, Saperstein, who knew the new league relied on Globetrotter doubleheaders to pay bills, threatened not to play them. Clifton's willingness to leave the Globetrotters stemmed from a salary disagreement. "He was paying the college all-stars more money than he paid us, and I happened to find out about it." Clifton didn't trust Saperstein and later accepted Irish's Knickerbockers offer as the lesser of two evils.

○

In the late 1920s, during the prime of Joe Lapchick's playing career, he and his Celtics teammates arrived early in Louisville, Kentucky, for a game the next night. With time on their hands, they decided to watch the Rens play the local collegians. As the Rens warmed up, Lapchick decided to go onto the court to greet center Tarzan Cooper. "How you doing, Tall Joe," Cooper responded to his friend as the men embraced.

The high school gym grew silent. This was Jim Crow country, where racial separation was strictly enforced. After a few seconds of stunned silence, the hecklers started with hoot calls and snide remarks, accentuated with words hyphenated with "nigger." Lapchick, who knew little of racial prejudice, was caught off guard. His job as a basketball pro was to entertain crowds, but his innocent contact with Cooper had disturbed them. Word of the "unforgivable deed" circulated in Louisville like church gossip. When the Celtics returned to their hotel, they were asked to leave. According to Rens coach Bob Douglas, the Celtics' game was canceled, and the team left quietly, narrowly avoiding an incident.

A few years later, Lapchick's barnstorming Celtics played the Rens in a segregated town outside of St. Louis, Missouri. As coach and manager, Lapchick paid more attention to the game's details. "Good game," Douglas said to Lapchick afterwards, as they shook hands outside the locker room. With bags packed for their next stop, the two seasoned travelers chatted while waiting for promoter Fred Gardner to pay them. "Here's your $500, Joe," Gardner said as he handed Lapchick an unsealed envelope with a stack of crisp $20 bills. Then he turned to Douglas to write a $500 check.

Lapchick sized up the situation. He would have no problem with the cash, but how would a black man cash a check in a segregated town? Lapchick anticipated only problems for him. "Fred," Lapchick called out as he walked toward him, "write me a check, I'll give the cash to Bob." A smile lit up Douglas's face as Lapchick handed him the cash. The Rens coach never forgot the considerate gesture of the tall coach from New York. Lapchick had made a friend for life.

Joe Lapchick never forgot the helpless feeling deep in the pit of his stomach thinking how Douglas and his team were forced to sleep in their bus rather than test travel accommodations in Jim Crow towns. Nevertheless, they played for the same folks who denied them a clean bed and a hot meal. Game site billboards blared assurance to white fans there was a "COLORED SECTION" in the balcony. The Rens mirrored the rise of professional basketball during the Golden Age of Sports from the 1920s into the 1930s and were considered the Celtics' closest rivals. Black athletes had previously integrated college sports and several minor pro leagues, and both the Rens and Globetrotters had toured against whites since the 1920s. But as late as the 1940s, they were still denied opportunities enjoyed by whites. In spite of the fact that the Rens were reputed to be the best pro team of the 1930s, society wasn't ready to accept them into the white world of sports. But that didn't stop Douglas from trying.

Although the new Basketball Association of America league excluded blacks, the established National Basketball League was already integrated and had signed two New York blacks in 1946, LIU great Dolly King and Rens star Herman "Pop" Gates.

In the fall of 1947, Douglas attempted to further integrate the more talented NBL with his black team. Would the league accept the Rens, even though the team had beaten the best white teams and in March 1947 in the Chicago World Tournament narrowly missed defeating the Minneapolis Lakers? Tired of touring the country in a bus for their bread, Douglas realized that with Brooklyn Dodgers' Jackie Robinson electrifying major league baseball, it was an opportunity of a lifetime, a chance to validate their claim to equality. The NBL owners met in Philadelphia. On their agenda was the admission of the Rens, with Douglas invited to sit in. Although the league was integrated, an all-black team scared some owners. As the discussion continued, it became obvious the Rens were facing heavy opposition. The owners feared the Rens would reduce white crowds.

Joe Lapchick, who had been waiting to speak, snuffed out his cigarette and strode to the front of the room. As a pioneer player and well-respected figure in professional basketball, Douglas could not have asked for a better character reference than the old pro.

Lapchick needed no notes or statistics, but was ready to pour out his heart. "I may be a newcomer to professional coaching," he humbly began, "but I support Bob Douglas's bid to play." He talked of the Celtics many battles against the Rens. "I may lose my job for saying this," Lapchick emphasized by knuckling the mahogany table that the owners encircled, "but I'd play against the Rens any goddam day. They're the best."

"How do you know that, Joe?" league official Ike Duffey asked. Lapchick told them how the Celtics, the best of their era, were played even by the Rens, in spite of some of the favoritism the Celtics received from officials while playing an all-black team in white towns. Having said his piece, Lapchick sat down by his friend to await the outcome.

After Douglas and Lapchick left the room, the owners voted against the Rens. Duffey gave Douglas the bad news. "Financial concerns" were given as the reason, but Douglas knew their day would come.

When the Detroit Vagabonds folded in December 1948, the Rens finally joined the NBL as the Dayton Rens. The Rens completed the remaining forty games but couldn't draw fans to watch an all-black team. In 1949, when the two pro leagues merged to form the NBA, the Rens' bittersweet experiment ended.

However, even though the NBL had previously integrated, the NBA owners agreed to an unwritten understanding that blacks would be excluded. Ironically, when the NBA printed its first game programs, it listed all the previous teams from both leagues, except the Dayton Rens. They were left out as if their games were never played. The Rens conveniently became invisible.

But as basketball became more popular in the postwar period, coupled with the success of baseball's integration, more talk centered around the possibility of blacks playing in the NBA. Ned Irish, sensing the financial advantages of integration and recognizing that this source of talent would help his team, favored the change. There were several players Joe Lapchick recommended who fit in the Knicks' plans, but the one name that kept popping up was Harlem Globetrotter Nat "Sweetwater" Clifton.

O

Eddie Gottlieb, head of the Philadelphia Warriors, took the Empire State Building's elevator to the eightieth floor and pushed open the door of room 8020, which read "NATIONAL BASKETBALL ASSOCIATION" and in slightly smaller lettering "AMERICAN HOCKEY LEAGUE." As he entered the NBA office of commissioner Maurice Podoloff, he wondered how many general managers would approve integration for the 1950–51 season.

Rochester Royals owner Les Harrison greeted him with an extended hand and a copy of the agenda for the March meeting of the NBA's governors. "Did you hear some teams are thinking of drafting Negroes?" the Rochester boss whispered. With the NBA draft six weeks away, this got Gottlieb's attention. Harrison listed several Eastern teams, with Boston and New York heading the list. "It can ruin us," Gottlieb insisted, as he walked to the more private conference room already filled with smoke and worry. Gottlieb scanned the room counting potential votes. The governors straw ballot would decide the league's integration policy, the meeting's most controversial issue.

Several general managers cut their financial laments short as New York's Ned Irish entered the room. Few owners cared for Irish, but the

New York czar was necessary for their financial survival. Although the owners knew the Knicks' value to the league and that it didn't pay to ruffle Irish's feathers, caving in to his demands was another story.

Maybe it was his Ivy League airs or lack of humor or just that he controlled their destiny. Whatever it was, he wasn't popular with the owners. But Irish didn't much care about high ratings. By March 1950, Irish viewed integration as the route to the Knicks first NBA crown.

As the remaining governors filed in and the meeting was called to order, the New York general manager waited impatiently for the agenda to swing to integration, and then on cue, sprang into action. "I want black players in our league," Irish curtly demanded. He let that sink in, and then continued badgering the owners. "If the Knicks can't sign Clifton, New York will withdraw from the league," he threatened. He pounded the table for emphasis as he finished his statement and then stormed out of the room.

Minneapolis's Max Winter was annoyed and let the governors know it. Fort Wayne's Carl Bennett tried to soothe his Midwestern neighbor. "You may be right, Max, but sooner or later, blacks are going to make it in this league," he countered. Gottlieb saw integration's financial risks. His ties to Abe Saperstein meant more than favorable dates, since he had an interest in the team that toured with the Globetrotters. The Warriors' general manager banked on Saperstein's team playing doubleheaders in his arena. Gottlieb hesitated to bite the hand that fed his struggling franchise. "Irish isn't the only one interested in signing blacks," Boston's Walter Brown informed the board. Brown was the spirited Celtics owner whose peppery coach, Red Auerbach, was in agreement. "The Celtics intend to draft a black, too," Brown confirmed.

Gottlieb realized with Irish and Brown for integration, Leo Ferris of Syracuse and Harrison of Rochester were likely to follow. He expected segregated cities like Baltimore and Indianapolis, along with Carl Bennett's Fort Wayne, would vote against blacks. Minneapolis, too, would likely side with its Midwestern neighbors and vote no. His vote made it five against. Gottlieb needed one more no to kill the straw vote. The two undecided votes were Mike Uline of the Washington Caps and Tri-Cities' Ben Kerner. The District of Columbia was segregated, but Kerner was hard to figure.

After a half-hour of heated discussion, Irish returned for the historic vote. The governors squirmed in their seats as Podoloff polled them. "In favor," Irish and Brown announced, loud and clear. Gottlieb and Winter's "opposed" was as emphatic. Kerner's no vote made Gottlieb feel the issue might be killed after all. The voting seesawed until Mike Uline voted "in favor," knotting the count at five. Gottlieb relaxed. He knew Fort Wayne, like all of Indiana, was a city that traditionally discouraged blacks playing with whites. When Bennett voted "in favor," Gottlieb was stunned. Integration passed six to five, opening the door to blacks. Podoloff made it official: the NBA, like major league baseball, would accept blacks. After the initial stir, Podoloff cautioned the owners not to announce the decision. "Accept integration as the new direction of the NBA," Podoloff decreed.

With the voting complete, Gottlieb reviewed his miscalculation. He could understand the Caps voting in the affirmative because he learned they had decided to draft blacks, and he was not shocked by Kerner's opposition. But he couldn't figure Bennett. Fort Wayne had no interest in black players, and yet, his vote turned the league upside down. Why? As the meeting broke up, the Philadelphia general manager buttonholed Bennett to vent his anger. Mild-mannered Carl Bennett had spent a lifetime in basketball as an NBL player, coach, and now the general manager of Zollner's Pistons. "Carl, you sonofabitch. You just ruined the league." Bennett was surprised by Gottlieb's outburst. "What are you worried about? We've increased the supply of quality players." Later, Bennett admitted that Zollner's eighteen hundred piston-plant workers had something to do with it. "How would it look if Mr. Zollner, owner of a racially mixed plant, voted against integration?" Bennett asked. It made sense, although Gottlieb was still boiling.

Bennett knew how important Irish was to the league. "Without New York," he felt, "the NBA would fold." Gottlieb wasn't buying any of that. "Yeah, but in five years," Gottlieb shot back, "the league will be 75 percent black," which, he predicted, would hurt attendance. Gottlieb touched a sensitive nerve for owners who wondered whether white audiences would support mixed teams. Gottlieb's prediction proved half-right. The number of blacks in the NBA increased to where today it's more than 80 percent. But he misjudged fan reaction, which grew as the game became more exciting. The new direction would also test Joe Lapchick. The old pro never coached black players, but he understood human nature. He knew what made athletes respond, and he planned to have Clifton click with the Knicks.

O

Joe Lapchick was explaining this to the small, barrel-chested Knicker-bockers PR man Lester Scott when his secretary popped her head into the office. "The boss wants to talk with you, Joe," she said. Lapchick looked up, dusted cigarette ashes from his suit jacket, and headed up to Ned Irish's office.

"What do you think of Sweetwater Clifton?" Irish asked before Lapchick had a chance to sit down. Sensing Irish's impatience, Lapchick went right into an evaluation. "We still need a big man, and I think this fellow from the Globetrotters is the answer." Lapchick went on to explain that Clifton owned the best hands in basketball. "How good would he be in our league?" Irish asked. "Plenty," Lapchick volleyed back. The Knicks coach knew Sweetwater handled the ball smoothly like a guard and could rebound with the young Harry Gallatin, the Knicks recent surprise draft pick. Clifton would have an immediate impact on the Knicks. "He's only 6'5" or 6'6", but owns those long arms that reach past his knees," Lapchick said, marking his trousers with his hand for emphasis. "Clifton can help us, and I recommend we sign him," he concluded.

Typically, Irish's mind was already made up, and he would send his trusted aid, Fred Podesta, to sign Clifton. Podesta would fly to Chicago to finalize the deal with Saperstein. The owner of the Globetrotters was willing to part with his high-scoring forward because of their financial differences. But there was another factor that made Saperstein cooperate.

"Now that the league approved integration," Irish thought out loud, "we have to get into the race." Both Irish and Lapchick knew the Knicks had been hurt competing against taller, more physical teams, and with last year's merger, they expected more of the same. Unlike football or baseball where there are more critical positions to fill, one key player in basketball could turn a franchise around.

Lapchick knew at least two other NBA teams interested in black players. Boston liked 6'5" forward Chuck Cooper from Duquesne University while the Washington Capitols, who had hosted a black college postseason tournament at Uline Arena, spotted a fleet-footed guard, Harold Hunter, from North Carolina College along with Earl Lloyd, a sturdy 6'6" forward from West Virginia State. Irish was not particularly interested in helping minorities. In the past, when black teams asked to use Madison Square Garden, or black college champions were suggested for the NIT, he was opposed. Irish was more interested in the tinkle of the turnstile and the number of black fans Clifton might attract, than whether an NBA city became integrated. Like most owners, Irish favored integration when the Knicks would benefit directly.

In 1947, Clifton demonstrated his ability in the World Tournament in Chicago playing for the Rens. He helped battle to the final against the powerful Lakers. In spite of foul trouble, Clifton led his team with 24 points in a close loss. At this point, his reputation was at its peak. Saperstein signed Clifton to a $10,000 annual contract; the highest ever paid a Globetrotter. When Irish heard of the rift between Clifton and the Globetrotters owner over money, he sent Podesta to meet with Saperstein in the NBA commissioner's office.

Clifton's contract was purchased in early May 1950, but the Knickerbockers front office didn't announce it until the end of the month. The letter to Irish closing the deal was dated May 3, 1950. "I have just purchased Sweetwater's contract for $12,500," Podesta reported. Saperstein paid Clifton $4,000 from the Knickerbockers money, but the Globetrotter still felt cheated. Clifton would later sign a Knicks contract for $7,500, more than the $5,000 Jackie Robinson received from Branch Rickey's Dodgers in 1947, but less than the reported $10,000 the Globetrotters owner paid him. The Knicks, along with Boston and Washington, had entered a new, untapped player market that would permanently change basketball.

O

"Clifton, Negro Ace, Goes To Knickerbocker Five," was the way the *New York Times* heralded Nat "Sweetwater" Clifton's entrance into the NBA in May 1950. Unlike the hullabaloo surrounding Jackie Robinson, Clifton's groundbreaking entrance was a small item in the back pages of the sports section. The media treated it as of little importance, hardly raising any attention in the sports world.

The press release listed Clifton as the third black to enter the NBA, but the first signed, all within days of each other. When Cooper was signed, the Boston papers didn't bother mentioning he was black. They either didn't know or didn't care. Jackie Robinson stole most of the headlines from pro basketball, a minor sport compared to major league baseball and college basketball. Since sports had been integrated in New England for years and game reports were sketchy, the significance was lost. However, in spite of its patriotic tradition, Boston had a history of intolerance toward minorities in sports.

For years, most accounts of NBA integration were inaccurate. Cooper was treated as the first black to play. In the 1980s, *Sports Illustrated* clarified the issue: Washington Capitols' Earl Lloyd played first, Boston's Cooper was drafted first, and the Knicks' Sweetwater Clifton signed first. A fourth player, Hank DeZonie, played only five games later that year for the Tri-Cities Hawks. What caused confusion was that Lloyd entered the military after playing his first seven games, and by January the Washington Caps folded.

While Cooper made his Celtics debut on November 1, 1950, in Fort Wayne, Indiana, history was actually made the day before in Rochester, New York. On Halloween night, October 31, 1950, a Sports Arena crowd of 2,184 watched Earl Lloyd and his Washington Caps lose to the Rochester Royals, 78–70, after trailing by 21 points with eight minutes left.

Again, the local newspapers, unaware of the game's historical significance, made no mention of Lloyd being the NBA's first black. Lloyd scored 6 points and remembered no incident. "Rochester was a small, sleepy upstate town, where in the wintertime nobody hated anybody," Lloyd recalled. "Besides all the public schools and local colleges were already integrated." On November 4, also in Fort Wayne, Clifton was the last of the three to play.

Fort Wayne, Indianapolis, St. Louis, and Baltimore were segregated NBA cities, but racial prejudice also extended to early season exhibitions played in the South to help cover expenses and popularize the game in new markets. Shortly after Clifton joined the Knicks, the team journeyed to Raleigh, North Carolina, to play an exhibition against the Rochester Royals before a sellout crowd to welcome North Carolina State Wolfpack's favorite son, Sam Ranzino. Clifton's poor treatment was lost in the ballyhoo over Ranzino. "He wasn't allowed to stay with us in our hotel," reserve forward George Kaftan recalled. Although this was an early taste of bigotry for Sweets, it was not the league's only experience with segregation.

In 1952, the Syracuse Nationals scheduled a preseason game in South Carolina. Because of the state's segregation laws, Coach Al Cervi told Earl Lloyd to stay home to avoid problems. At the time, Lloyd looked at it as a chance to rest. "But when I examined it later in life, I was disturbed," he recalled, feeling rejected by his own team. "If I'm part of the team, don't schedule a game where I'm not welcome," Lloyd reasoned.

While touring with the Globetrotters, Clifton learned to adjust. "In Birmingham, Alabama, we would play an afternoon game for whites,"

Clifton recalled, "and at night for blacks." What he remembered most of those games was a rope separating blacks from whites. "At some games they put a rope down in between, but we wouldn't play until they removed it." He didn't mind separating races, but "just didn't like that rope in between." Clifton smiled with satisfaction, realizing it was the closest he came to protesting. Globetrotter Marquis Haynes remembered playing in Jackson, Mississippi, to an exclusively black audience. "We had to have a black referee and a black scorer." The only white face was the sheriff's, who was there to make sure no other whites were present.

Of the three original black players, Chuck Cooper had the most difficulty with racial intolerance. While Lloyd grew up with it and Clifton had traveled with sports teams in segregated cities, Cooper was raised in Pittsburgh, an integrated Northern city, and was unfamiliar with segregation. Lloyd sensed the problem. "When Chuck or Sweetwater played in my town, I picked them up and provided dinner and company," he recalled. The same treatment was afforded Lloyd.

A widely publicized racial experience involved Cooper during his freshmen year at Duquesne. In December 1946, the school was forced to cancel a home game with the University of Tennessee because the Southern school refused to compete against a black. When he played for the Celtics, Cooper faced similar bigotry.

Little effort was made by the Knicks organization or its players to fight for Clifton's traveling rights. The team, however, tried to soften the injustice. "The Claypool Hotel in Indianapolis and the Lord Baltimore in Maryland," teammate Ray Lumpp said, "were two hotels that turned Sweets away." His teammates offered to go to another hotel, but Clifton discouraged the idea. Society was less conscious in the 1950s of blacks' daily problems. Clifton was no crusader. He simply wanted to play and have fun. He was the NBA's "ideal" black: talented, reserved, and rarely complaining about racial slights. "I didn't go out there to change anything," he said. In most cases, Sweets solved his own hotel problems on the road by staying with friends. While Clifton never complained about being separated on trips, Lapchick tried to make Clifton fit in with the team.

○

Ernie Vandeweghe invited Harry Belafonte, the handsome black entertainer, to drop into the Knicks dressing room before a game. Lapchick took the opportunity to make Clifton feel part of the team. As coach and chief chemist, it was Lapchick's job to blend a predominantly white, suburban, middle-class team with Clifton. "The trouble with you, Sweets, is that you think you look like Belafonte," Lapchick quipped, "but you're the ugliest guy I know, ugly enough to make the all-ugly team." Sizing up his coach's mood, Clifton shot back, "I heard you, and think you would be the coach of that team."

Lapchick once told his son, Richard, of a conversation with Bob Douglas in 1947, when he had stood up for the Rens manager and his dream of blacks playing in a professional league. "I know now there are whites," Douglas told the coach, "who would risk everything for blacks." In 1950, Lapchick was ready to make Douglas's dream a reality. As coach of a black player, Lapchick could help clear the way for others. When Clifton reported to the Knicks in late October of 1950, after playing baseball with the Cleveland Indians organization, Lapchick was anxious to start what could be the Knicks finest season. In Sweetwater, Irish had acquired an experienced physical warrior who played two major sports, was a war veteran, coped with bigotry, and had survived. Lapchick's job was to make the new black forward blend by treating everyone as professionals, with no prep school rules. As coach he knew each player was different.

"Some you pat on the ass, others you kick in the ass," was a reality Lapchick learned about coaching. He allowed Clifton flexibility to function freely. However, while the coach respected Clifton's maturity, he asked Sweets to act professionally. But there were humorous times when their signals got crossed. Lapchick had called an 11:00 A.M. practice for Sunday morning in their Bear Mountain preseason facility. About 11:30 A.M., Clifton came jogging onto the court. "Where were you, Sweets?" Lapchick wanted to know. "Coach, I was getting a haircut," the powerful center answered, with the team howling in the background. Clifton learned to take care of personal business at more opportune times.

The team accepted Clifton's special rules. He was older, had been through segregation problems, but he never let the coach's considerations interfere with his play. His teammates realized he could handle himself. "Sweets wasn't much for rules," Braun recalled, "but no one thought much about it, or held it against him, as long as he showed up and played hard." They understood the unique circumstances and had no animosity toward Sweets's privileges. Basketball in the early 1950s was a white man's game, with most of the Knicks having little experience with blacks. The

McGuires, guards Dick and Al, swing man Vandeweghe, center Simmons, and Lumpp came from mainly white, suburban Long Island. Gallatin, who attended college in Missouri, grew up in a small town in western Illinois unsympathetic to blacks. Only shooting guard Max Zaslofsky and Vince Boryla had inner city experience. And Lapchick's experience with blacks was more as a pro player.

His teammates judged Clifton by his ability and quickly accepted him. When they traveled, he was always welcomed in their card games. Fans, too, took to Clifton. His easygoing manner made him a hometown favorite. But his acceptance did not stop racists from cranking out their venom.

As Lapchick watched Clifton in practice, he determined that Clifton's adjustment to the NBA, unlike Cooper's or Lloyd's, was focused more on learning to play hard. After two years of soft competition rigged for Globetrotters showboating, Lapchick was asking Clifton to play the best big men in the league. Sweetwater was expected to understand unwritten rules of conduct that professional players followed. And, as for most newcomers, there was a kind of hazing period, where his opponents tested a rookie's manhood. His first year with the Knicks presented questions that had to be answered. One involved Clifton's toughness.

O

"Can you fight?" Joe Lapchick asked Clifton during an informal conversation in the train's smoking car as it rumbled along from Chicago to Fort Wayne, Indiana, for an early season game. "I'm terrible," was Sweetwater's misleading answer. Lapchick, understanding the laws of survival in the NBA, urged Clifton to defend himself. "You have to challenge these guys or they'll push you right out of the league," Lapchick warned. The new Knick, trying to avoid controversy, told his coach he didn't want to fight, never mentioning that he had sparred with heavyweight champion Joe Louis and with Bob Satterfield in Chicago.

"Sweets didn't have a mean bone in his body," teammate Braun remembered. However, the muscled forward was soon forced to act. Clifton's test came later that first year during an exhibition game in Albany with Bob Harris of the Boston Celtics, a newly acquired 6'7" Oklahoman noted for his aggressive play. More comfortable in the league by midseason, Clifton tried demonstrating his ballhandling on Harris. "I did a little fancy Globetrotters trick," Clifton explained. "You know, a twist where I threw the ball around his head fast."

Harris, annoyed with Clifton's theatrics, threatened the sad-faced Knick. The old Globetrotter placed the ball over the Celtic's head and drew it back, which was funny when he was on tour but now only angered Harris. As Clifton went up for a shot the Celtic buried a hard elbow into the Knicks forward's gut that ignited the altercation. But when Harris then used the word, "nigger," Clifton polished him off with a professional one-two, left-right combination. "He looked like he was gonna hit me," Clifton recalled, "so I hit him first and knocked him out." Other black players understood his feelings. "Only one thing made Sweets react," Earl Lloyd later explained, "and that was 'the magic word,' a no-no; even from your own teammates it was not tolerated." Clifton was one of the strongest opponents Lloyd ever played against. "He was a sleeping tiger, better left alone," Lloyd said, "but if aroused, he was a fierce fighter."

The Celtics initially raced from the bench to help their teammate, but when they saw how easily Harris was handled, they thought better of it. "All you could smell," Lapchick remembered, "was rubber burning," the screeching halt the Celtics bench made as they saw Harris hit the deck. Celtics teammate, "Easy Ed" Macauley saw the damage Clifton inflicted with two quick punches. "Harris's face was puffed up for a week," Macauley remembered. Clifton immediately had the league's respect. "After that, no one wanted to fight him." Seeing how effective he was with his fists, people later asked Clifton why he didn't fight for a living. He smiled and answered innocently, "My mother wouldn't let me."

Braun viewed Clifton as a "helluva fighter," but one who preferred playing to fighting. Knickerbockers pundits, however, were convinced that Clifton added the physical presence most pro teams had, but the Knicks had lacked. Clifton became a dominant force that caused opponents to think twice before challenging the undersized Knicks. Al McGuire often played recklessly knowing he had the physical backing of Sweetwater. "Once the league saw what Sweets could do, no one wanted to mess with him," McGuire admitted. Detroit Pistons forward George Yardley, who played with Clifton his last year, supported McGuire's assessment. "I never saw him fight," Yardley admitted, "but there were stories." The league rumor was, "You could fight with anyone, but never Sweetwater."

Cousy also understood Clifton's strength. "He physically dominated games based upon what he could do if he got mad," recalled the Celtics great. Few seemed to want to find out what might happen at that point. Clifton helped the Knicks compete favorably. Even without taller, bulkier players, the team held its own.

O

Segregated accommodations were not the only difficulties facing blacks. Subtle efforts were made by some owners to limit them in the league. While integration increased the talent market, fear that blacks would reduce attendance still lingered. As a result, a frame of mind developed encouraging blacks to play hard while being denied stardom. Popular sports in America had developed a consensus of purists who reacted unfavorably to change. From its conception through the 1950s, basketball was viewed primarily as a white man's sport played in a traditional setting. As a result, NBA owners, fearing rejection at the box office, considered Globetrotters play unacceptable.

The owners had selected the three original black players carefully. Cooper, Lloyd, and Clifton were sensible choices who didn't demand the team's spotlight. Clifton, the most flamboyant, accepted a more limited offensive role, while making a name for himself by becoming one of the better rebounders in the league, averaging from nine to eleven his NBA career. The ex-Globetrotter learned quickly. "At the time, the NBA wasn't making any black stars. You already had to be made." No permanent black star appeared in the NBA until Bill Russell arrived in Boston in 1956. He was too good to be denied the spotlight. However, in spite of their talent, top players like Russell and Minneapolis's Elgin Baylor faced racial problems into the early 1960s.

The original blacks were expected to fill "blue-collar" roles, which attracted less sportswriter ink. They were hired for defense, setting screens, rebounding, and, as Clifton described it, "playing it straight," meaning no Globetrotters showboating. But the Knickerbockers needed Clifton to rebound and defend against big inside players. With Boryla and Zaslofsky, they had pure shooters. Clifton, however accustomed to scoring and ballhandling, cooperated but quietly rebelled.

When interviewed in the 1980s, Clifton still voiced unhappiness over the Knicks' restrictions. "I played by the rules they set up, I didn't have any self-respect in those days," Clifton remembered. "No fancy stuff. They didn't want me to show anybody up." Clifton was discouraged from fancy play, which he interpreted as limiting his skills.

Sweetwater was used to entertaining fans in a special way. When Globetrotters circled to the rhythm of "Sweet Georgia Brown" performing ball tricks, audiences knew it was showtime. Clifton believed showboating added deception to his game, but Knicks management disagreed. Ned Irish, in particular, wanted none of the Globetrotters perception rubbed onto the Knicks, a style he considered a mockery of the game. This disagreement, more mental than real, never spilled out into the open. It was, however, a problem Lapchick had to work around for team harmony.

Clifton perceived Knicks restrictions as a form of prejudice. In Lloyd's estimation, "Sweets felt hornswoggled," deceived by the demands of a white league. He believed he should have been free to "show all his stuff." Clifton would have liked to speak out, but the times weren't yet right for that.

Tension between Clifton and the Knicks organization resulted from his Globetrotters experience. Sweetwater, who possessed one-hand ballhandling skills associated with future NBA greats Connie Hawkins and Julius Erving, found it difficult to separate showboating from more traditionally accepted NBA play. But the league wasn't ready for a flashy black player.

White fans, nevertheless, enjoyed the popular Globetrotters, while some felt a feeling of control, of safety, watching blacks behave like clowns in a stereotypical manner; like court jesters entertaining royalty. The Globetrotters seemed orderly, and white crowds didn't want NBA play compromised or blurred by Clifton's parody of their game.

Joe Lapchick, a traditional pro coach, wasn't receptive to Globetrotters clowning either, preferring the quality play of the Rens. To Lapchick, Clifton's fancy play could upset the team's rhythm. He, however, respected Clifton's skills when used within his pro system. His concern had nothing to do with race, but everything to do with the team's success. "The Knicks had a style and a plan," Clifton figured, "and I had to go along with it." Teammates saw another hazard to showboating. "We didn't want to show an opponent up in those days," Braun pointed out, "since the Knicks played them eight times plus playoffs, and we didn't need them ticked off at us." It would take Clifton several years before he would "arrive as a pro," according to Lapchick's later assessment. It took time for the creative forward to overcome the handicap, as Lapchick described it, from a "theatrical career" with the Globetrotters and "achieve professional basketball maturity."

Ironically, while Clifton's flair was discouraged, the rules for some white players were different. Boston's superstar Bob Cousy immortalized the "behind the back" and "faked pass," which allowed him to stand out. Coach Auerbach believed it was fine to be flashy—as long as the Celtics scored. No such consideration was given to Clifton by the Knicks management. Irish wanted him to play within white standards. However, while Irish discouraged showboating, he insisted Lapchick give Clifton extra playing time, especially for home games, to boost attendance. New York was more of a cosmopolitan city than Baltimore or Fort Wayne and especially St. Louis. Irish had seen how Jackie Robinson attracted Dodger fans from the heavily populated Brooklyn neighborhoods. He envisioned large numbers of African-Americans following Clifton's play in the Garden.

Another unwritten rule maintained by certain NBA teams involved a quota system. Basketball, like baseball, had no official racial limits, but it followed tradition. However, when early rosters are studied, it is obvious the NBA maintained quotas, which acted as a silent solution to owner fears of saturation. "Count the NBA's black players," Lloyd pointed out, "from 1950 to Bill Russell's entrance in 1956." The number never totaled ten. Lloyd insisted there was a team quota, and the number was one. Cousy, who broke into the NBA with integration in 1950 and was Cooper's roommate, had heard rumors. "I'm sure owners sat around and talked about limiting squads," he recalled. Cousy knew restrictions were possible. "You hear whispering about a color quota having been set to achieve balance," he said. The great playmaker wasn't imagining things. But as a mature athlete, Sweetwater had experienced segregation traveling with professional baseball and basketball teams. Lapchick's flexible rules eased the friction and created a comfort zone for Sweets to meld with his teammates.

O

Clifton understood his historical role, and as a pioneer black in a society that at best was indifferent to his entrance into the sport's largest market, it would be up to the critics to evaluate his contribution. As the halftime buzzer sounded on March 29, 1953, the Celtics left the Boston Garden floor leading New York, 45–31. For Joe Lapchick, everything that could

have gone wrong in the Eastern Division playoff game did. With the capacity crowd of 13,909 "bristling with hostility and yelling itself hoarse,"
as *Herald Tribune* sportswriter Leonard Koppett described it, the energized Boston Celtics jumped to a commanding first-half lead. As the
Knicks dragged their tails into the cramped locker room, Lapchick realized they would have trailed by more if Sweetwater hadn't snatched a
loose ball and slipped it into the hoop seconds before the buzzer.

Celtics talent worried the Knicks. Their trio of Bob Cousy, Easy Ed
Macauley, and Bill Sharman were among the NBA's leaders in most offensive categories. Cousy was best in assists, Sharman, first in free throws and
a leader in field goal percentage, and center Macauley second in scoring
to Minneapolis Lakers' George Mikan.

Lapchick also fretted over Vandeweghe, the team's most versatile
forward, delayed until the second quarter by weather conditions while
landing in Logan Airport, as well as having to deal with a weakened Al
McGuire, Cousy's defensive nemesis, who was forced to wear a mask for
a broken jaw. On top of everything else, midway into the second quarter,
Celtics enforcer Bob Brannum flattened the Knicks' top rebounder Harry
Gallatin after the two fought for a loose ball. The Knicks, to boot, hadn't
beaten the Celtics in four tries on their home parquet floor.

At halftime, Lapchick decided to play his shock troops that Vandeweghe described as the "No-Good Knicks," a strategy that could rattle
the Celtics and motivate the Knicks. The unit emphasized speed and defensive confusion that hopefully would create chaos and get the Knicks
back into the game. The Knicks needed a spark after a flat first half—
some adrenaline. The Vandeweghe crew included Braun and Simmons
along with Sweets and Al McGuire.

With Gallatin ailing, the burden of controlling Macauley and rebounding fell squarely on Clifton. As a three-year NBA veteran, Sweets
accepted whatever role was needed to win. It was the playoffs, where each
play took on greater proportions. Averaging a steady 10 points and rebounds a game, Clifton could disappear, seem disinterested, and be content to fade into the background when a victory was secured, leaving
others to score glory points and grab headlines.

A powerful and intelligent athlete, Clifton, whose worn body language betrayed his age, forgot fatigue this March afternoon. With his
strong third quarter and aggressive defense, the Knicks scratched back
into the game. Clifton shut down Macauley and fired bullet passes to

McGuire and Vandeweghe. The Knicks' offense now reenergized, outscored the Celtics 22–11. At the end of the quarter, the Knicks trailed 56–53. The Celtics were simply outplayed in their own backyard, and the partisan crowd sensed it. The momentum had shifted to New York.

As the team huddled around an excited coach, Clifton, who rarely spoke, caught everyone's attention. Looking directly at Lapchick, he offered a forceful solution. "Give me the ball, and let me see what I can do." The coach, looked into his eyes, and said, "OK, Sweets, the ball is yours."

Both teams traded baskets at the start of the last quarter, and then Clifton took over. With 3:15 left, after battling what seemed an eternity, the Knicks took their first lead. Sweets trailed a fast break, cut to the basket, took a low bounce pass from Simmons, and scored on a neat, twisting layup, putting the Knicks on top for good, 68–66. As Clifton ran up court dripping with perspiration, he nodded a rare smile of appreciation to Simmons. Lapchick, too, smiled, as he ground a half-smoked cigarette into the floor in front of the bench. The defense from his shock troops was working.

After Sharman's free throw cut the lead to 1, Clifton took an inbounds pass from Vandeweghe, spotted an open man under the basket, and fired a perfect strike to Simmons for a 3-point lead. Sweetwater's all-star play in the last sixty seconds was closing the door on the Celtics. After missing a free throw, the ex-Globetrotter stole the ball from Macauley and flipped a blind pass to Vandeweghe for another easy basket. Then as the clock ticked away, Clifton drove the middle of the court, spotted Boryla open near the basket, and delivered another 2-point assist, sealing the win.

Cousy instinctively tried one last desperate attempt to close the gap before the Knicks could recover on defense. Sharman whipped the ball to the Celtics playmaker who pushed it to the basket. Momentarily caught off guard, Clifton threw himself into high gear to catch Cousy as he launched one of his patented running hook shots. Out of nowhere, Clifton's long left arm halted Cousy's shot in flight, and with a final effort, Sweetwater smacked it away and then retrieved the ball before it went out of bounds, as the partisan crowd howled its disapproval.

The Knicks won, 82–75, but the day belonged to the muted giant who let his play speak for him. Clifton had fueled the victory and shamed the Celtics before their sellout crowd. His performance also left Lapchick speechless and pleased with his warrior. With 16 points, seventeen rebounds, nine assists, and a bunch of clutch plays that never make a box score, Sweets had been magnificent.

Lapchick habitually awarded the game ball—reminiscent of a pitcher wanting the last baseball from a no-hitter—to the player whom he felt contributed most to a victory. If he had been in the Garden, and if it were the house ball, he would have honored his quiet leader. The coach didn't say a word to the perspiring Clifton when the game ended but waited until Braun and Vandeweghe congratulated him. Then Lapchick stepped on the court, and with a full house of white Boston fans watching, kissed the gentle giant.

"Clifton laid it on the line," Lapchick later summed up Sweetwater's effort to the *New York Post*'s sports editor Ike Gellis in the Knicks' locker room. "Sweets wasn't only a one-man riot act, he was all over the place and was never better," the jubilant coach explained. "He gave 'em a demonstration they will never forget."

O

After a lifetime of basketball, Clifton found himself with memories and travel scars but with little security. He had been careless with money, spending it foolishly on friends in Harlem nightspots or giving it away. Twice divorced, with a daughter and an invalid mother to support, Sweets settled in Chicago's South Side and drove a cab six days a week the rest of his life. The lack of money was an issue with Clifton to his final days. Like all pre-1965 NBA pioneers, Clifton had been denied a pension, but he took a stoic approach toward his predicament. "I'm not going to ask for anything," the proud former Knick stated. "If they want to give it to us, fine." The league took its time but eventually gave the veterans a pension.

When the 1965 NBA All-Stars threatened not to play the game unless they were given a pension, the league reluctantly agreed. Those who played after 1965 needed only three years in the NBA to qualify. No pension arrangements, however, were made for pre-1965 pros until 1988. Even then old-timers were penalized by a double standard that forced them to have played five years before gaining a pension. Clifton was finally eligible in 1988, but he died in August 1990 of a heart attack, a few months before the first $800 payment. According to the NBA office, payments were retroactively made to his estate, but Sweetwater never saw a penny of it.

After Clifton's death, Vandeweghe, who had once helped Clifton's daughter with a medical problem, tried helping again. "After Sweets's death, I sent my first year's pension payments to his family." Vandeweghe, a successful West Coast pediatrician, felt the Clifton family could use it. Prior to his death, however, Clifton seemed more concerned with respect than security. Resentment over forgotten promises was replaced by a need to be remembered as one of the NBA's first blacks.

While financial needs and historical disappointments ran through Clifton's final thoughts, his past athletic association with his Knicks teammates could not have been better. Through Lapchick's efforts and despite their cultural differences, the Knicks seemed in synch athletically. But bridging the social gap between Sweetwater and his teammates proved more difficult to accomplish.

During his last NBA season with the Detroit Pistons in 1958, George Yardley and his wife invited Clifton to dine with them. As he was leaving, Yardley said, "He told us that it was the first time he had been to a white man's home for dinner."

The times were different with whites not readily socializing with blacks. Few Knicks encouraged a closer relationship with Clifton, never realizing he would have liked one. Part of the problem may also have been Clifton's celebrity among New York's black community, which made him more independent. To the team he appeared more a cartoon character than real: a "man-child" to some, a "gentle giant" to others, not someone with whom to share their intimate feelings.

Another dividing factor was that Clifton was older than his teammates and enjoyed mingling within black nightlife. Sweets was by far the best-dressed Knick and never dressed casually in public. Appearance and status in New York's black society were important to him. Boryla was a Knick who knew Clifton socially. Occasionally, when on the road, Sweets invited him to dinner. "I was Polish and grew up in Indiana Harbor, in East Chicago," Boryla related, "an integrated area in the1940s before the subject was discussed." In his high school, whites were the minority, but they meshed harmoniously with Hispanics and blacks. When Boryla dined with Clifton, he was treated like royalty, "as if I were King Farouk, with meals that were memorable."

Vandeweghe, Clifton's roommate, remembered happier days, too. "Sweets on several occasions invited my wife, Colleen, and me to Harlem nightspots," for wonderful entertainment. "He always made sure we were treated properly."

○

In spite of league approval in 1950, it took time before the fruits of integration were appreciated. Clifton made an impact on the Knicks through his skills and popular Globetrotters reputation, and he was productive for seven years, scoring 4,819 points and grabbing 4,066 rebounds, solid numbers for the 1950s. Chuck Cooper provided an initial jolt for the Celtics, but steadily faded, while Lloyd was a solid performer throughout his eight-year career for Syracuse and Detroit.

Integration for many franchises was slow. There was reluctance by Midwestern teams to sign blacks. Fort Wayne, Minneapolis, and Indianapolis held out, not wanting to upset their racial balance. Few followed after the three originals because owners remained uncertain of public reaction. With the exception of the brief stay by the fourth first-year NBA black Hank DeZonie with Tri-Cities, the original three played in Northeastern cities.

Baltimore signed Don Barksdale in 1951, but life was challenging for him in a city with racial restrictions. Years later, Barksdale claimed the NBA's few blacks complained to management to no avail. In 1954, the Knicks traded with Baltimore for their black 7'0" center, Ray Felix, who was never a standout. Fort Wayne added Chuck Cooper in 1955, its first black, but not until 1956 did the Lakers sign black center Walter Dukes for one season, then traded him to Detroit. The Indianapolis Olympians, owned by former Kentucky University All-Americans who had been coached by Adolph Rupp, a reputed racist, never signed a black before they folded in 1953. Jim Tucker and Sihugo Green, both of Duquesne, added quality. Tucker joined Lloyd at Syracuse in 1954 while Green played with Rochester in 1956 and later with the champion St. Louis Hawks of the Bob Petitt–Cliff Hagen era.

The full impact of integration wasn't felt until 1956, when Bill Russell joined the Boston Celtics. He immediately changed basketball with his defensive skills and started an era of Celtics domination unmatched in NBA history. With the Celtics' 1959 championship team, the NBA became less conscious of its interracial makeup, and blacks were accepted more freely. The first potential black star in the NBA before Russell, however, was Maurice Stokes, a name associated with tragedy. Stokes, a 6'7", 240-pound forward from St. Francis of Loretto in Pennsylvania, was a first-round pick of Rochester in 1955, but during a plane flight in his third successful season, he contracted a rare form of encephalitis. The debilitating disease ended his career and took his life while he was still in his thirties. Globetrotters star Marquis Haynes never tested the NBA. Haynes claimed he was offered $35,000 from the Philadelphia Warriors in 1953, one of the largest contracts for the times, but he turned it down.

Basketball experienced little of the tension major league baseball faced crossing the color line. Baseball was filled with a Southern tradition opposed to mixing races, while basketball was more a Northern sport started in New England and often played by collegians more tolerant of race. Baseball's experiment with integration was an obvious success, with fans not only accepting blacks, but teams like the Brooklyn Dodgers, Cleveland Indians, and New York Giants all doing well at the box office as well as on the field. As baseball benefited from integration, the NBA became more interested in integration's financial potential.

The NBA was fortunate that the first three blacks that integrated the league assumed some of the responsibility Jackie Robinson had shouldered. But the greater racial challenge was left to future civil rights activists and NBA stars who would build support and open more doors in the 1960s. Integration might also have gone differently if the first black was either Russell, Oscar Robertson, or even Wilt Chamberlain, all-stars with fan and owner support to publicly fight discrimination as Russell's book *Go Up for Glory* indicated. Russell, in particular, had the mental toughness to challenge racial bigotry, and he did.

Whether Clifton was understood or not, the Knicks were ready to improve on their past efforts. Clifton had raised the ability bar for the Knicks and helped them challenge Minneapolis and Rochester. While New York fans waited patiently, Joe Lapchick had assembled what he felt was his best team to win the elusive NBA crown.

O

It had not been easy getting to the playoffs in 1953. The East had three of the four best NBA teams with Syracuse and Boston their usual menacing selves. But first the Knicks had to get past Clair Bee's Baltimore Bullets. After a relatively easy win in New York, 80–62, the Knicks traveled to Baltimore to play in the Bullets' barnlike Coliseum before twenty-five hundred unruly fans.

While the final score registered 90–81, it was far from an easy game. In the back of the Knicks' minds had to be the fact that the team had beaten the Bullets twelve times in a row, but in the middle of the first quarter, star playmaker Dick McGuire sprained his ankle and was removed from the game. The game would seesaw until Bullets forward Don Henriksen scored the go-ahead basket at the end of the third quarter, 60–59. But the strength of the Knicks was their scoring balance and their ability to feed the hot hand. Vandeweghe would score 18 of his 19 points in the second half that, along with Boryla's 20 points, would lead the Knicks to a victory and a chance to move up the playoff ladder.

After defeating Baltimore, the Knicks took on the Boston Celtics in a best-of-five-game semifinal series. After a hard-fought game in New York, where the Knicks squeezed out a 95–91 win, the Celtics bounced back with Easy Ed Macauley and Bob Cousy scoring 21 points apiece and leading the way to a trouncing of the Knicks in Boston Garden, 86–70. It would prove to be a night where everything went wrong.

The Knicks knew it would not be their night when Vandeweghe's flight was delayed by weather and prevented the medical intern from reaching Boston Garden until the second half. Coupled with Vandeweghe's travel woes were Dick McGuire's sneakers, which he had forgotten at home. After wearing and discarding an uncomfortable pair, he was finally able to get into sneakers that fit, but by then the Knicks were trailing. The Knicks did regroup and, after trailing by 14 points, managed to cut the deficit to 1 point, 37–36, but that was as close as the more than thirteen-thousand-plus sellout crowd allowed the Knicks to get.

A few days later, with Vandeweghe and McGuire's sneakers in tow, the Knicks coasted to an easy 101–82 New York victory and returned to Boston Garden, leading two games to one. The Knicks found themselves again trailing by 14 points at halftime. This is the game in which Clifton demonstrated his value to the Knicks by leading the team back again before a sellout crowd. The 82–75 victory clinched the semifinal series for the visitors and set up the meeting with the Lakers.

Everyone on the Knicks had posted a good season. There were six Knicks in double figures, and even Max Zaslofsky who was hurt and played only twenty-nine games averaged more than 10 points. The McGuires, not noted for scoring, did well, too. Team assists demonstrated their strength. While Dick McGuire led the team, Clifton and Braun each registered more than two hundred assists.

Although the Lakers had the huge, physical front line of Mikan, Pollard, and Mikkelsen, they were slow-footed. Even though they won four of their six meetings, they had trouble with the Knicks' quickness. The "monster" team, however, showed signs of slowing down. Two seasons earlier, Mikan scored more than 28 points a game and almost 2,000 for the season, while in 1953 his game average dropped to just more than 20, totaling only 1,442 points. While the Knicks blew past Boston, the Lakers seemed tired struggling with the Pistons, winning the final game to survive.

The fast-breaking Knicks with balance, youth, and versatility caused mismatches for Minneapolis with Simmons and Boryla. Smaller, more mobile, they could pull Mikkelsen and Mikan away from the basket with perimeter shooting. The time was ripe for the Knicks' first NBA championship. As the plane banked into the Minneapolis airport, Lapchick imagined the warm feeling an NBA title would give Ned Irish. Things had been uneasy between them, but winning a championship would heal old wounds for the aging coach. The media consensus was that this team could do it, and besides, Lapchick was wearing his lucky brown tweed suit.

Lapchick could not know that the April 1953 playoffs were his last chance to snatch an NBA title. He came close the previous year, pushing the Lakers to an unexpected seventh game. This was Lapchick's most successful team despite being one of the youngest in the league. They not only won the Eastern Division, but also posted a 47–23 record, one victory fewer than the Western champion Lakers. This was their year. "Give me one more chance, just one more chance," Lapchick thought, as they prepared for the 1953 playoffs.

Chapter 11

A Lack of Communication

As the DC-4 climbed into the clouds above LaGuardia Airport, Joe Lapchick settled back with a Fletcher Pratt Civil War book, *The Monitor and the Merrimac*, which he probably wouldn't finish until after the playoffs. The Knicks were headed to Minneapolis to face the Lakers, a team that added to his insomnia.

The first two final games were played in a St. Paul's armory instead of Minneapolis's auditorium. The first was a close battle into the fourth quarter. But the Knicks showed unusual out-of-town fortitude with a 30-point quarter that blew the doors off the Lakers, 96–88. The Knicks had won the key first game. Even after a 2-point loss in game two, the Knicks were confident and in a festive mood as they prepared to take the series back to New York. Splitting with their archenemies had the Knicks a little giddy. Al McGuire confidently addressed the Laker press, declaring that the Knicks would not be returning to Minneapolis and arrogantly implying a three-game Knicks sweep in New York.

It was crucial that Harry Gallatin and Sweets Clifton stay out of foul trouble, but that wasn't going to be the case. As each took turns sitting out portions of the next three games with fouls, the Lakers were charged with renewed energy. Even the smaller 69th Armory court worked to rest the Lakers' aging legs while defusing the Knicks' fast break. The combination proved lethal. After splitting the pair of games in St. Paul, the rejuvenated Lakers arrived in New York and helped dismantle the home team. The third game turned into a rout, 90–75, and put the Lakers up two games to one in a best-of-seven series.

Lapchick knew the team couldn't survive a third loss and had to make its move now. The Knicks played with a certain level of temerity that at the end cost them the game. Trailing late into the fourth quarter of a close game, Vandeweghe got fouled and tied the score with a free throw, 62–all. The two teams would be tied at 63, 65, and 68 before the Lakers pulled away for good. With the score 71–69 and a handful of seconds left, the Knicks controlled a tap at their end, but Gallatin was forced to rush a shot that missed and caromed away, only to be retrieved by Clifton as the buzzer sounded their defeat.

The Knicks were hanging by a thread, trailing three games to one. The team again came out flat for the fifth game and found themselves trailing most of the first half by 20 points. Down 9 at the half and realizing the desperate position the Knicks were in, Lapchick ordered the pressing team into action, and it again got them back into the game. Battling with all their strength despite the loss of Braun on fouls, who was followed later by Boryla and Clifton, the Knicks cut the Lakers' lead to 1, 85–84, on a Dick McGuire free throw. But that would be all the Knicks would score as they went down in defeat, 91–84.

In retrospect, poor Knicks play led to three home losses that made the Lakers champs again. "Maybe Al McGuire got the Lakers angry," Boryla suggested. McGuire's euphoric postgame comments may have stirred their sluggish opponents. "Well, I guess he was right," Boryla said with a smile. The Knicks never did go back to Minneapolis.

Lapchick's Knicks never got to the finals again, and his last chance for an NBA crown drifted away. In spite of the loss, Lapchick remained positive, reminding his players that they showed their mettle being in the final with the NBA's best and had never given up battling the champs to the wire.

O

Joe Lapchick had joined the Knicks with unlimited enthusiasm. His team accepted him as an older brother with paternal instincts. The press as well as his peers welcomed him warmly into the pro ranks. All went well except for his relationship with his boss, Ned Irish. Lapchick and Irish were proven warriors, with Hall of Fame credentials. Their problem boiled down to a lack of communication. Aloof and lacking warmth, Irish was difficult to work with because he was used to giving orders. Lapchick, too, tended to internalize his emotions, but he relied on mutual trust and respect. He was used to behaving graciously and assumed others would act accordingly.

Character issues also divided them. With Lapchick his word was sacred, not having to think when answering questions, delivering the truth willingly. Irish at times treated truthfulness as something that could be manipulated to serve his purpose.

Another sore spot between the two was the coach's contract. Irish agreed to pay no player more than his coach, and Lapchick took Irish at his word. In 1949, when Lapchick found out that Boryla had signed a more lucrative contract, Irish denied it. But secrets have a way of surfacing. Players joked about being handed their checks in the locker room while Boryla's was in a sealed envelope. When Lapchick found out he became angry. This double-dealing caused friction. It was not the money, but Irish's insincerity that bothered Lapchick. It also bruised his pride, making him feel less important and second rate, and it upset the support necessary for a coach to maintain authority over his players. The coach viewed the salary as the pecking order of the team. Irish's duplicity also helped cause a rift between Boryla and his coach. In frustration, Lapchick turned some of his anger on the player. "No player is worth that much," Lapchick repeated. To prove his point he played Boryla for long stretches until he tired.

Much of Irish and Lapchick's differences stemmed from Irish's personnel decisions. As president of the NBA's pivotal franchise, Irish liked playing with power. But his problem was that he made poor player choices, often overruling his coach's recommendations. Lapchick never pretended to understand finances, but he possessed better credentials than his boss to judge basketball talent. As coach, he knew the direction he wanted the team to take and believed selecting players should be part of his job.

Irish knew Lapchick represented positive public relations, and that along with his pro ties, he was the best choice for the Knicks when the league started. However, Irish understood little of technical basketball; as a businessman he judged talent by its ability to bring fans to the Garden. The Knicks were a business with attendance the yardstick of success. If a local player could draw fans, Irish was interested. Lapchick believed a player's college popularity or social class, though important to Irish, didn't guarantee ability or chemistry. He looked past Irish's turnstile philosophy and searched for the skills and character in an athlete that produced mental toughness. What ate away at Lapchick was the free hand Red Auerbach had in Boston. When the Celtics coach recommended a player, his owner had faith in his judgment. Lapchick could recommend and offer input, but final decisions were Irish's to make. Both men needed to soften their position, but they rarely did.

Irish didn't always strike out. His interest in Boryla, Vandeweghe, McGuire, and Gallatin demonstrated some ability. But Irish had problems with impulsive and often emotional decisions, like Wat Misaka. At other times, Irish showed more serious errors in judgment. In the spring of 1948, both the Knicks and the NBL's Syracuse Nationals drafted NYU's skinny, twenty-year-old, 6'8" forward Dolph Schayes. When he asked for $1,000 more than the rookie cap of $6,500, Irish balked. Schayes went on to become an all-time NBA great. The NBL's Syracuse, exercising what now seems like brilliant judgment, paid Schayes the $7,500. With Schayes the Knicks could have dominated the NBA in the early 1950s.

Irish's judgment got worse. Lapchick loved Tommy Byrnes's hustle. Irish, with hometown markets dancing in his head, traded Byrnes for the Indianapolis Jets' Ray Lumpp, a former NYU favorite. Lapchick was furious. The coach knew that successful teams were triggered by chemistry created by players like Byrnes. Irish had no idea how valuable the former Seton Hall forward was or how he fit into the coach's plans, only that Lumpp was a local NYU graduate who might bring in more fans.

Byrnes was Lapchick's type of player, a hustler who made things happen. Lumpp was a good lefty scoring guard, but Lapchick preferred Byrnes. Some players click for a coach while others, even those with loads of press clippings, never cut it. It's difficult to understand unless someone has experienced the chemical reaction from a winning combination. The 1969 championship Knicks traded for forward Dave Debusschere and gave up two players who didn't fit. Byrnes was the player Lapchick wanted, the one who sparked his team, but instead he got Lumpp. "When I arrived in New York," Lumpp remembered, "Lapchick made it a point to tell me he hadn't made the trade." Lapchick believed in being up-front with his players. The Byrnes-Lumpp trade typified the way Irish operated.

The Knicks also missed 6'7" LIU All-American Sherman White, who was caught shaving points. White would have been the Knicks' territorial pick in 1951. Instead he went to jail, and along with him went Irish's hope for an NBA crown. Schayes and White could have made the Knicks a dynasty.

O

Joe Lapchick approached the 1955–56 Knicks season with an uneasy feeling that he would be fired. As he paced and chain-smoked in his Yonkers attic retreat, he reflected upon how things had soured. The Knicks' attempt to rebuild had stalled, and after three frustrating shots at an NBA crown, followed by two successive first-round playoff defeats, Knicks boss Ned Irish felt a coaching change was in order.

Lapchick knew his differences with Irish would have disappeared if the Knicks had won a championship. But instead, the team's decline added to his difficulties. As he approached his ninth Knicks season, the old pro felt his run was coming to an end, and circumstances were forcing him to move on. Most of the recent tension centered on management's interference with Lapchick's coaching decisions. Like most coaches, he worked best when left alone, but with Irish's second-guessing, that was impossible.

As he flicked an ash from his cigarette, he thought back to the Wat Misaka decision, but especially the Tommy Byrnes for Ray Lumpp trade, which made him sick for weeks. In 1954, Irish tried unsuccessfully to solve the Knicks' chronic center problem by trading for Baltimore's 6'11" Ray Felix. On a last place team that would fold the next year, Felix dominated as its leading scorer and rebounder, and he was voted the 1954 NBA Rookie of the Year. To Irish, Felix was the answer, but Lapchick wasn't so sure.

Lapchick warned that Felix was "too slow and had bad hands," but this was ignored by Irish. Felix was an awkward big man who duckwalked up and down the court and whose reaction time was seconds slower than desired. The center's hands concerned Dick McGuire, who rarely voiced criticism. "Ray, you're the only guy I know born with no hands," McGuire once mumbled after a sure-basket pass whizzed through his fingers. But in retooling, Irish and assistant Podesta insisted they had delivered winning talent.

Besides his physical shortcomings, a four-week holdout for more money got Felix off on the wrong foot. It was time he needed to adjust to the Knicks' offense as well as the new twenty-four-second clock. Felix's plodding didn't make Lapchick forget the loss of veterans like Vandeweghe, Boryla, Fred Schaus, and Simmons. Schaus was a forward obtained from Fort Wayne the previous year, and he had fitted into Lapchick's system. By the end of the 1953–54 season, Vandeweghe retired, Boryla left for business, Schaus went into coaching, and Connie Simmons was packaged with Al McGuire in the Ray Felix trade. As Lapchick's pro coaching days entered the last leg, Irish stocked up on untested rookies: Gene Shue, Jack Turner, Bert Cook, and even Ray Felix, the holdout, lacked the cohesiveness necessary to win. Irish defended his acquisitions, stating they were the best available. With four veterans gone, Lapchick's eight-man rotation floundered.

Seven-foot Walter Dukes—another futile attempt to solve the center problem—was a different story but with a similar ending. Dukes led Seton Hall to the 1953 NIT championship and was the Knicks' first-round draft pick. Irish again exercised poor judgment by refusing to pay Dukes what he wanted, forcing him to sign with the Globetrotters. After two years of travel and bad habits, Dukes finally joined the 1955–56 Knicks. Then, on the second day of practice, he tore his knee cartilage. By the following season Dukes was gone, traded to the Lakers and then to the Detroit Pistons. Ironically, he developed into a fine player, rebounding and scoring respectable numbers. His worst season by far was with the Knicks.

The 1953–54 season ended with the Knicks winning the division. But a crazy round-robin playoff eliminated the team, and the players and Irish were only too willing to blame it on coaching, leaving Lapchick feeling betrayed and unsupported. After Boston knocked the Knicks out of the first round playoffs in 1955, Irish targeted whomever appeared in his sights.

Some of Lapchick's disputes with Irish may have been fueled by the coach's popularity with the press. His success to an extent resulted from the national attention Irish brought to basketball and the extensive media coverage he received. Everyone wanted to play in the Garden, and Lapchick not only played the best teams in the media capital, but also developed into one of the country's most respected coaches. But out of these opportunities grew deep-seated differences.

While sportswriters wrote positively about Lapchick, his close friendship with them made Irish uneasy to the point where he was uncomfortable and frequently uncooperative. Irish's envy later turned to anger when sportswriters took Lapchick's side in their confrontation. But there was another side to the story. In the 1930s, Irish had been a local sportswriter who distanced himself from other sportswriters when he became successful. They, in turn, had long memories and never forgot the snub.

In his quest for honesty, Lapchick often told sportswriter friends what was going on between him and Irish. At times, information classified as "off the record" and often uncomplimentary to management found its way into the newspapers. Irish believed Lapchick's statements were harmful. The reality, however, was that no matter what Lapchick said, Irish's unfavorable impression forged over the years had influenced sportswriters. During Lapchick's last year, Irish publicly berated Lapchick, and this escalated into a war of words.

"Irish says I have a strong bench," Lapchick fired back, "better than last year, but I disagree." Shue, a fine future player, would take time to mature. Turner was out of the NBA the following year, and Felix never developed enough to help. But Irish used Felix's shortcomings to hammer Lapchick. He was quoted in the sports pages, saying "this great coach" was unable to improve the big center's play. Explosive, crude, and arbitrary, the Knicks general manager knew how to get under a coach's skin. "I can fault the players as much as the coach," he stated publicly, aiming his wrath at Felix with a few rounds left for his coach. "But how can he [Felix] improve without teaching?" Irish questioned.

When asked by the press how he planned to improve the Knicks, Irish directed his final invective at Lapchick. "I can see no way of improving in the coaching department," which left Lapchick bleeding inside. As Lapchick began to doubt himself, he realized Irish's chips at the team's foundation now appeared as giant cracks ready to destroy what he had built so carefully. Bristling at Irish's criticism, Lapchick became defensive. Defending himself in the press made him a winner with his sportswriter friends, but it only distanced him from Irish. He was losing control of the team and felt the inevitable process had begun. The barrage of criticism was wearing Lapchick down. It couldn't last much longer.

As the Knicks continued to play poorly, Irish surrounded himself with what he considered a group of technical advisors ready to analyze Lapchick's coaching faults. Sportswriters privately labeled them the "Nuremberg Jury" after the famous World War II tribunal. The group watched with folded arms anticipating the team's mishandling. It became another reason why Lapchick wanted out. He had successfully coached the Knicks without a losing season. "What did Irish want?" Vandeweghe asked. The answer was a championship.

While Irish looked to improve his Knicks, the NBA struggled to make pro basketball more appealing. The game was still deliberate, producing low scores. Excessive fouls to offset stalling also dragged out games. The last five minutes could last half an hour. Fans were bored. The game lacked the climactic finish of baseball's home run or football's touchdown. Nothing worked until Syracuse's owner Danny Biasone suggested a shot clock that would force a team to give up the ball after a period of time.

In 1954, the league adopted a twenty-four-second shot clock that solved game delays and created energy. It did more to save the new league than any other change. The clock corrected the need to foul for possession and proved to be a major adjustment. While speeding up the game, it limited play options. For example, there might only be time to make a fast break or to run a quick play, and this produced side effects.

The system Lapchick had sold his players—careful ballhandling and strong defense—became diluted and permanently replaced by all-out speed and scoring. In the past, the Knicks ran successfully, but if the fast break wasn't there, they waited for a good scoring opportunity. That was unlikely to occur with a twenty-four-second clock, which demanded a quicker offense. Lapchick's game centered on precision ballhandling and a patient offense that needed time to develop. The premium was now removed from ball possession and shifted to athleticism.

The twenty-four-second clock stimulated play, but it also helped shorten Lapchick's pro coaching days. With an aging team and coach hampered by inexperienced rookies and an ineffective center, Lapchick's ship began to spring leaks. As he approached his mid-fifties, he also found it more difficult keeping up with the game's changes. In Lapchick's world, a coach's word counted and camaraderie was the basis of team chemistry, but these elements were changing, too. As the salaries of star players surpassed those of coaches, and jet travel replaced trains, team camaraderie would fade. For Lapchick, the power structure of professional basketball was shifting. Coaches no longer had the authority and importance they formerly held.

Lapchick was unhappy that the game and the times were changing. The game he helped develop was becoming a different one. In his waning days, he talked with original Knick Lee Knorek about players going their own way and socializing less. Although basketball was still light years from its present international status, it was pioneers like Joe Lapchick who had initially sold its merits to the press and helped place the NBA on the map.

Irish's differences with Lapchick seemed endless. While the general manager continued second-guessing, whether from less talent or the disappointment of never having won a championship, the team stumbled. Lapchick's coaching was never about clever maneuvering, but when the Knicks fell short of a championship, Irish and the players blamed his lack of "technique." As the Knicks continued to struggle, Irish looked to make a change. Lapchick was getting older, and players were questioning his judgment. As veteran players become more familiar with a coach, they learn to deflect blame to him, and most pro coaches eventually lose effectiveness. As Irish's criticism of Lapchick mounted, players picked up on management's lack of confidence and used it as an excuse for their mediocre play.

The 1950s weren't much different from today when it came to placing blame on a team that was not playing well. In Lapchick's case, Irish's public hammering in the sports pages not only weakened his credibility, but also his will to hold onto his world. Like animals in the wild, players instinctively recognized he no longer had his former clout. When that became obvious, it was over for the old Celtic. While Lapchick's feud with management smoldered in the sports pages, Irish asked Vince Boryla to travel with the team. The former Knick, an Irish favorite who scouted the West, was seen as the likely replacement for Lapchick. Boryla knew Irish wanted to replace Lapchick and privately agreed with the move. He was less concerned with the old coach's problems and more willing to help solve those of the Knicks. Rumors claimed Boryla wanted Lapchick's job. While he wasn't deliberately trying to undermine Lapchick, his close relationship with Irish had that effect.

If Lapchick had thoughts of getting out, they now crystallized. Irish's message was clear. While Boryla shadowed the team, Lapchick admitted off-the-record to the media that he had reached the end of the line. Sensing his fate, his pride refused to let Irish fire him. Lapchick, sensitive to the stormy climate and realizing that his coaching magic no longer worked, felt his time was at an end. He used to say, "When basketball is no longer fun, its time to get out." He did, beating Irish to the punch.

On January 27, 1956, the Knicks front office hastily called a press conference. When Lapchick entered the room, the *Post*'s Ike Gellis hushed the other sportswriters as if they were at a wake. The room clearly reflected Lapchick's gloomy mood. He looked defeated; the ready smile was gone. For a man in his mid-fifties, Lapchick's weariness was apparent. He seemed older than his years, drained by his efforts in the early NBA. When posing for a picture with Ned Irish before the press conference, the old coach tried to smile and radiate a casual image as he clutched a cigarette, but it didn't work.

He looked leathery and twenty years older than his nearly fifty-six years. The lines on his face traced the long miles he had traveled selling basketball around the country. His face revealed a man who was suffering from insomnia and who had spent the past five months worrying about what was now happening. His pro career was over, and he knew it. The photo revealed no relief from the weight off his shoulders, only the hurt that he failed at something he loved. He appeared to have fought a serious illness and lost. Lapchick was, according to sportswriter Red Smith, "all chewed up inside." Irish had beaten him.

With notes in hand and dressed in a fastidious gray woolen suit, dotted blue bow tie, and white shirt, Lapchick performed one of the most painful chores of his life. After a few amenities, he looked directly at his sportswriter friends and announced, "I am resigning as coach of the New York Knickerbockers," ending forever his ties with professional basketball. He cited poor health and too many sleepless nights for his decision. Inwardly, he had enough of Irish's interference and lack of appreciation. Years later, in a letter to Knicks trainer Don Friedrichs, Lapchick expressed his true feelings. "Ned does not reward men who are proud of their job and give it all they got. He just takes them for granted."

In spite of Lapchick's bitter ending, his nine years with the Knicks were positive and winning ones, having amassed a record of 326–247, second in wins only to Red Holzman. As a legendary figure, Lapchick also allowed the new league to lean on his reputation at a time when it was desperately needed.

When Lapchick announced that he would step down, friends around the league honored him as he made his last visit as the Knicks coach. Boston's Walter Brown and Eddie Gottlieb from Philadelphia rolled out the red carpet for their old friend. When a New York committee asked if it could stage a "Joe Lapchick Night" at Madison Square Garden, Irish turned down the request. He was not going to be embarrassed into praising Lapchick before firing him, and he didn't want to risk being jeered in his own house. While Lapchick's future seemed uncertain, like a proud general after a losing battle, he carried his head high.

The next day the unemployed coach reviewed recent events in his Yonkers attic retreat. Like when replaying a loss, he wondered if he could have tried harder to work with Irish. As he reflected, his wife startled him. "Joe, phone call," Bobbie called up. "It's Walter McLaughlin from St. John's."

Chapter 12

The Wake
of a
Nightmare

When Lapchick was looking to leave the Knicks, he heard St. John's was unhappy with its basketball team's performance and was thinking of replacing Coach DeStefano. When Frank McGuire left St. John's in 1952 to coach North Carolina, the athletic moderator Father Honsberger had offered Lapchick the job. Lapchick turned it down but recommended freshman coach Dusty DeStefano, whom he felt would do a good job. DeStefano immediately took the Redmen to the final of the NIT before losing to Seton Hall. After an outstanding 17–6 first year, DeStefano did no better than break even over the next three seasons. St. John's, not used to mediocrity, became fidgety. The coincidence seemed prophetic. The idea of returning to college coaching seemed a welcomed solution to his problem.

As DeStefano prepared for the 1955–56 season, he hoped his team would do well enough to protect his job. Returning were big men Bill "Zeke" Chrystal and Mike Parenti, along with playmaker Dick Duckett, fresh from serving in the military. The team leaders were free and easy types who needed a firm hand, one that the good-natured DeStefano lacked.

The team was mediocre at best, ending the season with a 12–12 record. The Redmen would alternate wins with losses, and then go on a three-game win streak only to be followed by three consecutive losses. But the team's best demonstration of its mediocrity occurred against Wagner.

Late in February, St. John's played Wagner from Staten Island in its DeGray Gym and acted as if it were scrimmaging in a school yard. At the half it was up by two, 46–44, and demonstrated little interest in stopping the Seahawks' offense. The game came down to the end with George Blomquist, a replacement guard, sinking a buzzer shot to win the game, 92–90. The team continued to slide, losing seven of its last nine games, including the embarrassing loss to Wagner, a team St. John's had always easily beaten but under DeStefano lost to twice in the past three years.

As the team floundered, DeStefano knew he was in trouble. "We just seemed to run out of steam," 6'5", burly reserve center Pete Carroll later said, describing how the team played during the clutch part of games.

DeStefano knew of St. John's penchant for success. "My job is on the line," he pleaded with the team in the locker room before practice one day. The coach's pleas were ignored. The team continued its tailspin, and DeStefano waited for the tap on the shoulder, which eventually came. In the midst of the losing streak, while walking out of the Garden locker room to play Manhattan College, Father William Casey, the athletic moderator, told the worried coach that his contract would not be re-newed. St. John's went out and lost again by 2 points. The only unan-swered question was who would replace DeStefano.

Rumors had been circulating after Lapchick resigned from the Knicks that he would become the new St. John's coach. "I had gotten a call from Ned Irish," DeStefano confidant Bill McKeever claimed, "telling me to warn Dusty that Lapchick was after his job." St. John's in-terest in Lapchick at this point, however, seemed mutual. Early in Febru-ary 1956, as talk of a new coach continued to fly among the St. John's players, Lapchick appeared in his favorite Garden courtside seat for a Redmen freshmen game with Manhattan College, which preceded a reg-ular doubleheader.

The freshmen were thrilled. It made the team excited, and I felt honored that I might be playing for the Knicks coach the next year, the same one I saw on TV. I remember thinking I would have to be in good shape. Over the summer I worked hard to keep my weight down by run-ning three miles over the Kosciusko Bridge near my Greenpoint apart-ment and religiously doing 125 sit-ups by my bed each evening. In my mind, a pro coach would know the difference. Joe Lapchick, the Knicks coach, watching us play! He sat elegantly erect, legs crossed, a cigarette locked between middle and index fingers, with his other thumb under his chin, looking very businesslike as we warmed up. He wore a blue suit and white shirt, and he looked sure of himself, like an executive in a Trump boardroom, or as if he were about to order a meal in a sophisticated restaurant. He seemed to be a man used to having his orders followed.

The stands were practically empty for the 5:45 P.M. preliminary game, but for me, I was only aware of this neatly dressed, tall, thin observer, knowing I wanted so badly to impress him during this unstaged audition. We creamed Manhattan, and Lapchick knew he would have help. Before St. John's made the appointment official, Jack Kaiser, our freshmen coach, broke the news to us after the Fordham game. He confirmed that Dusty had been relieved and Joe Lapchick was the new coach. The buzz in the cramped, steamy locker room was electric. I was thrilled. I had always followed the Knicks, and Lapchick was this tall beacon of respectability whom I would now call coach. With all the contractual details completed, St. John's announced his return prior to the end of the season, as Lapchick had insisted. He wanted it known that he was returning to St. John's to reduce his coaching load. This was important to a proud man. Although the Knicks grind had taken its toll, Lapchick appeared to be landing on his feet, inheriting a group of talented seniors along with an undefeated freshmen team. Not everyone, however, was thrilled with the announcement of a new coach.

It didn't take long for Bill Chrystal and Mike Parenti to discuss their concerns about a new coach. They had their way with DeStefano for the past two years, but now the two were worried whether they could continue shaving points.

"Did you see the papers?" Chrystal asked Parenti as they left their law class at St. John's downtown business school. "Dusty is gone," he blurted out before Parenti could answer, "and Lapchick's got the job." DeStefano had coached them the past two years, and they helped turn his hair silver by the time he was fired.

"I hear Lapchick's tough," Parenti said. Both knew he was the big-name Knicks coach who it had been rumored would return to St. John's. "It may not be as easy as it was this year," Parenti whispered. "What the hell are you worried about?" Chrystal shot back. "What can he do? Besides, he needs us." Parenti nodded in agreement but was unconvinced as they headed to the campus cafeteria. With Joe Lapchick taking over for the 1956–57 season, they had to worry about their point-shaving scheme being scrutinized by an experienced pro coach.

○

The team finally met the famous coach at its first practice in the fall of 1956 at Flushing Armory. All eighteen of us trying out for the varsity encircled him as he spoke. He was serious but friendly. Neatly dressed in gray practice pants, blue sneakers, and a white T-shirt, he stood erect, legs oddly crossed like an ice-skater about to pirouette, with one hand cupping an elbow, eyes narrowed. What was striking was the way Lapchick, like a stage actor in the round, held our complete attention. Mouths slackened and eyes became riveted, centrically drawn to him; each player seemed to be holding his breath not to miss a word.

"Everyone at St. John's has made an old-timer like me feel right at home," Lapchick began, as he pivoted on his royal-blue Knicks high-cut sneakers trying to look into as many sets of eyes as possible. He looked tanned and well rested for the task ahead. I felt confident. He was a man to trust behind the wheel of our team.

What seemed strange was that without realizing it, most of us standing directly in front of him were mimicking his stance. Our arms unconsciously were folded in front of us as he spoke in an even and clearly modulated tone. He was setting the stage for us to perform at what he hoped would be peak efficiency, and he knew he had to win us over and gain our respect.

"As you know, I've been in the pros most of my life," Lapchick said, "and have returned to St. John's after being away from the college game since the 1940s." I wondered what he was driving at, why talk about the past? Then he continued. "As a Celtic, I never had a coach, we just helped each other." He spoke gently, never boasting. He was being himself. "I'm not familiar with all the college changes, and I'll need your help to make this a successful season," Lapchick emphasized.

Lapchick's quiet presence awed most of us. We had gone to the Garden to watch him and the Knicks. "There's this tall gentleman coaching them," sophomore guard Joe Daley recalled, "and a few years later, I'm walking into a gym with him calling me by my first name." We didn't realize it then but his point was typical of the man—straightforward and honest. Although he was back in college coaching and the game had changed over the past decade, he projected a confidence that he could work out the problems. He didn't stand up and brag about his reputation, didn't panic, but asked for our help. It was impressive to a nineteen-year-old.

Lapchick inherited what appeared an ideal team of nine lettermen, led by senior playmaker Dick Duckett and big men Parenti and Chrystal. From a 21–0 freshmen team arrived help in a solid starting five led by three All-City players: 5'10" guard Alan Seiden, 6'5" forward Buddy Pascal, and myself, a 6'2" guard. We each scored more than 400 points as freshmen and were itching to gain varsity stripes. Rounding out the freshmen squad was a pair of 6'5" forwards, Lou Roethel and Dick Engert. Both were smart players who could score points and rebound.

St. John's was forced to use Flushing Armory for practice since we had no campus field house. Flushing. It was well named. It would have pleased everyone if it were flushed into the bay. Armory officials did little to welcome the team. While Lapchick was jammed into a postage stamp office, players dealt with slippery floors that caused Lapchick to later remark that the team was "horizontal more than vertical."

Balancing the grim armory conditions were the occasional workouts at Madison Square Garden. All of St. John's important games were played there. College basketball had crashed with the 1951 gambling scandal, but by the mid-1950s, it struggled to recover. Sellouts of more than eighteen thousand, common before the scandal, were now reduced to three or four thousand. Lapchick, however, would fuel a revival. The Garden was half the fun playing for St. John's. Most of Lapchick's basketball life, as a player and coach, centered on the sport's most talked about facility, the one known as the mecca.

Chapter 13

The House
That Rickard
Built

On May 25, 1925, Madison Square Garden (the second of four arenas to bear that name) drew its curtains after thirty-five years. A fight card featuring lightweights Sid Terris and Johnny Dundee marked the occasion. Among the ten thousand eulogists who gave their final blessing was Mayor Jimmy Walker. Public figures from former president Theodore Roosevelt's sons, Kermit and Teddy Jr., to New York football Giants' owner Tim Mara also paid last respects. Ringside writers Grantland Rice, Rube Goldberg, and Damon Runyon, along with boxing favorites Jack Dempsey and Kid McPartland, were out for the finale.

The mastermind behind the third Garden was boxing promoter Tex Rickard. It remained the only major indoor arena in New York's metropolitan area through the 1960s. The Garden accommodated more than eighteen thousand fans for Knicks or Rangers games. Boxing and Barnum and Bailey's circus were features that also supported it. The new Garden took only 249 days to construct, and it would operate for forty-three years, until 1969.

On December 15, 1925, Rickard staged the Canadian-American hockey game that formally opened the Garden. The near-sellout crowd of more than seventeen thousand convinced him that hockey had a future. From this start the new Garden grew. It, too, would grow for Joe Lapchick and would have much to do with his future. Although he had

played with the Celtics in the Garden for Rickard in the 1920s, his reputation would be made in this building as a college and professional coach.
The Garden was Lapchick's stage to showcase his outstanding teams and
to test himself before some of the best critics of the game.

Lapchick's 1958–59 team entered the Garden by the main entrance
on Eighth Avenue, which was sandwiched between Adams Hat and
Nedick's. Fans surfaced from the Independent Subway, passed the Dav-
ega sporting goods store under the arcade, and walked into the rotunda
by the concessions. The theatrical marquee's bold black letters, "Zale vs.
Graziano," meant a toe-to-toe middleweight slugfest to a postwar crowd,
its way of paying tribute to the evening's event.

The rotunda had an enchanting character all its own. Before, after,
and especially during halftime of each game, it was the gathering place of
basketball aficionados. Anyone and everyone connected with New York
basketball congregated: players, coaches, scouts, well-wishers, media people, as well as sports eccentrics. Reputations were made and broken by the
buzz of gossip in no longer than the time it took to sizzle a hot dog. It
abounded with colorful characters. One of the more memorable ones was
Howie Garfinkel, alias "The Garf." Howie was an essential part of the
sport's eccentricities—fidgety, nervous-looking, and hard to miss in a
crowd. His well-oiled, parted black hair, medium build, and size were representative of New York's regular Garden clientele.

Garfinkel, who frequently punctuated conversation with an unconscious parody of old-time gangster actor James Cagney's elbow-jabs to his
hips, had been Syracuse University's student basketball manager. He received a good whiff of college basketball in the late 1940s and hadn't lost
the scent. His passion became his life.

Garfinkel, who initially seemed a likely target of prep school
pranksters, was a prototypical P.T. Barnum, shrewd enough to promote
his next venture before the ink dried on the current one. His intuitive
ability to judge high school talent led him to a schoolboy scouting service,
which complemented the nationally known Five-Star Basketball Camp he
still operates in Honesdale, Pennsylvania. His zaniness was most evident
at the camp, where he often awoke heavy metal devotees to 1940s Judy
Garland music. He further punished campers by demonstrating an old-
fashioned, twenty-five-foot, two-hand set shot. Garfinkel started out in
the 1950s racing to snare scholastic all-stars for the New York Nationals,

a youth club team he sponsored and coached. Amateur teams provided excellent training for schoolboys, but they also allowed Garfinkel to fantasize about being Red Auerbach. Instead of a victory cigar, Garfinkel chained-smoked over his players during time-outs. The Nationals were fun, Garfinkel unforgettable.

To the left in the rotunda stood Harry Gotkin. He was a distinguished-looking, gray-haired businessman with a neat, pencil-thin mustache whom we knew as "Mr. Gotkin." His nasal resonance caught one's attention because it sounded like a cross between a foghorn and a sinus condition that required attention. Mr. Gotkin was in his sixties and seemed out of place in the whirling world of Garden basketball. He looked like the New York textile executive he was, but basketball was the spark that ignited his life.

Scouting talent for former St. John's coach Frank McGuire was his love. When McGuire relocated to North Carolina, Gotkin joined him. To many high school prospects he was the "North Carolina man." Instead of ice cream, he distributed scholarships to talented city kids who knew little of the South but who quickly learned. Gotkin was drawn to basketball and to McGuire through St. John's, where relatives Hy and Java Gotkin had starred and where Harry had recruited. He was effective enough to help deliver to McGuire an all–New York schoolboy team that won North Carolina's first NCAA crown in 1957 with a perfect 32–0 record. Mr. Gotkin was a rotunda regular.

○

St. John's played all of its important home games in the Garden. The magic in the 1950s was performing in America's most famous arena. "Playing for St. John's was like playing Notre Dame football or for the New York Yankees," observed Normie Ochs, a former Redmen player.

Ever since my Brooklyn school-yard days, I dreamed of playing in the Garden, but reality was better than fantasy. Before each game the media, basketball fans, and the student body focused on St. John's Garden games. Every metropolitan newspaper covered them with action photos splashed across the back pages of the *Daily News* or the *New York Post*. *Herald Tribune* headlines paid tribute to "Joe's Day: St. John's, 55–51," while the *Journal American* informed the sports world that "Redmen Rally

Top Thrill of Lapchick Career." The excitement of playing in the Garden wasn't like *seeing* a John Wayne film, but like *acting* in one.

Pregame excitement for a St. John's game with Temple started on a cold, bright February morning on the new Hillcrest campus. Players attended school with visions of basketballs whizzing through their minds. Fair-weather students, labeled "lounge lizards" by Father Francis Keenan, an economics professor, prowled the campus hoping for insider information on the game. Enough back pats were distributed to require a liniment rub. "How you guys going to do tonight? Are they as good as the newspapers say? Do you have any extra tickets?" The questions were distracting but appreciated.

After class, the team headed to the Hotel Abbey on Sixth Avenue and Fifty-second Street in Manhattan and arrived about 2:30 P.M. It was exciting just going to a hotel. I had never stayed in one, but as a member of the team, I now did it a dozen times a season. We tried relaxing in our rooms waiting for our meal. Most of us undressed and got off our feet, saving energy for the anticipated forty-minute battle. Some watched television; others glanced at newspaper coverage.

Room assignments were a science difficult to figure but generally made by seniority and compatibility. Coaches believed proper pairings helped team chemistry. On some trips, starters were matched to ensure rest, relieving worry over an underclassman's addiction to Late Show films or Jack Paar's talk show. As a senior I roomed with my neighbor Butch Dellecave, a sophomore. The science of roommates also matched Dick Engert with talented Tony Jackson. Engert was a married, twenty-five-year-old senior while Tony was a sophomore. The senior's maturity and leadership determined the assignment.

The meal was served promptly at either 3:30 or 4:30 P.M., depending on whether we played the first or second game. Tie, shirt, and suit jacket were required. The advantage of playing first guaranteed starting on time. Sometimes the first game went into overtime, and the team set to warm up waited anxiously in the runway. Playing earlier allowed for a quick shower and a chance to watch the second game with friends and family. Early newspaper deadlines forced morning dailies to frequently feature the first game, another bonus. With Lapchick, St. John's was guaranteed full coverage. The press seemed to print every word he said. Athletes believed ordinary objects had magical effects on their performance.

I remember injuring my knee in high school and having to wear a large, spongy knee guard. The first time I wore it I scored 28 points. It stayed on the rest of the season.

Athletes are superstitious and upset by broken routines, but our coach was worse. Lapchick wore the same brown tweed sports jacket, striped tie, and loafers for weeks through a win streak. Some players had favorite socks or carried lucky charms. Each of us looked for extra help. The hotel meal had its own ritual with a well-done steak, salad, baked potato, and a scoop of vanilla ice cream. We could have coffee or tea, nothing else. Some players had little interest in food. Center, Lou Roethel got queasy and often threw up. He was a worrier and uncomfortable until, like most of us, the game started.

Athletes, like actors, lived for "good reviews." The early game allowed us to read them with breakfast. "He's tough, but fair," was Duckett's evaluation of the *Daily News* top sportswriter, Dick Young. "If you're mentioned, you did something good," he emphasized. Young once described Duckett as "a mesh man" for his floor leadership, a subtle compliment. We dreamed of playing well enough to be noticed by someone like Young. The *New York Post* was a popular read. Its in-depth style was consuming, especially if Milton Gross wrote in his column that one of us was "a mainstay of the Redmen team." A girlfriend or a mother clipped that kind of quote for posterity's scrapbooks.

After the meal we rested, some nodding off to the drone of television news, others discussing the sports pages' pregame stories. Exactly ninety minutes before game time, the team received a wake-up call from trainer Jack Gimmler. No other calls were allowed. Smiling Jack was a robust 6'1", solidly built, 200-pound bundle of positive advice and laughs that helped relax us while in the whirlpool.

Gimmler, a St. John's Prep and University graduate, was a New York City fireman until he injured his knees in the line of duty. As a result, he developed a walk that closely resembled John Wayne's short, hip-swaying gait that director John Ford encouraged the famous actor to use. It made this huge man look as if he were trying to avoid stepping on some unguarded pigeon droppings. Although Jack's roots were New York's, there was an unusual New England timbre to his voice. After a questionable call, Jack stood up on the bench and was heard throughout the Pittsburgh field house shouting at the referee: "Faantaastic!"

Gimmler offered plenty of advice and solutions to our problems before we left the whirlpool. He was great at finding lessons in what he described as "human nature." The wonderful thing about him was he usually made sense. That and his big smile helped generate the confidence we took onto the floor.

We dressed, grabbed our tan leather bags, and walked the few blocks to the Garden in small groups, usually stopping at St. Malachy's Catholic Church on 49th Street. As we entered the dimly lit church, we were comforted by the smell of incense and novena candles. In the quiet church, muffled bargains were made. Some prayed for playing time, others hoped for double-figure scoring.

We entered the Garden by the 49th Street player entrance, produced a game ticket, and were told, "Room thirty-four," by the businesslike guard. The high-ceilinged dressing room was large and rectangular. Clothing hooks lined the wall with planked benches built under them. The walls were painted bright green to eye level and then topped with white. A trainer's table for taping ankles jutted out in the middle of the room. Each player's dressing area was decorated with pregame gifts that magically appeared: new white, cushioned woolen socks and a boxed supporter. The room smelled of analgesic balm and citric acid from sliced oranges for halftime. Water was still the popular drink. Gatorade hadn't been invented.

There was a lot of locker-room activity. Managers were filling water jugs, stacking towels, checking for paper cups. Players were stretching, adjusting warm-ups, or tightening laces. Lapchick anxiously paced the room as if measuring it, all the while holding a lit cigarette. On the other side of the room, Father Casey was encouraging a player as he pointed and slapped a rolled-up game program in his hand for emphasis. After dressing, with a few minutes left before Lapchick's pregame talk, we passed basketballs or dribbled around to loosen up.

When the old pro coach spoke, it was something special. He rarely delivered emotionally energized pep talks, but instead quietly summed up what to expect and how he wanted us to approach our opponent. It was a few simple points, but they would last in our minds throughout warm-ups. "Keep them off the boards" and "Look for good shots" were ways in which he got us focused. "Get back on defense," a main concern, was added. There was never confusion. Simplicity was part of his motivation. After Lapchick's talk, Father led the team in prayer. He ended with, "Our

Lady of Victory," with the team chanting, "Pray for us." We charged out of the locker room, gliding past the battleship-gray runway up onto the well-lit, green-bordered Garden floor for warm-ups.

A hush, then a rising "oooh" sound welcoming "the Redmen." The crowd's buzz was quickly deafened by Indian tom-tom pulsations from Gladys Gooding's organ. As we ran single file past the scorer's table, friendly cheerleaders greeted us. The game concentration intensified. By then we became aware of our opponent's fight song. Some actually spurred us on. St. Joseph's "When the Saints Come Marching In" was the best one next to Notre Dame's. There was a sense of importance during warm-ups. I thought of neighborhood friends who missed the thrill of playing before a Garden crowd, who never heard trumpeted introductions or experienced the bright lights on our flashy red-and-white uniforms.

As we loosened up, the Garden floor provided a spongy welcome. For an era unfamiliar with slam dunks, it felt good soaring to the basket and not colliding with school-yard poles. Thin wires ran from the backboards to the end promenade, allowing a less-obstructed view. There was a soft, flexible quality to the slightly movable rims that allowed a ball to teeter and made every shot feel good, as if it would swish through the basket. It was a home-court advantage to those who knew the rims, a confidence visiting teams lacked.

It didn't take long to get to know the courtside regulars. The best metropolitan sportswriters and media people lined the court opposite the benches. Ike Gellis of the *New York Post* traded stories while Murray Janoff of the *Long Island Press* moved out of the way of Dick Young, from the *Daily News*. They milled around, clanking typewriters, papers flying, and smoke whirling. It all evaporated into the heavens when official John Nucatola threw the ball up at center court to start the game. John Goldner, Ned Irish's assistant, a tall, slim, distinguished, and sad-looking man who wore sunglasses, added a mysterious touch. He usually roamed near the dressing room runway and the perimeter of the playing floor, looking ominous, as if he were trying to unravel some mystery.

Public address announcer John Condon warmed the crowd with his broad Irish smile and wit. With a clear, powerful voice, he had a way of making even lopsided games exciting. "Basket by Pascal the rascal" or "Bucket by Duckett" was how he fooled with our names. There were no airs about him, being cut from the same "regular guy" bolt of cloth as Lapchick and many of the sportswriters. He was genuinely happy to see us. "We're all in the same boat," he seemed to be saying. "Why not have a good time." While Condon was warm, his boss Ned Irish cruised silently courtside like a stevedore lugging weighty problems on his back.

As the lights dimmed, highlighting the portable green-bordered, lacquered hardwood floor, the organist forced the spectators from their seats with the National Anthem. Like actors on a Broadway stage, we waited impatiently for Condon's introductions. When the starters were announced, my adrenaline told me it was game time. Years later films showed cheerleaders slapping the floor during play, spinning in whirling-dervish motions, but they never attracted our attention. Our focus was on the game; everything else was blurred. There were no Dean Domes or Meadowland Arenas, only Madison Square Garden.

It was the perfect place to watch rising NBA stars. We saw snarling, future Boston Celtic Tommy Heinsohn and his Holy Cross team battle legendary Bill Russell and K. C. Jones's undefeated San Francisco Dons. When we tired of West Virginia's Hot Rod Hundley's antics, we enjoyed playing against another Mountaineer, the Cabin Creek All-American Jerry West. It was also fun playing against future NBA stars Johnny Egan and the humble Lenny Wilkens.

And then there was Coach Lapchick, who completed the Garden experience. He remained hidden in the locker room, smoking Old Golds while the team worked up a sweat. A few minutes before the starting whistle, he crushed his cigarette under a brown loafer, stood up straight, walked through the runway to the bench, and made the first of many trips to the watercooler. He was as ready as were we.

Lapchick was Mr. Basketball to us: an obvious part of the game's history, a pioneer figure. From the beginning we respected him. There was no doubt about that. He and the Garden were made for each other. But woven into the fabric of Madison Square Garden and college basketball were prickly jabs that left even an old pro like Joe Lapchick bleeding.

Chapter 14

Betrayal of Innocence

When Joe Lapchick returned to St. John's in 1956, he never suspected that he might be entangled in a point-shaving scandal, one that challenged his character to its foundation. Like many Americans who drive drunk, smoke, or do drugs, certain athletes paid little attention to the harm of associating with gamblers.

It was January 14, 1951. Junius Kellogg, a competent 6'8" center for Manhattan College, waited for Hank Poppe in the college parking lot. Poppe and another former teammate, Jack Byrnes, were pressuring the big center to throw the upcoming DePaul game in the Garden. Poppe knew Kellogg was one of eleven children from a poor Portsmouth, Virginia, family.

"Take the $1,000. It's cash. You can use it," Poppe urged. Kellogg was confused. His team was heading for the National Invitation Tournament. In his dilemma, Kellogg turned to Coach Ken Norton. School authorities notified District Attorney Frank Hogan who encouraged Kellogg to continue the contact with his former teammates.

When Kellogg agreed to "do business," Poppe lit up. He then described how easy it was. "Miss a rebound, don't outlet any passes for fast breaks, be a little slower on defense, and just put a little more mustard on some of your hook shots." Byrnes reminded Kellogg that he didn't have to lose the game, only control the score. "Everybody's doing it," Poppe

191

encouraged. They agreed to meet on Tuesday before the game to set the final details.

Kellogg felt tight warming up. Poppe was sitting at courtside, close enough to get his attention. He got word to the Manhattan center that his team was favored and to win by fewer than 10 points. Kellogg agreed. Poppe smiled. "We'll meet after the game, and I'll have your money," was what Kellogg remembered. With all the pressure he played poorly, but Manhattan won 62–59. Poppe never showed up at the bar, but the police later arrested him and Byrnes. The 1951 scandal was off and running.

After the initial arrests, rumblings were directed towards New York's criminal atmosphere. "Out here in the Midwest, these scandalous conditions, of course, do not exist," legendary coach Phog Allen of Kansas University, insisted. "But in the East, the boys, particularly those who participate in the resort hotel leagues during the summer, are thrown into an environment which cannot help but breed the evil which more and more is coming to light." Allen's remarks, made before several Kentucky and Bradley players were caught throwing games, had the support of most of the basketball world ready to dump exclusive heaps of blame on the big-city environment and its gamblers. Kentucky's coach, Adolph Rupp, was another big-city basher. He swore, "His boys couldn't be touched with a ten-foot pole," when questioned about the scandal. Both coaches were mistaken.

Kellogg's cooperation was only the beginning. Later, on October 19, 1951, while watching a college all-star game in Chicago Stadium, a pair of New York detectives arrested two of Rupp's untouchables, Ralph Beard and Alex Groza. Another former Kentucky teammate, Dale Barksdale, was collared in his home in Louisville. Hogan's long net had finally caught up with them. After questioning, they admitted dumping games while in college and were barred from the NBA for life. Before Hogan's investigation was complete, more than thirty-three players from seven colleges were charged with fixing eighty-six games, and many others escaped detection.

"I'll never get over it until they hit me with a spade," pretty much described how former Kentucky All-American Ralph Beard felt after being caught in the 1951 scandal. Even today, more than fifty years later, he dreads the basketball season and having to relive the mistake that never gets any easier to accept. What he remembers most were the lost opportunities. But before the scandal, things were different.

Beard was thrilled with launching a professional career in the new NBA. His college team was so good it entered pro basketball as a unit. Along with fellow All-Americans Alex Groza and Wah Wah Jones, they formed the nucleus of the 1949 Indianapolis Olympians, which was partially owned by them, something unheard of in pro basketball. By the end of their first year, Groza and Beard were selected first-team all-pros, with their careers set. But that was all ended by the scandal.

Although Kellogg was the catalyst, the scandal focused on CCNY and Coach Nat Holman. What followed was a cacophony of accusations, with hand-wringing denials by young men whose lives were never the same. All the newspaper photos seemed alike: hands covering expressionless faces, hats pulled down over dispirited eyes. CCNY's Floyd Layne, Ed Roman, Irwin Dambrot, Ed Warner, and "Fats" Roth became household names.

In the past, St. John's University's basketball team had skirted the muddy waters of gambling scandals. When the first major college scandal broke in 1951, Bob Zawoluk, St. John's star center, was pictured with small-time gambling figure Salvatore Sollazzo in New York's Copacabana nightspot, and he came close to admitting his involvement. But nothing ever materialized, and the investigation was dropped. Rumor had it that New York's powerful Cardinal Francis Spellman had interceded for St. John's. Sportswriter Dan Parker of the *Daily Mirror* had passed innuendoes in the early 1940s about local collegians shaving points. There are no statistics, but the consensus is that only a handful of fixed games were ever exposed.

It didn't take long for gamblers to figure how easy it was to fix games. Athletes who shaved points rationalized that games didn't have to be lost, just kept within the point spread. Rumors had circulated in the 1940s that college games were fixed. If Madison Square Garden and other big-city arenas staged thrown games, the "out-of-town" rehearsals were in the Catskills resorts.

○

A casual postwar ride on a sunny summer day north on Route 17 into the Catskill Mountains led naturally to a number of New York's finest resorts. City businessmen sent their families to country clubs like Kutsher's, The Nevele, Concord, and Grossingers and followed on weekends to enjoy relief from the steamy hot city. While the Catskills became famous for its summer resorts, it also developed a subtle reputation as the breeding ground for point fixing.

By the mid-1940s, the GI Bill was filling universities with veterans, and college basketball was packing Madison Square Garden. Since many Catskills vacationers were passionate basketball fans, hotels entertained nightly with games by college players. As interest grew, hotels competed for national stars, paying them high salaries to join their staffs. After a full day in the sun, patrons flocked to the cool outdoors to watch collegians battle. The games averaged crowds of two or three hundred and were officiated by top college and professional officials like Lou Eisenstein or Hagen Anderson.

Some of the game's greats came to play, from George Mikan, Klein's Hillside's athletic director in 1947, to Wilt Chamberlain, who in the 1950s became the world's tallest bellhop for Kutsher's. Grossingers, one of the biggest hotels in the Catskills' Borscht Belt, attracted many fine New York players, often assembling teams capable of beating the best colleges. Most athletic scholarships covered basics, but the summer was the time for them to earn spending money. The unsupervised setting, however, encouraged gamblers to flock to the resorts. Hotel owners were careful to pay players for waiting on tables or assisting with their recreation programs, but it was obvious why they were paid well. As competition for stars heated up, some received as much as $1,000 to $1,500 a summer to play. "I was being paid $100 a game by the Knicks in the late 1940s," Ernie Vandeweghe recalled, "but when I was in college, Kutsher's offered me $125 a game."

Part of the Catskills entertainment was betting on a game's combined score. Some players were encouraged by gamblers to control the score and in turn share the winnings, which could be worth a few hundred dollars. Vandeweghe remembered his hotel playing Grossingers and leading convincingly at halftime. However, someone asked whether the players expected to be paid. They got the message and lost the game. In the Catskills the home team always won. With a professional future in medicine, Vandeweghe was never lured into the world of gambling; however, others were less fortunate. The resorts contaminated many young athletes with "on-the-job training" for fixers who believed it would work as easily at school.

For many New York athletes, bookmakers were neighborhood friends who knew them by name. Jack Molinas, one of the more notorious figures of the era, grew up around gamblers as a youngster in his father's restaurant in Brooklyn, where he learned about bookmaking. He was familiar with point spreads while at Columbia and got involved when he played in the NBA.

This was the sports world Mike Parenti and Bill Chrystal entered when they enrolled in St. John's in the fall of 1953. Like those who threw games before them, they never believed they would get caught. The pair had vague memories of local stars disgraced in the early 1950s, but they never took them seriously. The two had other plans.

O

A preseason poll in 1956 ranked St. John's eighth in the country. Lapchick exuded cautious optimism, but other concerns ticked away like hidden time bombs. Reminiscent of his Knicks days, Lapchick saw the team as talented but lacking a dominant big man. Parenti had previously scored well, but he lacked mobility and intensity. While Alan Seiden and Dick Duckett were a quick backcourt, Parenti, Chrystal, and Buddy Pascal were a slow front line. Lapchick hoped good defense and a comfortable freelance offense would inspire team play.

While Lapchick tried pulling loose ends together, it didn't take the team long to recognize that Lapchick's way of conditioning was running his "nutcracker" drill several times during and especially at the end of practice. The drill combined ballhandling with endurance, requiring three players to weave up and down the court four, six, or even eight times. But when Lapchick ordered, "And Two," the last two sprints required perfection—no fumbles or rule violations. The secret to survival was teaming with better ballhandlers. It was wise to avoid taller, slower players who tended to be clumsy and found the drill difficult to master. If it broke down, Lapchick's axe fell. "And Two!" And the last two sprints were repeated. As turnovers piled up and stamina drained, tempers drew short. When we finally reached the finish line, most of us collapsed, already dreading tomorrow.

Lapchick began to realize a preseason squad labeled "can't miss," showed a lack of togetherness. The team was made up of six seniors, six sophomores, and two juniors, with the seniors and sophomores having little in common. Most of the seniors went to the Brooklyn business school, while the sophomores attended the new Hillcrest liberal arts campus in

Queens. The Brooklyn seniors rarely socialized or talked much with Hill-crest sophomores. Duckett, Chrystal, and Parenti, the dominant Brook-lyn faction, differed from the cocky sophomores. They clashed like *West Side Story*'s Jets and Sharks, fighting for a piece of the playing turf. Older, and appearing out of shape, Duckett acted and played independently, with Parenti and Chrystal following his lead.

After carefully scouting last year's team, Lapchick ordered Duckett and Chrystal to lose weight. By the end of the summer, he felt he had made a dent in their conditioning. When practice started, Lapchick told the press he was pleased with their effort. But when the season began, the two still seemed overweight. As the season progressed, Parenti and Chrystal became more of the coach's concern. Bill Chrystal and Mike Parenti liked doing things for kicks. While Chrystal came from modest means, Parenti's middle-class family was in the wholesale food business. Chrystal went to local public schools, while Parenti attended St. John's Prep, where he ex-celled on the freshmen basketball team until he was asked to leave because of poor grades. Parenti entered New Utrecht High School where he teamed with Bill Chrystal. After Chrystal graduated in January, Parenti led the team to the 1953 Public School Athletic League championship.

Chrystal and Parenti were lethal weapons. At 6'5" and 220 pounds, Chrystal was a mass of strength and muscle capable of scoring inside and out. If he had a weakness, it was foot speed, but he more than made up for it with quickness and sheer power. He was a force to deal with on and off the court. Chrystal's cracked front tooth mirrored his personality. It was the kind of angled split that when coupled with cobalt-blue eyes and combed wavy hair, lent a Stallone, tough-guy arrogance to his smile. He had the daring to take chances, to do things on the edge, feeling he'd never get caught. It was rumored that he cheated on exams, stole from school lockers, and snatched goods from unsuspecting store clerks just to prove he could get away with it. Senior Harry Pascal once caught Chrys-tal stealing from a friend's locker. The 6'1" honor student insisted he re-turn the stolen property, which Chrystal did.

Parenti was different, less intimidating in spite of his bulky 6'7", 245-pound frame. Some teammates saw him as talented but unwilling to work hard to improve. Mike was more the follower. Chrystal played cold-bloodedly, like he wanted to trample an opponent; Parenti, as if he would help him up. He had a less-defined build with a soft shooting touch capa-ble of scoring big points with double-digit rebounding. After averaging

22 points and fourteen rebounds a game as a junior, he was touted by sportswriters as a preseason All-East selection with pro possibilities.

While Chrystal and Parenti were seasoned players, their leader was senior floor leader Dick Duckett, the balding Korean War veteran. Duckett and Chrystal, who both liked smoking cigars around the team, were cousins whose fathers were New York policemen. If the group strayed into some school or locker-room prank, Duckett would have joined them. Parenti and Chrystal, however, had other ambitions, but could they get away with throwing games under Lapchick's nose?

O

As the season grew closer, Lapchick remained apprehensive, and while questioning the desire of some of his players, he worried that he might be part of the problem. Recognizing that the college game had changed, becoming more complex than his first tour before the war, caused him to inwardly doubt himself. He was not a coach who went home to study new formations. As he examined his future, he began to feel his age. While coaching St. John's and the Knicks into the mid-1950s, man-to-man defense with few tricks was the standard. But when he returned to St. John's in 1956, zones were not only legal, but strategists like Temple's coach Harry Litwack were mastering new combination zones, a sophisticated maneuver for the 1950s that confused Lapchick. Combinations broke the defense into two parts with the two front guards playing a zone while the three baseline defenders matched up in a man-to-man formation. It created a zone look with man-to-man principles. It was effective because it was not widely understood and upset a team's offense.

Shortly after the coaching change, St. John's assigned head baseball coach Jack Kaiser to work with Lapchick. Kaiser, an excellent baseball man, was limited in basketball. Unlike pros, college kids needed hands-on instruction, more "nose-wipes." Since St. John's made no provision for an experienced assistant, the head coach did all of the coaching.

Several weeks into practice, however, former Redmen and NBA pros Al McGuire and Fuzzy Levane arrived during practice to help. McGuire, who was beginning a coaching career at Dartmouth, often showed up before important games to go over scouting reports and discuss game strategy. Lapchick admired the former Knick and thought his upbeat style would help. Traditionally, Lapchick played veterans, but several weeks before the first game, he decided to stir up the three lackadaisical seniors by starting sophomores Seiden and Pascal.

One day after practice Seiden tried discussing with Duckett some problems he was having in his guard play. The senior made it clear he didn't want to "talk shop," preferring to leave basketball in the gym. Seiden, an all-out player, didn't like that. The sophomores were more serious while the upperclassmen seemed to lack intensity and leadership. "Shouldn't they be the leaders?" Seiden asked.

St. John's opened the 1956–57 season in late November winning three soft games along with our first Garden date against a stronger Rhode Island team. "Let's wait until we play somebody," Lapchick warned the enthusiastic press after the team set a Garden record of 115 points against Rhode Island. Utah, a team we should have beaten, handed St. John's its first loss a week later in the Garden. We were flat, lacking cohesiveness, playing almost like strangers.

All the fire and confidence we had in walloping Rhode Island the week before disappeared against Utah. The game was an eye-opener, and for the first time Lapchick suspected something was wrong. St. John's, an 11-point favorite, lost, 79–71. He listened to his sportswriter friends whispering bookmaker rumors that certain St. John's games were "off the boards," which was bookmaker talk for a rigged game. He left the Knicks for what he believed was a more relaxed situation, but instead he walked into what could be a nightmare. Uneasy, and with no proof or smoking gun, Lapchick faced a dilemma. In spite of his misgivings, he hoped he was wrong and worked to motivate the team.

Seiden took the Utah defeat hard. "Lapchick wasn't much of an 'X and O' guy," he said. With a minute left in the game and the score tied, the team huddled around him. Seiden, too, was caught up in the fantasy that Lapchick was a miracle man, expecting some brilliant strategy from the former pro coach. He didn't get it.

When a team lacks cohesion, it causes a coach to wonder why. As Lapchick prepared for the Holiday Festival, he realized the team's chemical imbalance. They just didn't blend. The underclassmen resented Parenti and Chrystal's underachieving efforts. They appeared to be unreliable "big shots" who wore expensive clothing and smoked big cigars. Duckett wasn't playing up to his potential either. Being overweight and distracted didn't help. The seniors, on the other hand, saw the sophomores as an inexperienced bunch that got in their way.

The week before the Garden's Holiday Festival, the team's practice was sluggish. The biggest riddle remained our floor leader, Dick Duckett. In practice he was outstanding, by game time his talent evaporated, and we privately labeled him a "Two O'Clock Player." He was like a baseball player who hits balls out of the stadium in batting practice but looks lost when the umpire cries: "Play ball!" The team knew Duckett was talented; he could scoot past a defender on a drive with his quick first step or could curl his tongue onto his upper lip and fire a quick, perfect, two-hand set shot. His true strength was his passing. When in the flow of the game, he was a dangerous passer who could distribute the ball with the best. When he was right, he played levels above anyone in the gym.

As St. John's prepared for Brigham Young, the team was rated a strong but unstable tournament contender. Before the game, Lapchick, engulfed in clouds of cigarette smoke, appeared uneasy, pacing the dressing room floor and frequenting the john. However, when he delivered his pregame talk, he was composed. The Redmen lived up to their unpredictable billing by getting blown out. BYU out-shot and, as sportswriters described it, "mostly out-hustled the Brooklyn Indians." Parenti and Chrystal's rebounding and defense were nearly nonexistent.

The next day, Lapchick didn't come to practice and, in his place, appeared Al McGuire. Lapchick hoped some of McGuire's tenacity would rub off onto the team. The young coach sized us up, wondering if we had any guts after the night before. "Your sweat socks should be the only dry part of your bodies," he scornfully shouted at us, implying that players who play hard should be a pool of sweat.

But then he got to the essence of the practice. The substitute coach simulated conditions that caused quick reaction. In one drill, he lined us up and randomly rolled a ball in front of a player, who was expected to aggressively pounce on the loose ball, something missing the night before.

Although St. John's won both consolation games, Lapchick was uneasy. He never forgot the painful memories caused by point-shaving in 1951. Nat Holman and Clair Bee were close friends whose coaching careers were shattered. It frightened him to think his career could go up in smoke from some kids going bad. Gamblers, like K-9 dogs, had an uncanny sense of sniffing out financially strapped athletes who might throw games. Lapchick's lack of confidence in the seniors was a sign they were involved. This doubt eventually reached the team, and whispered accusations continued to be leveled toward them.

Although there was a lack of chemistry, like a parent's denial of a child's misbehavior, I was oblivious of my team dumping games, but like the coach, the team felt something was wrong. As the season progressed, I was splintering bench time and lost much of my focus. Most of the team knew little about gambling. I was totally naive about point spreads or where to even place a bet. My father never gambled, and I didn't have money to lose. But there were other more sophisticated athletes who did know gamblers and were willing to risk fixing games. As Lapchick rubbed his chin with apprehension he wondered, "Could these guys be in the tank?"

○

Before the January trip to the Midwest, Lapchick, with lines of worry wrinkling his face, sat the team down during a Flushing Armory practice and told us of the suspicions bookmakers had about our games. Although he smiled when he told us he knew we "wouldn't fix a game," inwardly he wasn't convinced. He felt helpless confronting a team suspected of not playing to win. Lapchick called an 11:00 A.M. practice for New Year's Day. Most teams relaxed after the holiday's late night revelry, but because the team was leaving the next day to play Bradley, he wanted to test the team's resolve. "I remember the strong beer smell," Engert said. The seniors didn't try to disguise how they had spent the previous night. Practice slowly melted into shooting drills, rather than any serious scrimmaging, with little accomplished.

On January 2, the team bused to Idlewild Airport for the trip to play Bradley and St. Louis. I was thrilled to be the first in my family to fly. My mom, fearing the unknown, warned me not to go. I kissed her good-bye, told her not to worry, and headed to the airport, feeling like Columbus sailing uncharted waters. It was a smooth TWA flight to Peoria, Illinois, probably the best part of the trip.

Shortly after we settled in our hotel rooms, the sophomores spurred by Lapchick's talk, tried stirring the team's lethargy. "Let's have a meeting in my room," Seiden suggested. "Why not," I said. "The way we're playing we've got nothing to lose." The team showed up at 4:00 P.M. for what was the equivalent of a family intervention. As the most outspoken sophomore, Seiden tried to sum up our feelings. "We're six and two, and lost our two toughest games. But we're not playing together." We all knew the team should be undefeated, that both losses were winnable.

Duckett listened, shifting in his seat while Chrystal indifferently folded a Peoria newspaper. "We can make the NIT," Engert chipped in. "As a sophomore, I would love the chance to play." In his second year, Engert was older, a married veteran who felt he could talk up to seniors. Parenti looked up and mumbled a weak agreement.

The underclassmen were looking around, waiting for the seniors to show leadership, to give the rest something to rally around. Instead Duckett, the oldest and most experienced, seemed content going through motions that were rapidly losing steam. Raising my voice in frustration, I yelled, "What the hell is going on out there?" That got Parenti and Chrystal's attention, almost like a lion tamer snapping a whip that annoys the powerful beasts in the cage. They wanted me to stop bothering them but couldn't physically flick me away. As we went around the room, each of us said what was on his mind, mostly complaints about our lack of team play and few solutions.

"Does anyone care about winning these games?" Hughie Kirwan wanted to know. "We look out of shape," the scrappy junior guard "put on the table." Kirwan liked to win. He had played for St. Ann's in Manhattan and, like most of us, knew only success. He felt alone as he looked around the room. "Wait a minute, Hughie," Harry Pascal countered. Harry was the well-spoken, clean-cut, older brother of sophomore Buddy Pascal and the team's best student-athlete. He had our respect. "This is our senior team, and we are not here to lose."

I summoned enough courage to stand up, looked Bill Chrystal in the eyes, and said what had been bothering me. "I can't feel you on the court." Quality team play grows from knowing each other's moves. When I had a chance to play, the seniors were like strangers, no "feel" or electricity. "Feel" in basketball was a "hand-in-glove" fit, a by-product of chemistry. Some players blend well, a sense found among winners. Others, for many reasons, don't.

"Feeling" was an odd word, but it came from a gut reaction, one I spontaneously brought up. Effective play in most sports occurs when teammates appear to play effortlessly, making it look simple. We've all seen it: a fluid double play or the natural motion between a quarterback and his seeing-eye receivers. We watch in amazement as to how it was performed. But it is also obvious when that magic is not there. That chemistry happens when team members become familiar with one another. There seems to be an unrecorded telepathic language between players that triggers success on the court. A player knows when it happens; he can feel it. But as hard as Lapchick worked, there was little of that on our team.

Parenti, Chrystal, and Duckett were strangers to us on the court. There was suspicion dripping from our relationship. We not only played poorly, we also didn't trust them. In the hotel room in Peoria that January afternoon, I couldn't put my finger on exactly what was causing it, but it was obvious that I wasn't getting much help figuring it out.

I could tell I had Chrystal's attention the way he slammed the newspapers down and turned to face me, looking like he was about to rip my head off. He hesitated, then smiled and burst out laughing, but he never answered my emotional plea. The room grew silent, and for the next few tense seconds, which seemed an eternity, no one spoke. The team was as confused by his "don't give a shit" attitude as with his play. By laughing in my face, it was clear there was no leadership in the room. If there were, someone would have gotten up, grabbed Zeke by the shirt, throttled him, and told him off. But, like mice avoiding a hungry cat, we crawled away, realizing any hope for progress was destroyed by Chrystal's reaction.

Teammates usually form close bonds. During a six-month period we spend much of our time together, playing, having sports fun, or talking about the team. To accuse a teammate would be like calling the police on a family member, something difficult to do. The following night we piled into a bus that took us to the Bradley field house. It seemed strange warming up because it was the first time any of us ever had to climb up three feet from our bench to reach a raised, stagelike playing floor. But the higher floor did little to elevate our play.

Chrystal and Parenti sleepwalked through another game, while Duckett was again ineffective, missing open layups and passing like he was playing in a youth league. Led by 6'7" future NBA forward Barney Cable, Bradley, spurred on by our lackluster performance, blew us out by 19 points, 97–78. We lost to St. Louis, too, but the Bradley game was the more vivid loss. It was the first major trip for the sophomores, and we were disappointed. The seniors didn't seem to mind.

After the Bradley game, Chrystal and Parenti led us to a local bar in Peoria where they celebrated. Beers for everyone. It surely wasn't the mood of the younger players. "I couldn't believe Duckett's attitude," Hugh Kirwan remembered. "He didn't seem concerned that we had just gotten beat. These guys are in a bar laughing and celebrating, and we embarrassed ourselves." A short while later, the younger players separated and returned to the hotel. For the point-shavers the party went on. Why not, it was a good night; they had fixed the score, and years later we would read that Parenti and Chrystal split $2,000 for their lack of effort. After the trip, the team won three of four, getting torched only in Morgantown, West Virginia, by high scorer Hot Rod Hundley and his Mountaineers, 105–72.

Early in February, we played a mediocre George Washington team in the Garden. The Redmen were 14-point favorites but struggled to win. It was a game where Seiden unknowingly became part of the fixers' strategy by being repeatedly fed the ball because he wasn't hitting his shots. With thirty seconds to play, however, Pascal stole the ball at half-court and passed to Chrystal for the deciding basket, allowing St. John's to squeak out a 63–62 victory. By staying below the spread, the dumpers were financially successful again.

St. Joseph's was another dumped game played in the Palestra in Philadelphia. St. John's, a slight favorite, fell behind early by 18 points. Senior guard Walter Brady got the call from Lapchick and brought the team back with some fine outside shooting. As the game got close, Chrystal, looking frantic, called time-out. As the players were walking to the bench, Brady questioned the call because the Redmen had momentum while St. Joseph's was wilting. Chrystal grabbed Brady by the shirt and pulled him aside. "Shut up, I'm the captain," he shouted at him. St. John's went on to lose by 12 points.

Years later, Brady ran into Chrystal in Brooklyn. Zeke, who needed a shave and was dressed carelessly, invited his old teammate for a drink in a local bar. The years had not treated Chrystal well. He had aged and lost much of his hair as well as his arrogance, and he talked openly of his misdeeds. He brought up the St. Joseph's game.

"Remember the time you got sore because of the time-out?" he asked. "I had to tell Parenti not to give you the ball because you were scoring and keeping us in the game." Brady, who by this time was a successful insurance executive, felt pity for his old teammate. As much as Chrystal's scheme had ruined the season, he couldn't lash out at him. "For the next ten years," Brady recalled, "I couldn't watch a college game." It was too disappointing for him to think that his teammates had thrown games.

Joe Lapchick's low point occurred during the closing minutes of the Manhattan game in the Garden on February 28, 1957. The coach was unnerved by his realization that the team was dumping games and felt stymied by their actions. It affected him to the extent that he began to lose control of the team. Walter Brady was a take-charge type who sat next to Lapchick. The senior guard gradually began to take over the coaching during the crucial moments of the game. With the score deadlocked, Brady turned to Lapchick and interjected his strategy.

"Coach, let's hold the ball for one shot. If we have the ball they can't score." Lapchick, confused by this time, turned to the team and fed them what Brady had suggested. What followed was a series of attempts to freeze the ball for one shot by having Duckett and Seiden stand near half-court and play catch for as much as four minutes before taking a last shot. During the critical stretch of the game, Brady also suggested player substitutions, which Lapchick followed. Brady repeated his "game plan" for each of the three overtime sessions, until Seiden finally hit a fifteen-foot jump shot from the right side with one second on the clock to win the game, 61–59.

After the game, Lapchick apologized to the press for holding the ball and making it an unpopular finish. He attempted to defend the ending by suggesting that colleges institute a shot clock, but then repeated that he needed the win. It may never have happened again, and only a few of the team members were near enough to realize what took place, but the Manhattan game had to be one of Joe Lapchick's most embarrassing moments in basketball. As the season was winding down, Lapchick was still puzzled by his team's play, uncomfortable with rumors spinning around the team. He had to get to the bottom of all this.

○

Mike Parenti was afraid he knew what Coach Joe Lapchick wanted to talk about. As he showered and dressed after practice at Flushing Armory, he tried to anticipate what Lapchick might ask him about what was taking place. The big center feared what his coach knew about the 1956–57 season. Maybe the police informed him, he thought. As he brushed back his receding, tightly cropped curly hair, Chrystal flashed past and stopped.

"What are you doing tonight?" his Brooklyn buddy asked while he packed his practice clothes into a bag. As they walked up the stairs from the dressing room, Parenti pulled Chrystal aside and whispered, "I think Lapchick knows." Chrystal gave him one of those "Are you shitting me" looks. "He doesn't know squat," Chrystal shot back. Parenti looked sideways at his friend but didn't feel relieved. "Coach wants to see me, now." A nervous look crossed his face. Chrystal stopped and faced his dumping partner. "I think you're crazy. Just play dumb. Call his bluff."

Parenti lumbered up the stairs and slowly walked toward Lapchick's miniature office. As he looked through the open door, he noticed the tall coach wore unfamiliar, dark, horned-rimmed glasses and was hunched over some papers in a folder.

"Mike, come in, come in, have a seat, and Mike, better close the door," the coach said a few octaves above a whisper. Parenti didn't like the feeling he was getting. It felt as if his coach wanted to ask serious questions, he thought.

Lapchick finally looked up from his desk, removed his glasses, and with Mike settled, looked right at him, wasting no time. "Mike, we've had an odd season. Good games and some horrendous ones, but one thing seems consistent." The coach stopped, leaving his player dangling on purpose. Rather than tell Parenti what that was, Lapchick rolled his thoughts up into a neat question for the big center to answer and had paused like a poker player to see if he would tip his hand. "Why do we seem to fall apart at the end of games?" he finally asked.

Parenti felt his worst fears materializing. Lapchick knew! I never wanted to be part of this from the beginning, Parenti said nervously to himself. Coach was blaming him for the team's poor showing at the end of games when Zeke and he melted the game away to collect their point-shaving money.

Parenti cornered, hesitated, then shrugged his shoulders and mumbled inaudibly, "I don't really know, Coach." By this point Parenti could see the welcome mat that was offered a few minutes ago had dissolved into something less friendly, more like a police-questioning. The coach's smile faded to a look of resentment.

Lapchick was eaten up by the season. A team with great preseason potential was mediocre at best. A star player like Parenti, who had scored bundles of points the year before, was reduced to carrying the scoring bags of sophomores Seiden and Pascal. What happened? Lapchick didn't know. But he didn't want to let him off the hook that easily.

"Mike, have you been approached by any, well, unsavory characters?" Lapchick wanted to know. Mike felt safer now. He was fishing around. Zeke was right.

"No, coach, but if any came to me, I know to report it to you." Parenti knew he had given the textbook answer, and even if there were a tape recorder nearby he was in the clear.

"That's right, Mike. I see you're up on the law."

The two volleyed for a few more minutes before Lapchick sensed Parenti was not about to make any confession to the brokenhearted coach. Parenti walked out of the room sweaty but temporarily relieved. Lapchick didn't feel any better. He never did get a straight answer that year.

As the season wound down, the athletic director hinted to the seniors that if St. John's defeated NYU in the last game, the NIT committee would consider them in spite of a 15–8 record. Seniors Brady, Bill Cowley, and Harry Pascal convinced Parenti, Chrystal, and Duckett to meet a few days before their last game. "If we beat NYU," Brady blurted out, "McLaughlin thinks we might get into the tournament." Pascal agreed. "We're good enough." For the first time that season, Brady felt the seniors were together as they bound their hands pledging victory. Three days later, St. John's lost to NYU by 12 points, 67–55. The dumpers won again. The season was over, and nothing was said about the year we had just experienced. It was just a bad dream to Lapchick and the rest of us, but as players, it was easier for us to put aside the bad taste than it was for our coach.

After the season, Seiden was working out in DeGray Gym in Brooklyn when Parenti dropped by to watch. When the scrimmage ended, he approached Seiden. As they chatted, the former teammate got around to the reason for his visit. "Alan, I can hook you up with a few guys to make some easy money." If "business" was to continue at St. John's, a player of Seiden's ability had to be recruited. "Mike, I'm going to pretend you never said anything to me," Seiden answered, "because if I thought otherwise, I'd have to turn you in." Seiden picked up the ball, turned his back, and continued shooting. Parenti started to talk, stopped, then left the gym. That was the last Seiden ever saw of his former teammate. He never reported the incident, and it was forgotten.

Lapchick was tortured with doubts of the previous season and found it hard to forget. Once burned, he would scrutinize players in the future more carefully. On January 10, 1959, during our senior year, after an 86–85 victory over George Washington in Washington, D.C., Lapchick and McLaughlin told Seiden on the train ride back that if St. John's had lost, the 5'10" guard would have been suspended because of gambling rumors that were circulating. Seiden was never implicated. Anyone who knew him understood his great love for the game and statistics. It wasn't in his makeup to hurt the team or his game. He wanted to win badly. His sights were set on the NBA, and dumping games was not in his interest.

Even after Lapchick had been cleared of any blame, when the point-shaving became public in May 1961, he was still uncomfortable with what Parenti and Chrystal had done. After the news was out on the dumpers, I dropped by St. John's to visit with my old coach. I found him in the basement of the new field house. I noted, even after all his success, Lapchick was assigned a small room without a door where he was answering mail before practice. It had an unfinished, whitewashed, cement-block look, with a light bulb dangling in the middle of the room like a scene from a 1930s gangster film. His wooden desk was vintage parochial school, the type used by the religious when delivering moral messages. In the words of an old comic, the room was so small he had to go outside to change his mind.

The conversation eventually turned to our 1959 championship season. As we reminisced, I talked about teaching and that I had gotten married. When I said most of us lived modestly as players and casually mentioned we "could have used money," Lapchick's face made a complete 180-degree change from broad smile to narrow-eyed frown. "What do you mean?" he asked. The tortured coach thought I implied our team threw games. Although I realized my mistake and wanted to apologize, I understood I created a doubt that would take time to erase. Lapchick had not forgotten the betrayal. He was still haunted by it.

O

Lapchick survived the 1956–57 season, ending with a respectable but disappointing 14–9 record. At the time, most on the team were unaware of his more serious problems. No public exposure of the thrown games was made until four years later, in spring 1961, when District Attorney Frank Hogan brought a new basketball scandal to light, which included Mike Parenti and Bill Chrystal, the two St. John's players among the fifty caught. Hogan's announcement was the beginning of college basketball's second round of disgrace.

Tim Cohane, sports editor of *Look* magazine confirmed: "The earliest reported fixes were five games played by St. John's in the 1956–57 season." Cohane computed that point-shavers Mike Parenti and Bill Chrystal each received $4,450 from gambler Joe Hacken.

Chrystal's father earned about $5,000 a year as a policeman, while the Parenti family's wholesale grocery business put them in the $10,000 range. Joe Lapchick was paid about $12,000 for coaching. The two St. John's fixers each made approximately an NBA pro's yearly salary. Parenti and Chrystal's point-shaving also earned them front-page photos in the *New York Times* on May 25, 1961, and listed each of the fixed games. The account named Joe Hacken and Jack Molinas as the gamblers who arranged them. While Hacken was the front man, Molinas was "Mr. X" of the '61 scandal.

When Jack Molinas was a Columbia freshman playing in my neighborhood tournament, he was lean and quick and always smart. Even then he was too smart. He led first-year head coach Lou Rossini's Columbia Lions to a 30–0 undefeated season, making him a first-round pick of the Fort Wayne Pistons in 1953. But that wasn't enough for Jack. He needed more action. The NBA finally fingered him for betting on Piston games. This horrified president Maurice Podoloff. Gambling issues could destroy the young league's credibility. Fresh in his mind was how it wiped out collegiate attendance. It took Molinas only twenty-nine games to be erased from pro ball. He had tried skating around the law but slipped and fell. Nonetheless, Molinas wasn't finished.

He became an attorney and practiced crooked law. He ran with the crowd parents tell their kids to avoid and was convicted as the key figure in the 1961 point-shaving scandal. Jack served hard time before he was murdered execution-style by gangsters on the West Coast. After his pro days, Molinas made sure he reached out to contaminate as many young athletes as possible, starting with the two willing St. John's participants.

In retrospect, the rumor was that more than five St. John's games were thrown that year. Brigham Young was another questionable one. Chrystal had admitted to Brady there were other games fixed during his career that were never reported, but there was no reason to verify every game. Five were enough for Hogan.

Dick Engert and Lou Roethel later discussed games they thought were dumped. Engert correctly believed the St. Joseph's game was one, while Roethel felt Brigham Young was another. "I always thought the St. Joseph's game was fixed," Engert later surmised. "They couldn't catch the ball." He wondered how a ball that big could fit between a player's legs.

Seiden agreed, but with a different slant. "They kept feeding me; I was on my way to a 1–for–10 night. They knew I would continue to shoot."

Unlike Hogan's 1951 investigation, the 1961 gambling disclosures concentrated on jailing the fixers rather than the coaches or players. Hogan was most interested in prosecuting mastermind Jack Molinas along with his accomplices instead of the athletes. Lapchick was never identified with the scandal. None of the bad press about fixed games stuck to him. The time gap of four years from the time Parenti and Chrystal dumped games helped. It was also widely assumed that the coach at the time of the dumped games was Dusty DeStefano, who had coached the fixers the two previous years. When the story later broke, no newspaper clarified the error. When it came to St. John's involvement, the focus fell on Parenti and Chrystal, not on Lapchick or the university. The St. John's program was not marred. Life went on. Parenti and Chrystal cooperated with the district attorney's investigation and helped indict Molinas and Hacken, who were convicted and served time. The St. John's players escaped jail time but were disgraced and lost their jobs with Citibank.

Little was ever heard about either Chrystal or Parenti. At team reunions nothing was mentioned about the two, as if they had dissolved and blown away. Forward Bill Cowley, who was a senior on the 1956–57 team, believed Parenti was selling tools. The talk was that he had dropped out of sight. Someone thought Chrystal worked for the post office and later moved to California. That was the last anyone heard of him. I was later told that he died in San Mateo, California, in 1981 of a heart attack. He had been married, had two children, but was later divorced. Few of us ever knew how well the seniors could play. The next year, during the 1957–58 season St. John's scrimmaged Mitchell Air Force Base. Chrystal was on the team, and we saw then how well he could play. He was awesome; a physical man among boys and impossible to stop.

Duckett, the senior floor leader, was rumored to have been involved with dumping games during the 1956–57 season but was never charged. "You were such a talented player, Dick," I reminded him, "that it was an assumption most of the team later made." Since he always had the ball in his hand, it was an easy conclusion to reach.

Duckett completely denied any involvement with point-shaving and repeated it for good measure. "I was as upset about what happened as you guys were." Both Parenti and Chrystal also denied Duckett's involvement during their grand jury testimony. Ironically, immediately after the season,

Duckett was voted the MVP in the Garden's annual East-West all-star game and toured against the Globetrotters. He was also good enough to play the next season in the NBA with the Cincinnati Royals.

"What did you think was going on?" I had to ask. "I couldn't figure it out," Duckett replied. He, however, did have something to lose. He was talented enough to make a living from pro ball. But his chances were weakened by the scandal. Everyone was a loser that year.

○

Today, Mike Parenti is in his mid-sixties, weighs 238 pounds, and has lost much of the brown curly hair that occasionally got in his eyes, but he still sounds the way he did more than forty years ago.

"Hello, is Mike Parenti there?"

"Hey, this sounds like Gus Alfieri," Mike answered. I was surprised he had that kind of memory, but maybe it was just his caller I.D.

Mike Parenti lives in a secluded upstate New York community in a house he built on the fifteen acres of land his father willed to him from what they used for hunting. "I'm going to need knee replacements soon," Parenti said. Another price paid for all that pounding on asphalt courts.

"I dumped games because I was depressed my senior year," Parenti rationalized. The former center, who had been the team's leading point maker as a junior and among the nation's top twenty, suddenly found himself denied the ball. "We had five shooters out there," Parenti recalled from preseason practices. "The sophomores were putting up shots as well as Duckett and Chrystal." He claimed that not much was left for the All-East center. "I realized there was no pro ball for me," and with that conclusion, he became open to making money.

"When you're down," the former center rationalized, "you're susceptible to gambler talk." Chrystal, who "was always looking for action," had a contact from high school who hooked them up with gambler Joe Hacken.

"At first, all we had to do was keep the score under the point spread," Parenti remembered. "But once we lost a game, there was no turning back." The two waited for the right games and did their business.

Life went on after the scandal. "I married a wonderful woman and we have three good sons and three lovely grandchildren," Parenti proudly admitted. Much of his life was spent in Bensonhurst, Brooklyn, where four consecutive, two-family houses were filled with relatives whose extended Italian roots went back to Tuscany and Sicily. "We loved each other and acted as one."

"We were always tasting each other's dinner meals and visiting with relatives," Parenti recalled. It was a way of life that many immigrant families clung to in the past. "My family is gone, but no one can take away my kids," a heritage he believes will live forever.

After the gambling investigation, Parenti drifted for a while and then took a job with the post office and eventually became the Postmaster of Queens, New York, a position he held until he retired a few years ago. But until I called, he had not spoken to anyone from St. John's in more than forty years.

"I was just thinking about you and your father two weeks ago," were the first words out of Mike's mouth when he answered. Parenti was close with his father and regretted hurting him with all the sad front-page news. "Like your father, my dad loved coming to games and was proud of me," Parenti poured out, "and I let him down."

Mike brought back memories of my father, a 5'7", medium-built man with a mustache who knew little about sports but enjoyed the games. I remember him coming with me to the Manhattan Hotel in the city my senior year after I had made the All-Metropolitan team. They had all the players together, and my father was asked to sit with the celebrity guests. He sat next to future all-time NBA great Oscar Robertson, who was honored by the New York writers as the best visiting college player. Pop was thrilled. I wondered how he would have felt if I had dumped games and it became public. Mike had to face that at home.

I thought about Mike Parenti after I spoke with him. Did he ever think about the consequences of his actions? By the mid-1950s when he and Chrystal were fixing games, it was not something new. There was the Brooklyn College shocker in 1945, as well as the massive scandal in 1951 that shook the foundation of college basketball and frightened every NBA franchise. "I have paid the price, I'm sorry for the heartaches I caused," Mike concluded.

But I thought about how good the 1956–57 team could have been. Playing straight, we could have been with the best in the country and proud that we were all from New York. We had everything needed for success. Chrystal and Parenti were athletes of little character who selfishly placed their own interests before the team's. We practiced to play our best, and they gave only a half effort. Their only excuse was that they were young, but so were the rest of us. It was disappointing to think about what might have been.

○

Why didn't Lapchick act on the suspected point-shaving? He was the coach and could have exposed them. He did bench those he felt were involved, but placing blame and accusing college students of a crime was not as easy as it seemed. It was difficult for a coach or university administrator to absolutely determine which players were throwing games. There were no rulebooks or court precedents to guide them when facing what seemed apparent. If suspects were benched on instinct, a coach could be open to criticism, and yet the question remains: What does a coach do when players don't measure up to their potential and rumors get heavier than ice in the winter?

Shortly after District Attorney Hogan's announcement of the second scandal, Lapchick was interviewed by a South Bend, Indiana, sportswriter. "Why couldn't coaches sense something was wrong?" the writer asked. "Many of them did," Lapchick answered. "But a basketball team is built on loyalty and integrity." Lapchick found it difficult to distinguish between a player who was having an off night or was "pulling his punches." What seems obvious may not be. Even when conditions are ideal, a player can "Stink up the place," while another could have unfavorable factors work to his advantage. Lapchick admitted being suspicious of some players. "But what can you do?" He talked of speaking "point blank" with them, which he did. He did bring up the subject with the team in general terms and would with future teams. He had been burned, and he didn't want St. John's or his reputation smeared. He felt, however, the "fellow on the take" was not about to give an honest answer.

"What about benching the suspected dumper?" the sportswriter asked. Lapchick tried warning that the team was being watched. He couldn't bench suspects on rumors or gut feelings. "Only if you're sure," Lapchick warned. "What are you going to tell his parents? That their son is dumping games when you have no proof." If Lapchick benched suspects, he would also be open to criticism. The press would want to know why the benched players weren't playing. If he did act, he would be judging them guilty before they had a chance to defend themselves. These were questions that might force a coach to publicly accuse players, and this could cause team chemistry to dissolve.

Adding to the uncertainty was the stellar play of some past fixers. LIU All-American Sherman White, who was caught fixing games during the 1951 scandal, played at a top pace, scoring and rebounding better than the nation's best. "How was a coach to detect point-shaving when the accused played so well?" Lapchick asked. There were other worries for Joe Lapchick other than determining who was dumping games.

Lapchick was unfolding the nightmare a coach faces during a season of doubt. To him the issue of throwing games boiled down to the question of certainty. Was Lapchick positive they were guilty? What if he was wrong? Hindsight makes those who dumped so obvious. Why not bench the suspects and take your chances? If the school and coach were proved wrong, Lapchick feared "being hauled off to court for slander or libel." Where could Lapchick voice his complaints? To an extent, his options were limited. When an athlete in the 1950s was suspected of shaving points, little could be done until due process procedures were enacted. Few college players were benched before an indictment. As a rule, no school or coach removed a suspect from the team prior to legal intervention. Parenti and Chrystal were not indicted and hadn't appeared before a grand jury until several years after they graduated.

There was also a tender side to Joe Lapchick that made it difficult for him to be vindictive, a stern judge over his players. He spent a lifetime worrying about others' feelings, fearful that he was hurting someone. He felt twisted inside over the pain parents of the accused would feel. He cried when he cut pros and hated when players that he was close with got traded. Accusing a player of a crime in print was not something he could stomach.

The simple solution was for a coach to remove the suspected players. He did. Throughout the first half of the 1956–57 season, he played more of his bench than he normally would have. When he suspected something was wrong, he made some lineup changes, but he had meager options sitting on his bench. Roethel broke his leg, and there were few others with experience. My teammates knew something was wrong. Players know when someone is "dogging it," and that feeling remained the entire season. We got used to losing key games. After the 1951 scandal, colleges and the NCAA discouraged and athletes no longer played unsupervised places like the Catskills, making it more difficult—but not impossible—for gamblers to prey on them.

On his return to St. John's, Lapchick saw his career fading. Who would hire someone touched by a scandal? He pictured himself as an out-of-work, aging coach with a limited education and no immediate prospects. Maybe Lapchick feared risking his job. He was human. The stigma of a scandal was difficult to erase. Holman was identified with the 1951 scandal for the rest of his life, but he never publicly discussed it. Holman sued CCNY to regain his job, but its program, like LIU's, was destroyed. His coaching basically ended when his team was dragged into the mud. That would not be the case with Lapchick, who was never identified with the fix scandal.

Clair Bee, who claimed he could detect a fix, stated publicly before the scandal broke that his LIU players were innocent. It's easy to understand a coach's denial. Lapchick, like others, saw himself as a father watching over his players. He was the grand old man, a legendary figure, highly respected. Would his boys fix games? Some observers saw a sellout by players as the least likely scenario for a coach to accept, and, yet, coaches were susceptible to betrayal.

In evaluating the gambling issue, Lapchick never abandoned his principles. As the coach, he could not act unilaterally but was forced to make the best of it. With either inconclusive evidence or schools pretending to be oblivious of what's going on, it was easier for a coach and administration to freeze in place and wait for the season to end.

In 1963, popular journalist Jimmy Breslin recorded Lapchick's dilemma with point-shaving in a *Saturday Evening Post* article. It was one of the few times Lapchick seemed uncertain. He again stated that coaches and school officials were helpless when it came to preventing athletes from fixing games. The process seemed as inevitable as today's illegal college recruiting or steroid use. "It is frightening," Lapchick admitted. "If there is anything akin to a blind alley, this is it."

"I don't know where it starts," Lapchick admitted, trying to rationalize the source of gambling fixes. It was concluded that big-city arenas with their gambling element attracted nonacademic athletes who fixed games, but Lapchick saw a change in the new round of fixes. "There were top students from small campuses involved in this one," Lapchick lamented, and they were masterminded by above-average students like Columbia Ivy Leaguers Jack Molinas and later Fred Portnoy. With all his experience, Lapchick admitted that he had no solutions. "All I know is it's widespread."

But not all of college fixers were good students seeking an education. Athletes who publicized their school through sports received a basic scholarship with few frills while the arenas and universities seemed to benefit. This perception encouraged athletes to seek ways of making money from their celebrity. It was part of the attitude that influenced St. John's big center in 1956.

O

Lapchick made it clear how important the "Scandal Book" was to him. Like a good physician, he offered the only preventive medicine he had. Joe Lapchick felt so strongly about the first scandal, that he assembled a scrapbook of newspaper clippings from 1951 that chronicled its path of destruction. He wanted his players to understand what happened when one became involved with gambling. He wanted his boys to be clean. Every player had to read and sign the book. But what he didn't know in 1956 was that he was showing the book to a couple of fixers.

I remember lugging home the large black scrapbook in my practice bag after a workout and going through it. The first few pages depicted players at police stations covering their faces. The book was riveting and sad.

Joe Lapchick carefully reviewed the 1956–57 season. It hurt knowing his team might not only have thrown games, but ridiculed what he most stood for. Those who shaved points caused the team's divisiveness. Chrystal and Parenti's guilt made them act aloof and distant, knowing they played to lose while we tried our best.

We became better informed on May 25, 1961, when we read specific facts about the dumped games on the front page of the *New York Times*. Unlike the rationale that dumpers only hurt gamblers, the seniors had to realize that they had also cheated their teammates, school, and most of all, their coach. But maybe Parenti and Chrystal hurt themselves most. Mike admitted going to the Garden to watch us play. We had two good seasons, and it must have hurt watching what could have been for him. He had to think whether the $5,000 was worth missing the thrill of playing your best and winning the NIT in the Garden. He, too, could have been a champ, as Marlon Brando said in *On the Waterfront*.

Last year's graduating dumpers became next year's recruiters. In the business world, it's called networking. It was a cycle hard to break until it was exposed. Those who had fixed games wanted to recruit the next batch of dumpers for more than a gambler's bird-dog fee. Recruiters wanted to subconsciously justify their insidious behavior, as if saying, "See, dumping games isn't so bad." There always seemed to be new recruits waiting to dip their paws into the pool. Fixer Joe Hacken was pleased to find some athletes showed character by turning his offer down, implying how rotten he felt about his business. In the end, it was college basketball's inability to patrol its waters that encouraged the scandal. The rationale that fixers only hurt gamblers never did stack up.

In a way Lapchick, too, joined the crowd of coaches who didn't point an accusing finger at suspected players and missed the chance to make a clear statement as he had done his entire life. Although he did nothing wrong and it may not have changed gambling on college games, pointing that finger would have placed Joe Lapchick in a pantheon of sports heroes. As it was, he was a good man, not a perfect one, who suffered pain for years after.

But there was a lot of Jack Dempsey in the old coach. Like the 1920s boxer, when knocked to the canvas, he always bounced up with the strength and resiliency to drag himself to the ropes and hold on until the bell rang. Then he could regroup, rethink his Rudyard Kipling philosophy, and face the next challenge. Joe Lapchick knew the sun would shine again, and he would work to keep it that way. He was a more experienced coach, and the scars made him tougher and better prepared for next season.

Chapter 15

Lapchick Bounces Back

They haven't looked good,
but they keep winning.

—Danny Lynch, St. Francis coach,
describing the St. John's 1957–58 team

The 1957–58 preseason found no sports publication praising St. John's. Even the Holiday Festival snubbed them. Like most coaches, Lapchick preferred being unheralded in the preseason, but he realized it was going to be a struggle to mold an inexperienced team into a winner. Last season's gambling nightmare was in the past, but questions lingered. The junior squad's undefeated freshman record seemed distant.

New York's college basketball would experience a transformation in the late 1950s, and unknowingly, Lapchick and his Redmen would help revive it. The 1951 scandal drove local talent to greener pastures. The recipients of many of New York's finest players were out-of-towners like former St. John's coach Frank McGuire, who had taken over at North Carolina. McGuire's Tar Heels' recruiting net snared Tommy Kearns, Pete Brennan, Bob Cunningham, Joe Quigg, and Lenny Rosenbluth. By 1957, these New York all-stars produced a 32–0 NCAA championship. McGuire's sophisticated recruiting system, headed by Harry Gotkin, broke metropolitan colleges' monopoly on New York talent, arguably the best in the country.

Despite the mass exodus, Thomas Jefferson's scholastic All-American Tony Jackson and 6'11" Leroy Ellis followed Alan Seiden and Buddy Pascal to St. John's. While McGuire basked in North Carolina's national glory, Lapchick and St. John's tried returning New York to basketball prominence.

The mediocre performance of last season's much-heralded St. John's team had tarnished Lapchick's return. He understood he would be measured by the 1957–58 team's results, and if it faltered again, he would be put out to pasture. Lapchick had a good-size scoring forward in Pascal and an aggressive pair of guards in Seiden and me. There was little overall size with only the two 6'5" forwards Lou Roethel and Dick Engert, but both were effective players. Lapchick knew he had to make do. The undefeated freshmen had to be welded into winners.

Seiden spent the past summer playing for Temple coach Harry Litwack in the Israeli Maccabiah Games, the Jewish Olympics. He liked Litwack and wondered what it would be like teaming with Guy Rodgers, their future NBA ballhandling wizard. He looked at his first two St. John's years as unproductive. Although thoughts of transferring passed through his mind, Seiden's heart belonged to St. John's. It was no time to quit. He had something to prove, too. Lapchick's concern was the other guard position.

I still had some growing up to do after my sophomore year. My focus the previous season was more on not playing than on the chaos the seniors caused. When I walked into an empty Flushing Armory for the first day of practice my junior year, I noticed Coach Lapchick dressed in practice clothes. He was alone on the court in Knicks high-cut, blue Kinney sneakers, taking old-fashioned, waist-high two-hand set shots. He looked like a good but old-time player. As I greeted him, he turned, smiled, and waved me over. After a few friendly exchanges his brow suddenly furrowed and the talk became serious.

"The onus," Lapchick reminded his stubborn player, "is on you." The word "onus" stood out as if I were wearing two different sneakers. I stopped to digest exactly what Lapchick was referring to, but the word stirred up last year's horror. As I quietly chewed on Lapchick's muffled ultimatum, his firm demeanor revived the nightmare of last season. Besides the suspected point-shaving, Lapchick was forced to deal with players like me who were disappointed with playing time. I had grown up dreaming of playing at St. John's, but as my sophomore season progressed, those dreams had evaporated.

Part of the problem my sophomore year stemmed from my well-intentioned father, who knew little of sports but was emotionally involved. He was proud of the action photos of his son in the newspapers where I'd be diving for a loose ball. A paint foreman, he would bring clippings to his job and pass them around. When my father heard enough complaints, he naively told me to, "Tell Lapchick to play you, or else!"

While the team dressed last year for the Brooklyn College game, I delivered a softer version of his advice, but as I tried to plead my case, Lapchick politely suggested that just before a game wasn't the right time to discuss it and that we would talk later. Frustrated, I pouted and purposely arrived on the playing floor late, sulking through warm-ups. The coach, aware of my tardiness and conduct, noted the breach in team etiquette.

Understanding what had to be done, Lapchick approached me during what was turning out to be a romp. "I'm putting you in, but I want you to hustle," he warned. We continued to bury Brooklyn, but I played without any passion. By this time, Lapchick was angry trying to motivate a young player, but he waited until late in the game to try again. This time he came smoking down the bench, towered over me, and barked, "Play hard or go take a shower!" He then pushed me toward the scorer's table, wishing he could shot put me out of his thinning hair.

I continued to loaf through the next few days of practice. Fear of failure was always present, and, yet, I stubbornly refused to knuckle under. It was a crazy ambivalent mind-set game athletes play, and it challenged a coach's patience. The idea was that the coach, sensing the player's mood and needing him, would acquiesce and allow the player more game time. That obviously was not the case.

When the team arrived in Philadelphia a few days later to play St. Joseph's, Lapchick called me to his hotel room, where he and team moderator Father Casey greeted me. "Gus, I can understand your feelings," the serious-looking coach began, "but your lack of cooperation is affecting the team." Father Casey jumped in with the finishing touches. "If you continue, we will be forced to remove you from the team." That got to me. I felt as if a Mack truck had run me over. As I drooped to my room feeling as if I had been expelled from school, I realized I wanted very much to be part of the team. I had taken my immaturity as far as it would go. I wasn't buffaloing anyone into playing me, especially not an old pro like Lapchick. I now understand he was trying to balance many issues of which I was just a minor sidebar.

As I now stood in that poorly lit armory for the first day of practice my junior year, Lapchick hoped there was no confusion about what he wanted, and what he meant by "onus." His one sentence had summed up my responsibilities. Playing meant a lot to me, and both coach and player wanted to get off on the right foot. I was focused on the new season and determined to please him. I never realized how important the coming season was to my aging coach.

Early in December the team traveled to Bridgeport for a game. I played flawlessly the first half, but early in the second half the game opened up and became a rout. As was Lapchick's style, he played everyone with starters never getting back into the game. My replacement, senior guard Hughie Kirwan played well. As teammate Lou Roethel and I waited in the New Haven train station to return home, Lapchick joined our conversation. "Gee, wasn't Hughie great tonight?" the coach directed to Roethel, but was meant for the probationary guard. The wise coach was sending a clever message: "Hey, Gus, you played well, but don't get complacent; Kirwan is ready to take your place if you do!" Lapchick had ways of teaching even while waiting for trains.

When St. John's was left out of the prestigious Holiday Festival, Madison Square Garden sent a clear message to Joe Lapchick and his team, as well as to metropolitan sportswriters. The talk was that this was not a quality Redmen team. If St. John's couldn't win with last year's heralded seniors, the pundits figured they would never make it with a bunch of undersized, unheralded juniors. Lapchick quietly disagreed and set out to disprove the implication right off. Starting with a fair but challenging schedule, Lapchick guided the Redmen through the end of January to a perfect 9–0 start, the only undefeated major college in the nation. Although often not pretty, the job was done. After St. John's defeated St. Francis, Danny Lynch, the Terrier coach, was asked to analyze his opponent. "They haven't looked good in any of their games, but they keep winning," Lynch accurately estimated. "It's not a big club, but it's resourceful."

The most satisfying win in the streak was the Rice game. St. John's was 5–0 a few days before Christmas. Rice was a Southwestern Conference team with three exceptionally tall players and was billed as our toughest early-season test. "They had a huge frontline," Engert recalled. Even *The Torch* panned us. By being so negative, our own school paper offended the players, which may have spurred us on. *The Torch* predicted the team would be fed "Bitter Rice." They were big, strong, experienced, and besides, they were "loaded." The student body was warned, "The outlook is bleak." The more we read, the more strengthened we became.

Rice *was* big. Temple Tucker was 6'10", but there were other giants as well. At 6'5", Engert and Roethel were our tallest players. But we were confident, and Seiden was quick to remind the press that as 21–0 freshmen and winners of five games this season, the team was undefeated. "Twenty-six games," the cocky guard shouted to sportswriters, "and on Saturday, it'll be twenty-seven!" Help also arrived from unexpected sources.

Lapchick had permission from the St. John's athletic department to hire a full-time assistant. He chose Lou Carnesecca, who was finishing an illustrious career at Archbishop Molloy High School in Queens. A winner, Carnesecca paid immediate dividends. The energetic coach suggested a spread offense, which turned Rice's size into a disadvantage. We "back-doored" them to death, penalizing an aggressive defender by changing direction and cutting to the basket behind him. On one play, Pascal faked coming to the ball, slipped, fell down, recovered, and still beat his man to the basket. Rice looked foolish and clumsy, as if out of its league, but the win helped build our confidence. St. John's ate up Rice, 80–67. At one point the margin was more than 25 points, but Lapchick refused to run up scores. Coach was chilled by poor sportsmanship. Pounding an opponent was undignified and embarrassing. When the Rice game was decided, Lapchick cleared his bench to allow the wire services to relay a respectable score to the opponent's home fans. He wanted the defeated team to salvage its dignity. Our team started to think maybe things were better than predicted.

On January 30, 1958, we took a perfect 9–0 record (the only major undefeated team in the country) to Pittsburgh to play the Panthers with 5'8" All-America guard, Don Hennon. It was a battle of All-America shooting guards. Our half of the equation was Seiden. We lost 86–73 with Hennon getting 25 to Seiden's 29. But Roethel's absence proved the difference. During the St. Francis game the week before, Roethel dislocated his shoulder and was sidelined for what Lapchick described as "the toughest part of our schedule." He knew a team with average height could not afford to lose a rebounder like Roethel. His absence was felt.

After Pittsburgh, St. John's traveled to the Palestra in Philadelphia to play Coach Harry Litwack's Temple Owls. Litwack, master of the then-revolutionary combination defenses, caused most coaches' hair to go gray. When Lapchick returned to St. John's in the mid-1950s, the college game had changed. Variations of the zone defense with all its chicanery made the game more analytical. They whacked us, 81–58. The next day Lapchick admitted he was puzzled by Litwack's defenses. The trip taught us the value of rebounding and defense. Team scoring didn't matter as much. But then our coach had always preached defense, rebounding, and ballhandling as the keys to the game.

Lapchick also learned from his Celtics days that it was difficult winning in an opponent's backyard because officiating played an even greater role in a game's outcome; television was still in its infancy in the 1950s. Lapchick's approach, later successfully adopted by Carnesecca, was to play a "half-court game" that forced officials and spectators to see all the action in a fixed area. It made it difficult for hometown officials to job visitors if the crowd's focus was on all of the game's action. But the strategy was not foolproof.

The previous year in Peoria, I had been awarded two free throws in a Bradley game. As I got set to shoot, two Bradley players on opposite foul lanes simultaneously reversed their body positions to distract me. The one standing up straight crouched, while the other stood up. The movement was a violation of the rules, and I complained to the official. Looking straight ahead and acting as if he did not hear me, the official whispered, "Shut up and shoot!" The two local referees were willing to let the Bradley violation go unnoticed. So much for out-of-town hospitality.

Dick Duckett told of a 1957 game we played against the St. Louis Billikens in Kiel Auditorium. We lost by 5 points, 82–77, in a game that was closer than the score. A few key calls by the officials near the end of the game tipped the outcome. Lapchick, who rarely complained, later banged on the officials' dressing room door to vent his frustration. At the end of the season, Duckett toured with the College All-Stars and the Globetrotters. When he asked for a few additional games in the tour, the man in charge agreed to Duckett's request. "I owe you one," he answered. "He turned out to be one of the officials from that St. Louis game," Duckett said. Large TV audiences today, however, help eliminate much of the home cooking.

In spite of recent losses, Lapchick developed a positive feel for his team of scrappers. They were far from perfect, but he sensed a winning chemistry. The momentum of the good start was carrying them. The 1957–58 team had a chance to find out what their coach was like. His first year was a scramble of stress and indecisiveness that weakened team harmony. But now, gone were the seniors who had other agendas. The new season was a fresh start for the team and coach. Lapchick knew competitive spirit pumped through an athlete's veins. His job was to harness and channel this spirit rather than have it become divisive. Pride fueled the tandem of competitiveness and individualism. He knew the team closely scrutinized his comments to the press and was aware of his praise and criticism. While encouraging pride, his job was to create a winning but physical balance using what he had lived by his whole life.

Mental toughness insisted on "taking it" and returning in kind, showing no pain and giving no satisfaction, even when crushed by defeat or injury. Your opponent should never think he had broken your spirit. It summed up how Joe Lapchick defined basketball and life. His job was simply to find players with it growing from their ears. "Injuries become a certificate of virility, a badge of courage," was sports historian Allen Guttmann's take on modern athletics. Guttmann had much in common with Coach Lapchick.

"During my coaching days, I taught players to be tough." Lapchick said he liked to link manliness to mental toughness. "Athletics, like no other field of endeavor, counts only the man and his performance." He saw basketball as youth's passage into manhood, an opportunity to prove oneself. He felt athletic injuries tested an athlete's manliness while instilling a sense of pride. Today's major college coaches are well paid. In Lapchick's day, he had to work in the off-season to supplement his salary. From March until October, he had to make ends meet while charging his batteries for next season. Players in the past learned to stay out of trouble and care for themselves, and no one monitored their grades. It was college, and Lapchick saw athletics as training for manhood.

O

The 1957–58 team was turning out better than expected. With average height and speed, the team was driven to prove its worth. Seiden and

Pascal were scratching out successful seasons while Roethel, Engert, and I performed specific roles. Kirwan, Joe Daley, and midseason transfer John Ryan provided bench help. After a mid-February slump with losses to Providence and St. Louis, the Redmen ran off four straight wins to earn a bid to the NIT, St. John's first since 1953. Lapchick wanted us to prove our 16–6 record was no fluke while helping to erase the memory of last year's disaster. As the juniors headed into their first postseason play they were ecstatic, ready to perform in what was then *the* tournament.

Lapchick had a funny way of pronouncing "tournament." He'd say, "*turn*-na-ment," with heavy emphasis on "turn." Whenever he talked about it our ears perked up. Going to the NIT was why we played. The NCAA, still in its infancy, lacked today's media hype. The NIT meant Madison Square Garden, basketball's best arena, the zenith of our careers. It's what players dream about. So when Lapchick said "*turn*-na-ment," we heard every syllable.

Five players usually dominated Lapchick's teams. But as St. John's entered the NIT, two starters, Engert and Pascal, were physical question marks. Fewer than three weeks earlier, Engert played the best game of his career against Richmond, scoring 19 points, but he broke an elbow. "I always kidded Dick about that game," Seiden remembered. "Once he proved he could score big numbers, we would have to get him out of the lineup." The team needed a healthy Engert, but by tournament time Engert's injury still limited his mobility and rebounding. Pascal was no better. He was suffering from emotional exhaustion, which forced him to play below par, and by the first tournament game, it got worse. Yet in spite of the team's weakened condition, we held it together.

While personnel problems danced in his head, Lapchick faced another dilemma. St. John's first-round opponent was Butler, coached by future Hall of Famer Tony Hinkle. Lapchick respected the Hoosier from his barnstorming days. "Coach Hinkle doesn't come to a tournament unless his team is good enough to win," he warned. The game featured a strong fast-break effort by the Redmen, who outran the running Indiana team. Hughie Kirwan's play from the bench along with Roethel's twenty-two rebounds helped dominate the boards and launch the running game that Seiden, Kirwan, and I completed. After a hard-fought game where Butler stayed within 2 and 3 points for much of the second half, St. John's finally broke away, winning 76–69.

Years later *Newsday* sportswriter Mike Candel asked, "Do you know who played for Butler?" I shook my head. "Bob Plump, the Milan High School star who made the winning shot in the film *Hoosiers*." He scored 13 points in a losing effort.

The team's attention shifted to its quarterfinal opponent. Utah was a cocky bunch bragging to New York newspapers that it would handle the Redmen. Their "Sheriff," Gary Hale, a 5'10" guard noted for defense, would "handcuff" Seiden. A pregame photo spread in the local newspapers of Hale in a ten-gallon hat, six-shooters, and riding britches added to the authenticity of Utah's claim. But in spite of Utah's boast, we came through in an unpredictable but dramatic fashion. After St. John's had led most of the game and was up 6 points with little more than three minutes left, we suddenly played as if we had never seen a basketball before. We treated it like a hot potato that would be better fed to our opponents. Part of the panic stemmed from an attempt to freeze the ball too early, which broke the team's rhythm and encouraged the Cougars to gamble on defense.

With thirty seconds left, after blowing our comfortable lead, the Redmen trailed by a point, and Utah had the ball. With the clock running down, we tried desperately for a steal. As Utah attempted to hold on to the ball, I took a swipe at a pass to the high post. Their big man, Carney Crisler, swung an elbow that caught me square on the left side of my jaw, a blow completely missed by the officials. I felt a back tooth explode as if middleweight Rocky Graziano had belted me. I lay, not moving, above the foul line for several seconds, which seemed an eternity, expecting a bell to ring. The referees eventually spotted me and halted the game, allowing "Doc" Gimmler to run onto the court. He cracked smelling salts under my nose, which got me to sit up with my hands over my knees, shaking my head. The elbow to my jaw was more shock than pain. Gimmler, in his excitement, asked, "What's your name, Gus?" I smiled, and we walked off the court.

I remember being a little woolly when I arrived at the bench. Lapchick tilted his head and narrowed his eyes, trying to determine if I was running on all cylinders. With time halted, he had the opportunity to decide to play or replace me. "I'm OK, coach. I'm fine," I said in a strong voice. He was convinced.

When play resumed, the ball was given to Utah to inbound from half-court. A blond, crew-cut sophomore named Keith Ancell froze, unable to find an open teammate, and was called for a five-second violation. Lapchick leaped off the bench signaling time-out. The unbelievable had happened; St. John's miraculously had the ball and a nine-second window of opportunity to overcome 1 point. The team ran toward the bench with new enthusiasm, a chance to pull the game out. As we huddled around our coach, he unfolded his strategy. He looked directly into my eyes and confidently delivered his orders while tapping me on the chest with an index finger. "Gus, take the last shot. You have the hot hand." With that directive he verbally sketched a loose play for me to score. Lapchick turned to Kirwan and instructed him to inbound the ball to me, with Seiden an option.

I never doubted his confidence in me. I had it, too. I didn't know what I would do after the inbound pass, but I knew something would open up. The Utah game was one of my best in college, shooting nine of twelve and scoring 25 points. Because the game was televised, I was helped by the extra time to warm up. Instead of fifteen minutes it was more like thirty-five before the center jump. I remember being exceptionally loose. The team clenched hands, shouted an emotional mantra of "Fight!" and moved from the bench to take its positions. As we digested instructions and headed onto the court, Coach Lapchick smiled, grabbed me by the shirt, and humorously whispered, "It's just like pissing off Pier Eight."

I faked one way and changed direction to catch Kirwan's crisp pass on the left side near half-court, the last nine seconds ticking away. As a lefty, my defender forced me to the middle of the court, and I instinctively bulled my way toward the foul line. Unable to penetrate further, I pulled up and launched a slightly off-balanced, floating, fourteen-foot desperation jump shot that caromed high off the back rim and toward a crowd of mixed players on the left side of the basket.

Out of nowhere, among the tall Utah rebounders, sprang Seiden who, with an extended hand, miraculously back-tapped the ball to Roethel. With only two ticks left on the clock, the bespectacled center wisely took one dribble to balance himself and flipped up a flat, crooked, twelve-foot angle hook shot that acted as if it were magnetized to the rim and dropped in. St. John's won, 71–70. The Garden erupted. As fans poured onto the floor, the team smothered Roethel as if he were a World War II hero back from a bombing mission, while Lapchick choked back tears of joy. The "not good enough" label that rejected St. John's from the Holiday Festival and had driven the team was suddenly lost in the excitement. Coach was thrilled and relished the win. We had reached the semifinals.

Even after a wonderful win, there was an attempt at the coaches' luncheon on Monday to discredit it. Coach Tom Blackburn of Dayton, our next opponent, sarcastically referred to St. John's victory as a "dying-swan act," which disturbed Lapchick. Blackburn felt my injury, which led to a mandatory time-out, was staged. "I have never in my life taught a kid to do a thing like that," Lapchick retaliated. "Alfieri got belted, and he's got a broken tooth to prove it." When later questioned about the incident, Lapchick responded: "We don't teach Barrymore at St. John's."

Before the semifinal against Dayton, an Associated Press photographer, thinking my injury was a shattered front tooth, asked for a picture as the team came out of the runway to warm up. A cracked side molar didn't interest him. St. John's had sent me to Lapchick's dentist in the city. The elbow from the Utah center had sliced off a large piece of a molar, and the impact created an indentation in the line of teeth along the left side of my jaw.

The bizarre Utah ending demonstrated the unpredictability of sports. An injury stops the clock and causes a turnover, which leads to a missed shot, a back tap, and a fluky, 1-point buzzer-shot victory. It falls in line with a bad call, a dribble off a player's foot, an inadvertent fifth foul. Lapchick was measured by victories and took losses personally, blaming himself for the team's shortcomings. He privately agonized with criticism and innuendos and would toss all night fretting over what he called his failures.

Coaches pretend losing is a learning experience, not a reason to leave a suicide note pinned to a hotel pillow. In his darkest moments, Lapchick found guidance from Rudyard Kipling. The poet suggested life involves risks, with losing being a part of it. He also advised to "lose, and start again at your beginnings," but "never breathe a word about your loss." Lapchick learned to present a confident visage to ward off sympathy. His pain was for later in the solitude of his room. He advised young coaches—thumb under your chin, head high, back straight, shoulders squared, and, most important, a big smile to relax everyone. He was a man with no damp handkerchief protruding from his pocket.

○

St. John's faced a bigger, taller, more physical Dayton team with undermanned board strength. Engert's elbow was still weak, and Pascal was scratched from the game. Sensing its shortcomings, Lapchick privately felt the team had reached the end of its rainbow. At the pregame talk, he focused on a theme he would often use. Lapchick was all smiles, filled with confidence. He knew we achieved what few expected, and he was proud of us; that alone was inspirational. We could see it in the twinkle in his eyes and by the way he joked with us.

He recited from his favorite Kipling poem, "If." "If you can talk with crowds and keep your virtue, or walk with kings—nor lose the common touch." He dwelled on walking with kings, telling us we were in a select circle by being one of the tournament's final-four teams. He was filled with positive enthusiasm and tried reaching inside the team to let us understand his feelings. We all glowed with special warmth from Lapchick's compliment that afternoon in the Garden dressing room. Engert knew. "He said the right things to turn you on in the locker room. If we were a football team, we would have broken the locker-room door down to get on the court."

It would have been a storybook finish if the Redmen ripped down the locker-room door that March afternoon and beat the pants off Dayton. It didn't happen. We learned character and humility that day. Despite playing without Pascal, and Engert's broken elbow from the Richmond game a month ago not healed, St. John's still played Dayton close in the first half, trailing 34–31. But Dayton's size proved too much for the Redmen, being out-rebounded fifty-six to thirty-one. Nonetheless, it took until late in the second half before we ran out of gas and the Flyers put the game away, 80–56.

Lapchick was still teaching the next day while preparing for the consolation game against St. Bonaventure. "Me and my big mouth," Seiden later recalled. "I went to Coach and reminded him that it was Kirwan's last game and that the team thought it would be nice if he started the senior." Roethel chuckled. "Lapchick listened to Al's suggestion," narrowed his eyes, thought for a moment, and said, "That's a generous, warm-hearted gesture, Al. He'll start for you tomorrow."

Lapchick rarely missed an opportunity to teach. He often talked of Max Zaslofsky, the old-time Knicks scorer. "We'd win by 20, but if Max got only 7, he'd be pouting in the corner. The next night we'd lose a close one, but when Max filled it up for 23 points, he was at the mirror, combing his hair, whistling a happy tune." Self-interest didn't make points with Lapchick.

The coach provided direction during the season. He took a team with scars from the previous year's scandal, when both Lapchick and his team were questioned, and turned the next season around with nine straight wins and an NIT bid. But the crowning glory was reaching the semifinals. He had nothing to be ashamed of and looked forward to the start of the Tony Jackson era.

O

On a sunny March afternoon in 1957, Lapchick, along with dozens of other coaches from top schools, was vying for the Brooklyn player's talent. The coach asked Seiden to accompany him to the Garden to watch the Thomas Jefferson all-star in the PSAL championship against legendary Boys High. Anthony Baxter Jackson sounded like a victorious Civil War general but was a young black athlete who, along with Joe Lapchick in the late 1950s, helped change college basketball in New York. Whether it was the presence of the St. John's coach at courtside or just butterflies, the All-American had a terrible game, shooting three for twenty-seven from the floor while his team lost. As Jackson struggled, Lapchick turned to Seiden and jokingly said, "I think we made a mistake," to which Seiden wisely answered, "I don't think so, Coach."

On a quiet April evening a few weeks later, Lapchick received a call in his Yonkers home from former playmaker Hy Gotkin. "It's all set, Coach," Gotkin announced. "Tony Jackson is a Redman." As he heard the good news, the phone, acting like a bar of soap, nearly squirted out of his hand. "I almost burst out of my skin," he later recalled. "I was so excited I couldn't wait to call the school," to tell the St. John's administration that Jackson had decided to enroll. Lapchick felt that in two years Jackson, with a team of experienced seniors, could restore St. John's basketball and big-time college crowds to New York. He smiled as he sat down to his evening dinner.

Chapter 16

The Fastest Guns in the East

"**T**he fastest guns in the East aren't cowboys—
they're Indians," wrote sportswriter Gene Roswell of the *New York Post*
after a St. John's win early in December 1958. After the previous year's
18–8 season, the team gained some national recognition, and Lapchick
smelled a winner.

Lapchick's lofty plans for the new season were heightened with the
addition from the freshmen team of sophomore sensation Tony Jackson,
who could shoot and leap with the nation's best rebounders and was the
keystone to a strong senior team. "He has tremendous spring, leaps three
and four feet into the air to take jump shots and grab rebounds," his coach
guaranteed. The young forward's shooting was pure silk capable of "lighting the sky" with soft, long-range jump shots. Everyone predicted he
would be magical.

The other major addition to the team was Lou Carnesecca. Crossing over from the high school ranks where he set all records at Archbishop Molloy, Carnesecca was part of the new style of scientific coaching
that was springing up. Jack Ramsey from St. Joseph's and future coaches
like Hubie Brown and Rick Pitino would change how teams prepared for
games. The fiery bundle of energy was exactly what the doctor ordered,
a perfect complement to the legendary old pro.

During preseason, Lapchick recognized the team was more polished
than last year's. The Redmen could run, score points in bunches, and make

free throws. But, most important, we could penetrate to the basket and draw fouls. With good ballhandling and adequate defense, the team had the necessities and heart to succeed. Lapchick predicted the team would be difficult to beat with Jackson and had a chance to win every game.

The *Long Island Press*'s headline was correct when it insisted "Lapchick Smiling and He Has Good Reasons." Lapchick was notoriously cautious, but he went with his instincts. Preseason sportswriter calls asked him to evaluate the team. "I think we are improved over last season," the old coach told the *Long Island Press*'s Murray Janoff, "and it may not show up in the win-loss column, but they're real tough and hard to beat," he added. His words proved prophetic. Instinctively, Lapchick had accurately evaluated his team.

The well-balanced team hinged on senior maturity and exceptional talent. Seiden was a hard-driving clutch player who spent much of his time on the free throw line. I had developed into a scoring point guard before the term was used. I made sure the ball was distributed to the right players and could accurately shoot a two-hand set shot as well as drive to the hoop. Roethel and Engert were bright players who knew how to score, rebound, and play defense. Their strength was boxing out opponents to allow Jackson to use his leaping ability to clear the boards. Jackson was free to play effortlessly.

The seniors relieved the defensive pressure from Jackson, allowing him to grow into his role. He was respected for his ability from the start and never denied the ball. But the young sophomore was more than a great player. He was a fine person and a good teammate who was fun to play with. The Redmen exuded their coach's chemistry and confidence, and when the team faltered, he reminded the players of it.

As the team prepared for its Garden opener against Providence, Lapchick faced a difficult decision. He was aware of the media pressure Jackson faced as a highly touted sophomore entering the national spotlight. Playing his first Garden game was like a Broadway opening. The coach had planned to start 6'4" sophomore John Caso, a rugged board man, but he had never recovered from a knee injury. Against better judgment, Lapchick went with Jackson.

A healthy crowd of fourteen thousand showed up for the early December Garden doubleheader. It featured Cincinnati and its All-American Oscar Robertson playing NYU with stars Cal Ramsey and Tom "Satch" Sanders, while St. John's showcased Jackson against Providence's sophomore sensation Johnny Egan and less-heralded but future NBA great Lenny Wilkens. While Robertson poured in 45 points in Cincinnati's nightcap victory, Jackson lived up to his billing by sinking 10 of 14 shots, scoring 23 points while grabbing sixteen rebounds. The Redmen cruised to an easy victory while Jackson's performance foreshadowed an outstanding season and helped big-time New York basketball take a stride forward.

The only blemish on our season was an early 5-point loss to Bradley, the Missouri Valley Conference power. Despite our strong start, the critics made St. Joseph's the Garden's Holiday Festival favorite. After two easy tournament wins, St. John's met St. Joe's in the final. Dr. Jack Ramsey was St. Joseph's coach and part of the new breed of scientific coaches whose defensive pressure had troubled St. John's in the past. But the old coach had grown, too. The Saint's press, once broken, helped open up the court and encouraged many fast-break points. Once Ramsey's team fell behind, it was forced to continue pressuring St. John's, which built up the score. The whole team had a great game, and after five attempts, St. John's finally won the Holiday Festival and national recognition, beating St. Joseph's 90–79 and mastering Ramsey's press and highly touted team. Lapchick liked the good feeling in the winner's circle posing with Jackson and the tournament director. It was the first tournament victory since Lapchick's 1944 surprise Gotkin-Summer-led NIT championship.

While the team played well against St. Joseph's, Jackson's stats were spectacular: 33 points on eleven-for-eighteen shooting, eleven for twelve from the charity stripe, and a game-high twenty-two rebounds. He was, unquestionably, the tournament's MVP. After the game, Lapchick could not resist talking up his overnight sensation. When questioned about Jackson's performance, Lapchick bubbled over with praise. "You haven't seen the end of him." Sportswriters naturally compared the Brooklyn sensation to Oscar Robertson. Jack Spratt, St. Joe's scrappy guard admitted, "Jackson gets up higher than Robertson." Tony was in good company. As a result of winning a big tournament, St. John's sported an 8–1 record and was listed among the country's Top Twenty, while everyone was buzzing about the Brownsville phenom. But just when it seemed the team was headed through the roof, reality set in.

Every sport's season has a life of its own. When things go well, coaches bite their nails and tread lightly, fearing the worst. After the Holiday Festival, signs of a letdown appeared. An early January Garden game with an average Temple team produced a lackluster 81–76 win. Suddenly, some players started believing their clippings and eased up on their effort. Just as suddenly, the team's roller coaster took an upswing. Fewer than three weeks after the brilliant St. Joe's victory, a rematch was staged in Philadelphia's Palestra. Lapchick didn't have to get the team pumped up. The game was a tonic, a meshing agent, and it produced our best effort of the season. We buried the Saints 97–72, committing only four turnovers, a miraculous stat in a forty-minute game. It was our high moment.

The polished performance elated Lapchick. "That [four turnovers] doesn't happen often in undergraduate ball," he pointed out, "where it's mistakes that beat you. Even the pros don't give you perfection." The newspapers distributed credit, citing scoring, rebounding, and assist leaders. Only later, after several of us became coaches, did we realize pro and college teams averaged fifteen to twenty turnovers a game. The victory provided the team with confidence and had everyone thinking big.

Ranked seventh in the nation and sporting a 12–1 record, we prepared for a midyear three-game Midwest trip. Lapchick believed teams had to face manly challenges to succeed. He knew adversity made teams "tournament tough," and he never avoided a difficult opponent. Problems in an opponent's arena despite Lapchick's half-court strategy appeared in our first game in Kiel Auditorium against St. Louis.

St. John's loss was helped by a questionable block call. Trailing by 4 points with fewer than ninety seconds left, Bob Ferry of the Billikens, a huge, 6'7" forward, came barreling down the court when I stepped in to take the charge. As I braced for the impact, the referee already blew his whistle and signaled a foul. While I dusted myself off, I realized he'd called a block on me and awarded Ferry two home-cooked free throws, which he promptly made to help seal the victory, 72–63.

Two nights later against Loyola in Chicago Stadium, we lost in double overtime, 95–85, despite Seiden's 38 points. Again, the defeat hinged on several dubious calls. We had a 66–62 lead with only seconds on the clock and decided to spread out our opponent. As we tried holding onto the ball, I jumped straight up to pass to Seiden. When I tried to return to the floor, the Loyola defender stepped in my path, and the official called the deciding foul on me. I fouled out, and Seiden would be called for a similar "charge" that helped Loyola to force overtime.

Lapchick's gentlemanly reputation was being tested. He rarely demonstrated his displeasure publicly or complained to the press. Conducting himself professionally, he preferred taking his lumps. Lapchick knew sportswriters could fill volumes with laments from losing coaches, and yet a loss on bad calls still singed him. What we as players always remember about the game was that a bench player named Frank Hogan, who never made our scouting report, scored 30 points, a total he would never see again.

The final game at Notre Dame in South Bend, Indiana, still evokes vivid memories. By this point, the trip was a disappointment and had shaken the team. Losing has an obvious way of upsetting a team's confidence, and ours was no exception. Notre Dame's old student center was packed with five thousand spirited but noisy fans in spite of the semester break. Near the end of a close game, Lapchick called time-out. The team huddled two to three feet away, but we could not hear him. Between loud cheers and radiating acoustics, he was drowned out. It seemed strange to see Lapchick's lips moving with no sound. Roethel still gets goose bumps. "As the game approached the last critical minutes, the entire student body stood up to sing the Irish fight song." We had no trouble hearing, "Fight, fight, for old Notre Dame." With the rhythmic cheers taking their toll on our composure and ability to communicate, we lost by 2 points, 72–70. We had opportunities, but no one took charge.

A clean sweep sent us home with our tails tucked between our legs and in everybody's doghouse. It doesn't take much to turn positive winners into doubting losers. A rash statement from an emotional coach or disappointed teammate can wipe out a season after a loss. Lapchick never showed any change in his demeanor, no anger or blame placed on anyone's shoulders. He taught patience and self-control that balanced with the unhappiness of a disappointing road trip. He guaranteed us that the sun would shine again.

When the team returned from the trip, with no league play to focus on, we prepared to play the metropolitan colleges for what was then a mythical title. Early February found the local teams waiting to tag St. John's. The team acted as if local games were unimportant. Lapchick knew better. After a sour practice with the team playing flat, he told us to take two days off, hoping to rekindle a tournament fire. It didn't happen. A complacent Redmen team struggled through several unimpressive wins, and after a relatively easy one over Richmond in the Garden, Fordham and Manhattan beat us in two hard-fought back-to-back games.

With five seconds left in overtime, junior guard Mike Pedone stole the ball from Fordham at half-court, passed it to me, and I drove to the basket. I had to get by tandem defenders, and the clock was ticking. I weaved around one and flipped up a spinning, underhand layup with a lot of "English" on it. It rolled around and off the rim, and the rabid Ram fans cheered our 2-point loss, 79–77. The Manhattan game was another frustrating overtime loss, 70–65. While we battled Fordham, our team let down and played like a mixture of oil and vinegar against Manhattan. We lacked spark and had gone sour.

Lapchick could accept losses, but he didn't like what he saw. Pettiness was breaking up a good team. The press sniffed trouble. "Selfish seniors, more concerned with press clippings than team play," was how the old pro described it. Even in the 1950s, with only eight NBA teams, college coaches had to deal with senior dreams of pro ball. Inquiry letters from NBA teams stimulated professional aspirations. They asked about military status and whether we'd play if drafted. Family relatives and acquaintances added to disharmony often pitting teammates against each other. We sponged up biased advice to shoot more, not pass, get bigger newspaper write-ups, and, in effect, short-circuit team chemistry.

Suddenly postgame stat sheets were scrutinized more closely for offensive distribution. The unspoken thought of "Was I getting my share?" was being felt in the team's play. The daily fuel of discontent in practice and games spiraled our play downward. Carnesecca was aware of an ongoing feud between Al Seiden and me. We were two competitive guards whose differences peaked our senior year. The natural conflict stemmed from a clash of personalities and style of play, but there was an underlying, almost subconscious competitive attempt to prove who was better. As the season was coming to an end, our dreams of being pros churned our emotions.

"Good teams have good guards," Jack Gimmler believed, "and they were two good ones who could score, handle the ball, and were absolutely dedicated." Lapchick's teams usually had one floor leader, but both of us were take-charge players, which fueled the conflict. Carnesecca saw the feud as divisive. St. John's excellent team was being torn apart by two of its best players who could not get along. He thought it was counterproductive and that it could destroy the team chemistry. Unknown to us, Carnesecca suggested Lapchick get rid of one of us for the team's good. Lapchick smiled, but never made an issue of the conflict. Ridding the team of a player might not solve the problem. "That would be the easy thing to do," he reminded his rookie assistant. "No, it's the coach's job to get them to play together."

The differences never disrupted the team. Lapchick acted as if the problem didn't exist, never "picked at it," allowing it to heal itself. When it came to playing, Lapchick sensed our love for the game would win out. And it did. Lapchick got us to play well together, never dragging our problems before the team or into games. Both of us wanted to win but needed Lapchick's direction. He had the experience, had been there, and knew how to win.

But, just prior to the NIT, our differences erupted again. Lapchick was attending the coaches' luncheon at Leone's while Carnesecca ran practice. Something long forgotten triggered old wounds and I went for Seiden. As I invited him to the locker room to settle matters, he exploded, said he had enough, and, ignoring Carnesecca's pleas, walked off the court. Lapchick never panicked, but he wanted the arguing to end. He understood how hope burned inside most athletes and often kindled unrealistic dreams. Much of it was healthy, encouraging players to give their best, like a bit actor hoping for Hollywood stardom. But when it became divisive and picked a team apart, it was time for the Big Indian to step in.

After practice one day, Lapchick took the team to a classroom and discussed St. John's bid to the NIT. After a few words about the tournament, he focused on how disruptive bickering affected our chances. With this in mind, he withdrew a two-foot piece of string from his coat pocket and pointed to Seiden. "Alan, you're the team captain, see if you can break this." The guard shuffled up to the desk, took the string, and with a big smile snapped it with a loud pop. As Seiden made his triumphant return to his seat, Lapchick removed from his other pocket five similar strings neatly twined and knotted at each end and called the captain back for a repeat performance. Seiden, still seeing humor in the exercise, tried with extra force—enough of it to wipe his smile away—but he couldn't snap the reinforced strings.

As the team watched, Joe Daley and Dick Engert in the back of the room started to laugh, but then the metaphoric message crystallized: a united team was difficult to dismember, while five selfish individuals were no threat to an opponent. The coach saw the gleam of his strategy in their eyes, and he drove home the lesson.

"You have been a selfish, self-centered lot the past three weeks," Lapchick reminded us. "If we allow it to continue, all our hard work was wasted." As he saw the seniors wide-eyed, he went on. "The beauty of basketball is five-man teamwork, not five individuals," he pointed out.

"When fingers on a hand are coordinated, they perform all sorts of miracles, from surgery to scoring graceful jump shots, but separated their natural teamwork is lost." Roethel shifted in his seat as Seiden nodded in agreement. It would be foolish to imagine five pieces of ordinary bakery string having an effect on our play in the NIT, but it helped us see our shortcomings and bury differences.

St. John's had a chance to clear its head before the tournament when it played its final game against rival NYU. Lou Rossini's team made a remarkable recovery from its poor start and was now a dangerous team capable of giving St. John's all it could handle. Cal Ramsey and Satch Sanders, a pair of 6'6" Violet forwards, along with a dynamic 5'6" lead guard Russ Cunningham were the players to watch. Ramsey was one of the leading scorers in the country, and Sanders would play thirteen years for the Boston Celtics.

"Lapchick calls me into his office to tell me how he wants to play the NYU game," Seiden recalled. "You have been asking to play the pivot," the coach reminded him. "Well, here's your chance." The All-American smiled and drooled in anticipation of posting the smaller Cunningham under the basket where he knew he had an advantage. After the opening tap, the strategy called for Seiden to pass to Engert and then buttonhook Cunningham into the low post.

"The game starts, I turn around," Seiden remembered, "and there's this big Satch Sanders staring me in the face." Rossini had benched his miniature guard and placed the long-armed forward on the elusive St. John's guard. While Seiden was taken out of his game, the team and Tony Jackson adjusted to the unexpected strategy. With the score tied and ten seconds left, NYU's Ramsey missed a layup. As Engert retrieved the loose ball, he whipped it up court to Jackson who caught it, looked up at the clock, noticed only three seconds left, and hit a spectacular twenty-two foot jumper at the buzzer for the win. It was an electrifying victory. For a team that had been flat for over a month, it produced the kind of adrenaline we needed going into the tournament.

○

With a respectable 16–6 record, St. John's was happy to again be in the NIT and play some of the best teams in the country. Bradley, rated in the nation's top ten, with wins over Cincinnati as well as St. John's, was also invited. We were predominantly a senior team that knew it was our last time around. Again, we were underdogs. In preparing for the tournament, Lapchick used subtle forms of psychology to motivate.

"A thin line separates greatness from mediocrity," he theorized. He reminded us of what it took to cross that line and be a champion. I never thought much about it. Talent was obvious—some had it, others didn't. It was easy to recognize star players, but what about the rest? Coach had placed a different twist on it. With more effort, an average player could approach greatness. Lapchick's mental challenge encouraged extra effort. It screamed out that greatness could be reached. Lapchick's psychological carrot dangled for the hungry to chase. We all felt that carrot was within our reach, ready to be snatched up.

We entered the NIT well motivated. After an easy win over Villanova, our best was required to beat a seasoned St. Bonaventure team. Tony Jackson demonstrated why he was an All-American, hitting key second-half jump shots down the stretch that regained the lead and buried the Bonnies. Providence, a team we easily beat in December, proved just as easy in March. After three tournament wins, St. John's entered the final for a rematch with Bradley. On an NBC nationally televised Saturday afternoon game, we had an opportunity to return New York and St. John's to national prominence.

As we warmed up, Lapchick paced and smoked in the locker room. He was almost fifty-nine and starting to feel it. The game could be his last chance to prove himself. Three years ago he left the Garden with his bags packed, looking to get away from the pressure of pro basketball. Now his team could "walk with kings" by winning a tournament the whole country would notice. He felt the chill and excitement of the game's significance.

We all realized the importance and finality of the Bradley game. There was no tomorrow for seniors, no time for pettiness. It left a lump in our throats, an eerie, disoriented feeling. Seiden sensed it, too. "There was a funny feeling in the pit of my stomach. All of us had it." It was never openly discussed but repeated afterwards. Engert agreed. "It was the most pressure I ever felt." The seniors knew it was their last game. Warm-ups, even shooting early in the game felt different. I remember shooting two free throws before halftime. Each one fluttered up and in, the way a player would react if playing tight. I had never felt as uncomfortable because my mind was riveted on the fact that this was undoubtedly the end, a feeling I never had or would ever feel again.

In an emotion-filled game, St. John's was down 7 points with nine minutes left. Lapchick, however, looked calm. He had been there many times, but each trip had its own memories. When Seiden picked up his fourth foul, the coach's heart took an extra beat, but he countered with the textbook strategy to replace him. He realized Bradley was capable of sprinting away with Seiden on the sidelines, but they were also smart enough to exploit his foul situation if he remained in the game. It was a roll of the dice either way. As soon as Seiden hit the bench, he bounced up almost immediately and approached Lapchick. "This is my last game, Coach, I have to go back in, Pedone can't do it," Seiden pleaded. Lapchick turned to the dark-haired guard whose unshaven intensity almost shocked him. Both coach and player knew this was that moment when games are decided.

Much of coaching is intuitive. Lapchick reacted instinctively by showing confidence in his warrior. If Seiden fouled out or was exploited by Bradley, the game could be lost. Most coaches learn to balance important decisions on a scale of percentages, but Lapchick often acted on gut feelings and took what the profession called a calculated risk. It was a risk playing Seiden, but one worth taking, he decided. "Catch your breath and go back in," Lapchick ordered. Seiden, who had been on the bench fewer than thirty seconds, streaked to the scorer's table to report into the game. "As we crossed, Pedone gave me a look," Seiden recalled. No player likes to be yo-yoed in and out of a game. Pedone wanted to play, too.

As soon as Bradley coach Chuck Osborne saw Seiden, he ordered junior guard Mike Owens to post him in the pivot to draw his fifth foul. The strategy backfired as Seiden carefully avoided fouling while Bradley's offense sputtered. Down the stretch he would make some clutch shots, and he went on to score 13 much-needed points.

Within the last minute, the score seesawed with neither team holding the lead. Finally, with a handful of seconds remaining and the score tied, Bradley stole the ball for one last shot. Dan Smith, a Yonkers resident, launched a twenty-foot jump shot as the buzzer sounded. It caromed high and away. Overtime.

With new life, and the New York crowd, St. John's quickly jumped on top in the five-minute overtime. Free throws by Jackson and me put us ahead by 2. As we continued to battle, we maintained a slim lead. Then with fifty-four seconds left, up two and in possession of the ball, Lapchick called time-out. His look exuded confidence, and he knew something would develop without a set play. "Work the ball until you find an opening," he encouraged and then sent us out. The ball was put in play, and we followed Lapchick's direction. With fewer than thirty seconds, *New York Times* sportswriter Louis Effrat recorded for history why we play championship games. "Then came the key to the game, the tournament, and the entire year for St. John's."

After carefully moving the ball, I knifed past my defender Gene Morse on the left side and drove baseline to the basket. Morse, realizing my intention, adjusted quickly and tried cutting me off. I had always loved driving to the basket. I had a wide body that made it difficult to stop me. I knifed past the Bradley defender, as I had done so often as a kid in my Greenpoint school yard, and floated up a soft left-hand layup off the glass that fell through the net easily as Morse belatedly swiped and hit me on the shoulder. Referee Nucatola signaled the basket good and his closed fist, a foul.

As I picked myself up off the Garden floor for the last time in my career, I realized the free throw could ice the game. Noticing my pregame jitters were gone, I walked to the line and calmly sifted the shot making the score 72–67. The 3-point play put us up 5, and the game was locked up. Years later Seiden agreed. "When Gus made that 3-pointer," Seiden reminisced, "Lapchick let out a sigh of relief. I think he also got a little shaky on the bench, as if he was going to pass out." The lead allowed Lapchick a chance to exhale mental relief. He was home. The players were mobbed as the buzzer sounded, but the most deserved tribute was for the Redmen coach, who was easily lifted off the ground and paraded around the Garden floor by well-wishers as unashamed, proud tears flowed down his cheeks.

O

"Congratulations, Joe," Madison Square Garden executive John Goldner echoed to the winning coach as he left the court. The St. John's Redmen had just won the 1959 National Invitation Tournament, defeating nationally ranked Bradley in overtime. The Redmen had won. He had done it. Lingering thoughts of being washed up faded into a quiet corner of his mind.

In the flush of victory, the *Herald Tribune*'s photographer called for one more locker-room shot. "This one with the whole team," the photographer coaxed. As the team gathered around their coach, he sat on the uniform-cluttered trainer's table, his legs on the floor, balancing the NIT championship cup clutched in one of his strong hands and the MacGregor X10L game ball palmed in the other, echoing the kind of enthusiasm winners shout, when it happened. Players' hands suddenly reached out of the jumble of tightly stacked players and touched their coach's head and shoulders, as if he were a religious relic with healing powers.

Most of us spent the past three years with him, but on this day of merrymaking and accomplishment, we fulfilled a subconscious impulse. Touching our coach, this man we had heard so much about, not only proved he was real but left us with a lasting memory. The moment was like taking a keepsake or a piece of memorabilia from a departed loved one. The affectionate touch had to last a lifetime. Many of us didn't realize its significance during the postgame celebration.

Jackson was again voted MVP, scoring 21 points and snaring twenty-seven rebounds. A fine day's work. "Tony's the best outside jump shooter I've ever seen. He's better from there than Oscar Robertson," Lapchick later admitted to the press. Bradley's coach, Osborne agreed. "I'd have to put him in the same class as Robertson." It was Jackson's day and tournament, although it was far from a one-man performance. Roethel, a smart player who seemed to get hurt when on the bubble of success, had a spotty season. But when he entered the NIT, knowing it was his last round, he made it count. The bespectacled center shot a torrid twenty-six for thirty-eight, just short of 70 percent from the floor, for 67 points, the best field goal shooting in the tournament. Engert, Seiden, and I played well, but when blended with Jackson's efforts and Lapchick's confidence and direction, it produced a championship.

After well-wishers and sportswriters left the locker room, Lapchick began to replay the game. He had used that intuitive sense coaches reach for in desperate moments. He believed in Seiden's strong will. He taught players to be coaches on the floor, to develop confidence in their judgment. Whenever he spoke about coaching, he quickly credited player talent. "Great teams have great players," he would say. He was not an "I" coach. Postgame press discussions centered on what players did on the floor.

The tournament was one of Lapchick's finest moments. He saw the championship as a team victory. But it was more than that. It was the first postseason title won by St. John's in fourteen years—since Lapchick's victory over DePaul in the 1944 NIT. With the Bradley victory, a new era of metropolitan basketball prominence loomed on the horizon, encouraging New York players to stay home in the future. Lapchick recognized the winning spark in others. With the photo shoot complete, he walked over to Seiden, who had played his final St. John's game, and awarded him the game ball, a tribute that the coach placed great stock in.

As the locker room emptied, Lapchick reached for his "winning" tweed overcoat and hat and made his way to the door when he noticed a favorite sportswriter from the *New York Post* sporting a whimsical smile. "I listened to your postgame praise of the team," Lennie Koppett confirmed, "but I saw the game from a different angle." Lapchick, leaning on the trainer's table, balanced his hat on his knee and gave his friend complete attention. "The real hero," Koppett insisted, "was the tall, lanky coach who led his team all the way back this year and who wiped away those years of disillusionment from Irish's Knickerbockers."

As Lapchick listened his eyes moistened, but he expanded on his feelings. "The NIT victory also helped erase a lingering doubt in the mind of yours truly." He thought a bit, and continued. "When I left the professional ranks, I began to doubt my coaching ability. I had to prove that I still had it." Winning the NIT proved he could still coach to someone with serious doubts—himself. He had worked hard for Ned Irish, only to have his "life broken" when Irish gave him no support.

Lapchick was approaching his fifty-ninth birthday, a time when most coaches play with grandchildren. He left the Knicks under fire followed by whispers that the "old man" couldn't cut it anymore. Koppett, more than any other New York sportswriter, understood what winning the tournament meant. He knew what Irish had done, and that Lapchick had momentarily found himself out of basketball for the first time in his life. It was difficult for him to describe his resignation from the Knicks. "How low was I? How low can a man be? I had so much to reestablish. With the Knicks I'd lost the reins." But he did not stay down. Three years later, Lapchick bounced back.

Few knew of his self-doubt after being forced out by the Knicks. The point-shaving rumors had also rattled him. The game had changed, too. And yet, in spite of that he kept his head. He was again the darling of New York's sports media. Both men understood what was buried out there on the Garden floor. It felt good for the proud coach to get all that hurt out of him. He felt free and thanked his friend for listening. Koppett smiled, then the men hugged and headed out the door to celebrate at Leone's.

The NIT championship was Lapchick's crowning glory. Bradley had a great reputation, and the victory helped restore New York basketball. It was the first big win Lapchick had since he left the Knicks; it was New York, The Big Indian, national television, and he did it with city players. It was wonderful for the game. He knew as they walked to Leone's he would never sleep that night.

Shortly after the NIT championship, Lapchick wrote to his seniors and team managers. Seiden's letter described him as having "the guts of a burglar." At the end of a game, with the game on the line, Seiden wanted the ball, had the confidence to take an important shot, something many star players on all levels avoid. An excellent free throw shooter, he shot best at crunch time. He still holds the St. John's free throw record. Photos show him taking headers while driving to the basket. He floated through the air, eyes glued to the rim with no thought of how he would make his reentry. "Did it go in?" was his only concern. The 5'10" guard had one of the best "first steps" in the game. It's the foot fake that frees the drive or pull-up jump shot. Watch tapes of Michael Jordan. It's how all the great ones operate. Few could react to Seiden's; it was a blur. He was a great guy to have on our side. Lapchick was right, a gutsy winner. But then shortly afterward, Lapchick took time in a hotel in Boston to write to me about his continued joy. The letter he sent to me stands by itself.

2 April, 1959

Dear Gus,

I have been kept very busy since that glorious afternoon when you and your teammates made history at St. John's. I want to take this opportunity to thank you for your contribution to the rebirth of the prominence of St. John's. It is a great school and one that we are proud of. I sincerely hope that we who remain can keep the name high in both artistry on the court and human behavior off the court. You have added fame and dignity to the many laurels that the University possesses.

Your two MVPs in the Saint Francis games were a remarkable achievement. Moreover, there were many games where you distinguished yourself, but I shall never forget the finals of the NIT. You made a bad play that hurt. Men with less courage would have brooded over the incident and only think of the bad play in the overtime. But you quite properly dismissed the incident and really bore down. Then when the clutch time came it was you who made the big play—the 3-pointer that made us an unprecedented three-time winner of the event. You were all guts and all man.

I sincerely hope that the lessons you learned on the court will serve you well in the life ahead. I know if courage to face a situation and gentlemanly conduct are the answers—then I am sure you have a good life to look forward to.

With warmest personal regards to you, your future bride, and your family I am ever,

Your Friend,

Joe Lapchick

By the fall of 1959, Engert, Roethel, and I had entered the teaching profession. Late in October another Lapchick letter arrived. He admitted having "thought of you and the team quite often." Then he brought up a euphoric dressing room statement a young twenty-one-year-old made after the NIT championship. I remarked left-handedly, "At least we didn't go out like bums," to a sportswriter. He again reminded me, "In the final analysis, you sure left your mark in St. John's." He closed by asking our team to stay close, not to drift away, and to "drop around at your convenience." The letters confirmed that season's importance. At the time, we were too young to recognize how much it meant to him.

Lapchick was picked to coach the College North All-Stars in Raleigh, North Carolina. More important was his selection by the Philadelphia sportswriters—a tough, critical group whose opinion carried weight—as their Coach of the Year. St. John's handled St. Joseph's easily in two games while defeating Philadelphia's Temple and Villanova. He was looking forward to a talented new bunch to accompany All-American Tony Jackson. Life was sweet again around the old coach's household. Lapchick could whistle a happy tune because he had passed another turning point in his full life—he knew he could still coach with the best of them.

When it was over, there was Lapchick—the first three-time NIT winner—the first coach to win the Holiday and Invitation tourneys the same year. Lapchick had passed "Go" on his second college go 'round. He was again walking with kings.

O

Tony Jackson scored almost 1,100 points over the next two years, but in spite of a squad of talented players around him, St. John's didn't make it past the first round in postseason play. By far, his best year was as a sophomore, where he helped a senior team win big.

Lapchick's 1960–61 club, when Jackson was a senior, was as strong a team as he'd coached since his return to St. John's. With the exception of a first-round loss to Wake Forest in the NCAAs, the Redmen's four other losses were narrow ones. When facing NCAA champion Ohio State in the Holiday Festival, Jackson played like a professional. The lithe shooter made everyone in the Garden know why he should be an NBA first-round pick.

By the time the NBA draft took place in the spring, Jackson, one of the nation's best pro prospects in 1961, had lost his luster with no team willing to risk a high draft on him. The Knicks decided to pick the St. John's star on the third round but never invited him to camp. Jackson's professional value dropped after District Attorney Frank Hogan's investigation into college improprieties revealed that gamblers tried unsuccessfully to draw the St. John's star into fixing games. Like Seiden, Jackson refused but never reported the attempted bribe. But when Podoloff heard of it, along with Connie Hawkins and Roger Brown's association with indicted gambler Jack Molinas, he quietly blacklisted all of them.

Lapchick was notified about Jackson prior to the St. John's awards banquet. Representatives from the university showed up at Lapchick's home, warning him not to give the All-American any awards because of the pending investigation. While the coach was upset by the news, Jackson never appeared and dropped out of school. In 1969, Hawkins was cleared and finished his career in the NBA, while Brown had a long and successful American Basketball Association career with the Indianapolis Pacers. It was rumored that the NBA secretly paid Hawkins and Brown for its wrongdoing. Jackson, however, only played briefly in the ABA, never in the NBA.

O

By the 1961–62 season, Joe Lapchick had molded an experienced team capable of playing with the nation's best. Point guard Donnie Burks teamed with fleet-footed Ivan Kovac in the backcourt, while 6'10" future

NBA center Leroy Ellis developed into a strong inside force. Willie Hall, a powerful bull of a 6'4" forward, gave the team board strength, while another future NBA star, Kevin Loughery, a Boston College transfer, acted as the catalyst that propelled the Redmen into prominence.

St. John's had compiled a successful 19–4 record that included wins over basketball powers like Oklahoma, Kansas, Creighton, and Marquette and was again invited to the NIT. After defeating Holy Cross, 80–74, and "holding" its outstanding scorer, Jack "The Shot" Foley to 35 points, the Redmen faced a tough Duquesne team led by 5'10" sophomore Willie Somerset that upset Bradley to get to the semifinals.

Fresh from the upset victory, the Dukes jumped ahead of the Redmen by as many as 16 points and held onto a 9-point lead at halftime, 36–27. St. John's fought back in the second half and eventually wrestled the lead from Duquesne. After a brief but physical brawl that broke out under the St. John's basket between Donnie Burks and the Dukes' Mike Rice, the Redmen settled down to lock up the game, 75–65, and reached the final against Dayton.

The Flyers had been to the NIT nine times, and Coach Tom Blackburn and his team came close but had never won the tournament. That would change. Dayton quickly gained the lead, and St. John's never was able to unseat them. The major battle of the game was fought between two 6'10" centers, with sophomore Bill Chmielewski outplaying the Redmen's senior, Leroy Ellis. Near the end of the game, Dayton built a 5-point lead into 10 points and coasted to the victory. Both teams had ten-game winning streaks, but Dayton was able to close its season with its streak intact. The big Dayton center was also voted the NIT most valuable player for a clean sweep for the Ohio school.

The Metropolitan Sportswriters Association honored Lapchick as its Coach of the Year, an award he treasured. In spite of the Dayton loss in the NIT final, the 21–5 season had everything a coach could ask for.

With the graduation of four 1962–63 starters and a weak underclass helped by the loss of key freshmen, Lapchick experienced the first losing season in his coaching career. It was a year where everything went wrong, from losing prospects to 6'7" forward Billy O'Sullivan breaking his wrist. The only consolation to the 9–15 season was that the nine daily metropolitan newspapers went on strike in December, and it lasted 114 days, well past the season. If the year was a horror, at least the coach and the players didn't have to read the bad news. But Joe Lapchick never lost faith or blamed his team. During the season, I visited with him at St. John's, and we had a chance to talk. "I never had a harder working bunch of athletes," he beamed with such enthusiasm. "And never had a better time coaching," he said with that broad, winning smile that could warm an igloo. There were others who saw things differently.

He was sixty-three years old, and some fans questioned, "What have you done lately?" Others were not so discreet. "At several home games, the St. John's crowd started to get on my Dad," Rich Lapchick recalled. Once, on a bus back from a loss in Philadelphia, he overheard a conversation suggesting he step down. Mixed with complaints were issues of Lapchick's health. Rumors circulated that he was not well. The coach knew how fickle human nature was, but being strong-minded, he dealt with aging his own way. He was fanatical about posture, believing a tall, hunched-over man made a poor impression. He was always well groomed and dressed fashionably throughout his athletic career. Approaching the inevitable end of his career, he did whatever it took to maintain his legendary reputation.

After a comeback season in 1963–64, when the team won nine out of its last eleven, including Loyola of Chicago, Creighton, and Syracuse, three top-twenty teams, rumor was that St. John's would complete its journey by sneaking into the NIT. The last game of the season was played against NYU, a team already picked and rated the best in the city. Lapchick had his team at a fever pitch, ready to show the selection committee that the Redmen were part of this town, too. St. John's, with the tournament on their minds, destroyed Lou Rossini's Violets, 71–51. The game stirred the old coach's pride, and Jerry Houston and Bobby McIntyre had that look in their eyes that this game might get them into the NIT. But that was not to be the case.

The NYU game was played in Alumni Hall and demonstrated the frustration of the whole season. Until game time, the team believed it still had a chance. The game ended with what the Redmen thought was a decisive win, loyal fans flooded the court yelling, "NIT, NIT," hoping the selection committee would hear them from Jamaica, Queens. Unknown to the rabid fans, Drake had been selected that afternoon as the last NIT team. But Lapchick wasn't satisfied. The next day's *New York Times* headlines captured the flustered coach perfectly, "LAPCHICK ASSAILS NIT SELECTIONS; SAYS TEAM RATED NOD OVER NYU." Lapchick pleaded that since his team totally outplayed NYU, it deserved to be in the tournament before Drake, and that the NIT committee had pulled the trigger before his Redmen had a chance to make their statement.

The coaches' luncheon took place at the Spindletop Restaurant, and for one of the few times in Joe Lapchick's public life, he demonstrated anger. "I have a grievance," he said, as he turned to speak. "This is the first time the best team in New York City was not invited to the NIT." With smoke pouring from his ears, he wasn't finished. "We weren't even considered, and that was an insult to my players," Lapchick finished jabbing his index finger at the podium, and then he returned to his seat.

Joe Lapchick was no fool. He could add and subtract well enough to know St. John's expected an annual trip to the NIT, and anything short of that was a disappointment. In his quiet moments, Lapchick worried that he would be relieved of his coaching duties. But he would have to wait for next year.

O

Scholastic All-American Lew Alcindor's name dripped desirously off the lips of every college recruiter in the country. Everyone wanted "Big Lew," whose 7'2" frame and talent guaranteed national prominence. Alcindor's coach, Jack Donohue, was one of two or three young coaches who practically lived at Lapchick's doorstep. Donohue sought his advice, and the old pro was a sucker for anyone who wanted to learn. Since he lived nearby in White Plains, he became Lapchick's frequent companion. When Alcindor became a senior, Lapchick felt confident he had a shot at the superstar. As The Big Indian prepared for the 1964–65 season, and in spite of the fact that he was approaching sixty-five, he felt strong. And then there was the fantasy, the dream of landing Lew Alcindor. With Alcindor he would have the makings of a national team with a rosy future— a future that was never to be.

Chapter 17

A Momentous
Occasion

"This is a momentous occasion, Joe." Father Walter Graham, the chairman of St. John's athletics, was nervously watching Lapchick sketch a flowery signature to his twentieth contract that sunny September morning in 1964. He smiled as he put the final curlicue to his name but didn't understand the fuss over signing a contract. As Lapchick looked up from the legal language, he noticed beads of perspiration on "the Padre's" forehead.

Father Graham swallowed and answered Lapchick's troubled look. "Joe, this is your last contract." Lapchick was stunned by the priest's words, numbed, as he fought to control his shortened breath. He wondered if his health problems, which he tried to keep secret, were behind this shocking announcement. "Come again, Father?" the tall coach asked, narrowing his eyes as if they could filter out the bad news.

Father Graham was a tall, thin, Prussian-like Vincentian priest who had climbed the administrative ladder at St. John's Prep. Many students remembered him as a stern teacher from their prep days, but a priest with a dry sense of humor. On this day, though, he wasn't trying to be funny and felt uncomfortable with the message he was delivering. Graham, struggling not to falter, answered. "You are aware of the university's mandatory retirement policy for staff members, aren't you? You'll be sixty-five in April, Joe. That will terminate your coaching position. This is your last contract," the priest repeated, with the jolt of a doctor telling

251

a terminal patient he has six months to live. What the priest wasn't telling the twenty-year St. John's veteran was that he had been told the aging coach was losing his touch and that the game had passed him by.

And then there was the question of losing assistant coach Lou Carnesecca. St. John's primary concern was retaining Carnesecca, who the university felt was getting itchy for a head-coaching job. The well-respected, dynamic assistant had made Lapchick's life easier the past seven years. He was expert in areas Lapchick was happy to have him perform. Lou liked to scout, recruit, and think the game through from a scientific perspective; Lapchick enjoyed creating team chemistry and putting everything in understandable terms, a formula that had proven successful for more than thirty years.

"If Lou wasn't given the job," Graham related, "he was going elsewhere to coach; he was anxious and people were talking to him." Carnesecca later swore he would have waited, that he wasn't going anywhere. He was a career St. John's man. "We wanted very much to keep him," Graham insisted. Under the direction and with the blessings of the president, Father Edward Burke, a decision was made on the pioneer coach's future. The university searched for the most palatable way of telling Lapchick he was finished and settled on the staff retirement policy. Its goal, however, was to make room for the new coach. What the university did not anticipate was the media upheaval that followed.

Lapchick had a seasoned team that was sure to better last year's 14–11 record. Then there was also the hope of 7'2" Lew Alcindor. Nothing was in the bag, but the kid liked him and knew Lapchick spoke his language. Lapchick had cultivated a strong relationship with the sensitive youngster, meeting him at Donohue's basketball camp in upstate Saugerties, New York, which his son Rich attended. Rich had come to the big center's aid when a white camper abused him with racial slurs, and the two remained friends. "Lapchick understood the problems tall players face," Lew Alcindor, later known as Kareem Abdul-Jabbar, recalled. "As a former player who people laughed at because of his size, I felt comfortable talking with him."

Look magazine had recently quoted Lapchick praising the seventeen-year-old Power Memorial All-American, who he felt could become the greatest player of all time. The magazine predicted the schoolboy star would attend St. John's. Years later, Abdul-Jabbar wrote of his feelings for Lapchick. "St. John's did a lot of winning, largely because of its coach."

Abdul-Jabbar had the highest respect for the basketball pioneer, recognizing that wherever Lapchick coached he was a winner, producing teams that were adaptable, aggressive, and smart.

But what interested the intelligent and sensitive youngster was that Lapchick was an honorable man who understood the emotional stress of being extraordinarily tall. "Coach Lapchick had obviously given some serious thought to me personally," he correctly surmised. "He was the first to put into words for me how the world alienates tall people."

Lapchick told him that society scales up its demands for tall people, which he learned from his own harassment fifty years earlier. "They expect more from a giant," he explained to the star center. Alcindor later claimed he would have stayed in New York if St. John's allowed Lapchick to coach. "I had the sense that he would have liked to stay on, that basketball was in some way not only his pleasure but his sustenance." But the whole Alcindor issue was lost when Lapchick left.

It had only been a few years before in March 1962 that Lapchick had been selected Coach of the Year, when the St. John's president flattered him with words he would not forget. "We are proud of your long association with St. John's," he had written. "Winning or losing," the letter continued, "you may be sure we feel you are doing the best thing for the students, and that we are commending your action." What caused Lapchick's welcome to sour so quickly? But then, maybe, it wasn't so sudden; maybe Joe Lapchick hadn't paid attention to the warning signs.

When Lapchick's teams won the Festival and the National Invitation Tournament in 1959—followed by the Kevin Loughery–Leroy Ellis era, with St. John's knocking on the door of national prominence—talk was of how wonderful he had done. But after that the team's talent ran dry. And when coupled with a few key injuries, it led to the 9–15 season in 1962–63. Suddenly the boo-birds were calling for Lapchick's head. Whispered voices talked about retirement, and leaks of his heart condition circulated, creating a climate that encouraged Lapchick to step down. But quitting was not his style.

The criticism after the losing season only confirmed Lapchick's awareness of the fickleness of fans. But he wasn't ready to retire. He took what was left of his program and battled back. The coming season included point guard Jerry Houston; 6'3" guard Kenny McIntyre, who could and would shoot successfully from any spot on the floor, while brother Bobby McIntyre was a 6'7", banging forward. The other forward was the quiet, 6'4" ex-Marine Bobby Duerr. The experienced unit in-cluded the prize of the group, 6'7" all-scholastic sophomore center Sonny Dove, who was ready to play. Lapchick believed the team had experience, size, and talent "to make St. John's proud."

For days Lapchick sulked at home, pacing his attic sanctuary. He dis-cussed his feelings with Bobbie and Rich. His son, a student at St. John's, wanted to launch a campus fight, but his father didn't want any of that. When his older son, Joe, a school superintendent in Aspen, Colorado, tried to convince him retirement was for the best, the hurt remained.

Shortly after the news broke, Jack Donohue visited his mentor. The Power Memorial coach seemed uncomfortable. He asked to speak pri-vately with the coach, and the two went into Lapchick's study. Rich later found out that Donohue was offered the assistant's job by St. John's. Dur-ing their meeting, Lapchick asked Donohue if Alcindor's name came up in connection with the job. Donohue murmured, "yes."

Donohue's memory of his visit with Lapchick was different. He claimed no one at St. John's offered him a job. "I don't remember any offer, no, I don't think so. You know how things build up." He insisted he had never spoken to anyone at St. John's about a coaching position. Rich, however, still believes there was a job offered. When asked how he knew, he answered, "My father told me that's what Jack Donohue had said."

It was easy to understand Donohue's discomfort. Lapchick had been his mentor, teaching him the finer points of coaching. Accepting a coach-ing position at St. John's after Lapchick had been dismissed would appear callous. He didn't get the job, so the facts were never confirmed. How-ever, years later, in *Sports Illustrated*, Abdul-Jabbar revealed that he never would have played for Donohue in college because of personal reasons. The article claimed Donohue had used the word "nigger" at halftime of a game to motivate the high school sophomore. Donohue accepted the Holy Cross job the next year while Alcindor enrolled in UCLA.

Lapchick began to see St. John's intentions were to force him out, sign Donohue, and hope to land Alcindor. He rarely got angry, but this was an exception, and he was livid. Emotions began to weaken his reason-ing. The understanding was for Carnesecca to replace him when he re-tired. *When I retire*, Lapchick thought, *not when I'm forced to retire*. That never was the arrangement.

Back in 1956, when Lapchick returned to St. John's after coaching the pros, he told the university, "Basketball has been my whole life, and I hope to go on coaching until I feel I can no longer contribute my knowledge of the game." No mention had been made of a mandatory retirement age of sixty-five. That was for university professors, he thought.

In March 1962, after an outstanding season, Larry Levine of the *Journal-American* interviewed Joe Lapchick, and he again spoke of his future in coaching. "I intend to remain at St. John's another four or five years, and then retire." He was having too much fun, and coaching still excited him. No one from St. John's corrected Lapchick's belief that the mandatory retirement didn't apply to him. St. John's, however, claimed that the standing regulation applied to all faculty and staff, which included athletics.

"'These Vincentians have short memories," Jack Curran, Archbishop Molloy High School legendary basketball coach, remembers Lapchick saying to him one day in his gym. "I had written to St. John's," Curran recalled, "about Molloy's use of Alumni Hall for our graduation, but they refused to help us." The St. John's basketball team had been using Molloy's facility to practice during the early 1960s before its new gym was ready. Lapchick's evaluation of the Vincentian's memory could have applied to his retirement.

O

The 1950s was a decade of relative calm, with Americans adjusting to a peacetime economy and an improved standard of living, but that changed in the 1960s. The Vietnam War joined hands with a drug culture that shook the foundation of America's way of life. Catholicism was jolted when the new Pope John took a revisionist look at long-standing dogma. In the 1960s, like the Twenties Jazz Age, Americans turned a deaf ear to attempts to restrict society's manners. Americans, especially college students, were questioning what had been taken for granted in the past. The fires of challenge were lit, and St. John's, too, experienced its period of rebellion.

Religious orders are built on faith and the obedience of their members, but it is difficult to apply the same standards to the secular world. St. John's hierarchy was used to acting unilaterally, and by not allowing Lapchick to discuss his retirement, he was treated as if he were a Vincentian. He was told he would no longer be the St. John's coach after the present season, and no negotiation transpired, something Joe believed he was entitled to after almost twenty years of loyal service. He did not want or like being discarded, and it hurt him mightily.

Lapchick's health was failing; he had a heart condition and suffered from stress-related ailments. But if it was his time to retire, couldn't the university have discussed it with him before the contract signing and allowed him to leave with dignity? It would have been more palatable. He was a sports figure at a school that respected basketball the way Notre Dame did football. Hadn't twenty years of dedicated service earned him that courtesy?

Some students questioned why Lapchick was being forced out at sixty-five while priests continued to teach into their seventies. Father Graham could only repeat the mandatory retirement rule. But Lapchick was unique, they would answer, an exception to the rule. Since Graham mentioned St. John's considered Lapchick staying a final year, the possibility existed. Although rumors claimed Father Burke was close to allowing Lapchick to stay on as coach, nothing came of them.

Not every university agreed with St. John's retirement mandate. Many preferred the age of seventy; others had no policy. It was strictly an internal decision, but even those universities with a fixed-age retirement made exceptions. However, by holding fast, universities could unload those past their prime. Ironically, several years later, St. John's made an exception for its athletic director Walter McLaughlin, who stayed on until he was sixty-seven. Coaches at St. John's were never protected by tenure laws and usually signed one-year contracts, which left them vulnerable. Their famous basketball coach was being treated no differently than any other athletic staff member.

Lapchick's influence with the metropolitan sports media, however, was so powerful, he didn't have to fight his cause. Friends like Dick Young, Ike Gellis, and Lennie Koppett did it for him. They clearly cited that an injustice was done, and because of public interest, Lapchick's forced retirement became the lead story for much of the basketball season.

○

"They should stop treating Coach Lapchick like a man, and start treating him like a human being," Sonny Dove, star sophomore of the St. John's team shouted into the CBS 6:00 news reporter's microphone. Dove was trying to stir up the campus over the shock of Lapchick's forced retirement. Despite its passivity, there was an element at school more willing to take up causes, and its leader was a rabble-rousing, student-athlete.

The varsity baseball catcher Mike Moloney was unique even for the 1960s in that this future congressional candidate from California had a flare for oratory that energized campus causes. But it was more than the spotlight that drew him to the Lapchick controversy. Mike had a soft spot for the old coach and would do whatever it took to help. Moloney jumped into the fight by stirring up a campus rally. The former basketball walk-on had a take-charge reputation and demonstrated it on one clear fall day.

"Lapchick was fired," Moloney shouted to the growing crowd of more than two thousand in the lounge of St. John's Arts and Science building, many of whom were standing on chairs encouraging the speakers who were goading the crowd to march on Alumni Hall. "We should have the guts to voice our protest," Moloney insisted, as the students agreed and fraternity brothers pumped the air with their fists. "Joe Lapchick," the firebrand reminded, "is the heart and soul of the Redmen. This is our chance to do something about saving Coach Lapchick's job," Moloney said. While students continued to flood into the now-overcrowded lounge, skipping classes to exercise their civil liberties, the rally's unofficial master of ceremonies introduced some basketball players.

Sonny Dove grabbed the microphone. "Coach Lapchick deserves better," Dove repeated. "Alumni Hall and Joe Lapchick," the students started to chant as they stomped their feet and jumped onto fraternity tables for a better view. Jerry Houston, normally quiet, suddenly seemed energized. "Coach not only taught me how to be a better player, but how to be a better human being." Kenny McIntyre added, "He showed me that there was more to life than just winning, but to learn how to accept losing." The students up front pumped the air and nodded agreement, and the sentiment was strong for some physical demonstration of their feelings. Moloney, who could "read" a crowd, sensed it.

The self-proclaimed leader moved toward the front door, waving his arms and urging the students to follow. "On to Alumni Hall," he said. "Let's hear what Coach Lapchick has to say." The throng followed its maestro out the main exit and down the road to Alumni Hall. As students milled around in front of the gymnasium, Moloney realized he had delivered an enthusiastic student body that was waiting for the "headliner" to come out and lead the demonstration.

But it wasn't Joe Lapchick's style to challenge his boss. As the students raised their voices and hopes, he remained inside. These were moderate times at St. John's, and yet, neither Lapchick nor the students would forget the demonstration. Joe Lapchick heard the protest from his office and wanted to join their rally and pour out his feelings, but he knew it would be considered inflammatory by the university and hurt any chance of his coaching in the future. The student protest would be forgotten. Lapchick knew he would get no help from a demonstration, but it felt good knowing someone cared.

"If Lapchick would have joined the demonstration," Moloney said later, "I think it could have turned the whole retirement business around." Rich Lapchick agreed. "If my father had come out of the gym and made an appeal, it would have played out differently." In spite of the fact that his father's firing had not swept through the entire campus, there were "pockets of seriousness" present that could have helped. "But my father did not want to hurt St. John's," Rich said. For the first time in his adult life, Lapchick would be unemployed with a small pension and no immediate prospects. He worried about his family. His son Rich was still a student, Bobbie had always been a homemaker, and now at sixty-five, he was left with limited resources. Rich later claimed his father had two firm coaching offers—Ben Kerner's St. Louis Hawks and a college offer from Notre Dame—but relocation seemed impractical to him.

St. John's was not "kicking him upstairs," but cutting him loose. Hurt, angry, suspicious of a plot, Lapchick laced into those around him. He wrote a letter critical of the athletic administration and circulated it among the staff. He was looking for support from his fellow coaches but received only sympathetic words. His angry letter proved ineffective.

The Big Indian was nationally known and respected, but he had few allies at St. John's. As a coach who appeared primarily only during the season, the staff knew more of his reputation than of him. The large student body had little to do with athletics, since many traveled to part-time jobs at the end of the day. St. John's was more the team of New York basketball fans and alumni than of the student body. There was also the issue of how much support Lapchick would get from an athletic staff with one-year contracts that was not used to challenging the administration. Lapchick's support came from his team, a circle of student leadership, and the sports media. But more than the coach's age fueled the issue of Lapchick's retirement.

○

It was a cold January Sunday morning in Milwaukee in 1963, and the St. John's coaches and team were heading to mass. Suddenly Lapchick grabbed his chest and "pulled into a doorway to catch his breath in the dry morning air," Lou Carnesecca recalled. During his last season at St. John's, Lapchick also had two heart attacks that were unreported. One of the angina attacks happened in the dressing room before the Miami game. But Lapchick brushed it off as nothing. Those around him were led to believe it was indigestion. He had also learned to apply mental toughness to health problems. "You have to beat fear or fear will kill you," he often said. He never let his condition take him out of coaching or interfere with the course of his life. "You have to stay on your own route," he would say. Although hushed up, rumors of his health circulated in St. John's athletic department.

Lapchick was never in the best of health, and he came from a family with a history of health problems. His sister Frances died in her late thirties, while his brother Ed had a fatal brain tumor at forty-six. Lapchick himself had lost a kidney during the war years and suffered from a career of stress that wore him down to the point where he would often check into St. Clare's Hospital at the end of a Knicks season to regain his strength.

Speaking at a sports banquet in Rochester after the 1965 NIT victory, he talked about his heart condition. He recalled how he had "damned near died on the bench." He had taken a physical exam prior to the 1964–65 season where everything was fine, but by the end of the season, doctors found scars from an angina condition, as well as indications that he had suffered several silent heart attacks. "The scars were all there." In reviewing his last season, he recalled having no problems throughout the six-week practice period. But with the first game, severe chest pains forced him to wait outside the locker room for fear the players would notice. However, by the second half of games the pain disappeared. Being a strong-willed, private person, he never talked about them.

During his Knicks years, questions about Lapchick's health often appeared in the sports pages. Some sportswriter friends created a humorous caricature of him as a tall, string bean of a coach wailing through a season of misery by pulling his hair out and suffering from "ulcers," which he never had. But lifelong habits of heavy smoking and drinking would catch up with him. As he aged, "he couldn't see well," trainer Jack Gimmler recalled. He had trouble reading the scoreboard without squinting, but he wouldn't wear glasses. At sixty, after a routine examination, a spot turned up on one of his lungs, and a lifelong smoker kicked the habit. But the coach's punishing lifestyle had taken its toll.

In a 1954 article, Lapchick discussed the pressures of coaching. "My weight, never great for a man 6'5", drops from 195 to 178 pounds. I no longer can get a full night's sleep. I have to rely on sedatives." To calm him down, doctors recommended he carry a small bottle of brandy. On the road, he listened to all-night talk shows or discussed eclectic subjects with sportswriters, because insomnia was another lifelong ailment. Lapchick's shyness caused him to internalize his feelings. During a close game, anxiety often produced abdominal spasms. At the end of his coaching days, the St. John's trainer supplied him with eight to ten aspirins before a game for his heart condition. He often attended functions at St. John's after he had retired from coaching. The brandy bottle would be replaced by a vial of nitroglycerin pills.

Throughout his coaching career, Lapchick suffered from what he called "nervous tension." He was often too emotionally involved with his teams. When he delivered bad news to a player—like being cut or traded—he took each decision to heart. He cared about others' feelings. "When a kid fails," Lapchick believed, "you can't dismiss it by saying, 'Well, he just went home.' He didn't just go home. In many cases, he was a hero in his hometown." Before the player left his town, they had a dinner for him and gave him a watch. There were write-ups in the local papers. Lapchick worried how the cut player felt when he got home. All these health issues just added to his woes.

O

Joe Lapchick refused to go public with the retirement issue. He never made formal charges against the university; he didn't believe in fighting for his job in the press and didn't want to be in the middle of a "pissing war." Lapchick smiled and did not ask sportswriter friends to fight his battle. But many did. They wrote columns with razor-sharp comments about their friend's dilemma. The sports media's new cause was salvaging their old friend, and Joe became their poster child. The attack on St. John's came from every major sportswriter with few exceptions. Newspapers, whether local or out of town, found it difficult to accept that Joe Lapchick, who looked and acted as normal and as pleasant as ever and who had just coached his team to a victory over the number one team in the nation, wasn't capable of coaching any longer because he would be sixty-five on April 12.

The university's cause was championed by Bernie Beglane, a sports-writer from the soon-to-be-defunct *Long Island Press*. Beglane claimed Lapchick had agreed to retire at sixty-five when he signed on in 1956, and that was the arrangement the university and its athletic department understood. "The commitment to Carnesecca was that he would get the job when Lapchick retires, and Lapchick was on record to that he wanted Looie to succeed him," Beglane insisted.

Momentum to support Joe Lapchick's cause was fed by the fact that he was well liked by the metropolitan press; also, his St. John's team was successful. This combination caused a media stir that couldn't be denied. Everyone was talking about the raw deal Lapchick was getting and asking what could be done. The barrage of media support for Lapchick would make its point.

Ed Shea, a St. John's graduate, sent a letter on January 28, 1965 to the *Daily News*; it was filled with words like "character," "legend," "humble," and "simple." Shea recognized that St. John's "leaked" the story that Lapchick was "over-the-hill" as a cover for what he believed was their duplicity. "He's getting the axe," Shea insisted. "As long as Joe Lapchick lives, he will be young. To destroy a man and a legend with a lie should not go unchallenged." He closed with, "The near-sighted administrators are doing more harm to St. John's than to Joe."

Sportswriters, who had covered his progress for more than thirty years and valued their relationship with him, tried to help Lapchick. Jerry Izenberg of the *Newark Ledger* felt St. John's was unable to appreciate the old warrior's value. "People like Lapchick work their whole life to gain knowledge, then we ask them to throw it all away for someone who doesn't know as much."

Jimmy Cannon unloaded both barrels into his February 1, 1965 *New York Post* column. "Why did St. John's have to target this man?" Cannon wondered. "He is basketball as no man is, and this includes Adolph Rupp, Bob Cousy, and Wilt Chamberlain." Would Lapchick be better suited to coach next year, Cannon wondered, if an error had occurred, and it was discovered that Lapchick was really only sixty-four? Cannon had known Lapchick for enough years to know his essence. "He is a good man, and his greatness as a coach is only a small part. But they don't want him any more because he's sixty-five. St. John's should be ashamed of themselves."

Caustic Dick Young of the *Daily News* hammered St. John's resolve, pointing to Lapchick's effectiveness. "St. John's believed being sixty-five is the worst sin in the world, and punishable by banishment from a life's work." Young summed up the complaint of most Lapchick defenders. "Lapchick earned the right to quit on his own, to make the decision himself, and they deprived him of it." Maybe one of the most astute comments was made by a St. John's senior in the school's newspaper. He pointed out that President Lyndon Johnson saw fit to overrule the mandatory retirement age of seventy to keep J. Edgar Hoover on as FBI director.

St. John's, however, never budged. The administration resented Lapchick's fueling the press with his feelings, which it perceived as a challenge to its authority. Father Graham in particular resented Lapchick's quiet resistance to the school's position. "I knew his reaction to our decision was very poor during the Holiday Festival," the administrator revealed. The priest took exception to Lapchick's "sounding off to the press, they were his buddies, he was bad-mouthing." The decision was made, and hell freezing over wouldn't change it.

While the university and its famous coach silently butted heads, Lou Carnesecca, his recognized replacement, was in an uncomfortable position. He wanted the coaching job but could do without the negative publicity it was causing. Carnesecca went about his work with his usual efficiency. "I never noticed any hard feelings between the two," was Houston's observation. Lapchick seemed as friendly and warm towards his assistant, and Carnesecca showed respect for the headman.

However, Carnesecca had heard rumors that made him feel unsure of his own future. Arthur Daley of the *New York Times* had casually dropped an item in his column that Jack Donohue and his star player were a packaged deal for St. John's. What if Donohue could deliver Lew Alcindor? Would St. John's hire him to gain the greatest player in the country?

The truth, unknown to St. John's University at the time, was that Donohue could not sell himself with his franchise player. Alcindor would not have joined his high school coach under any circumstances. The big player had an interest in playing for Joe Lapchick, as well as a strong friendship with Redmen forward, Sonny Dove. But once it became clear that Lapchick would not coach at St. John's, Alcindor, in his autobiography, said that, "The school [St. John's] lost much of its appeal."

Jack Donohue's name kept swirling around the St. John's situation, but nothing ever came of it. Rumors flew around the young scholastic All-

American. One had it that UCLA's John Wooden stepped in and snapped up the undecided center. Another even claimed the giant center was tied to a film contract that would eventually pay him $150,000. But the only certainty was that he would not attend St. John's.

Lew Alcindor finally visited the UCLA campus in the fall of 1964 and liked the warm weather and the comfortable, relaxed life on the West Coast campus, as well as the school's "very quaint-looking Midwesterner," Coach John Wooden, who called him "Lewis." But the tall center would wait until prior to his Power Memorial school year to end before he called a press conference to announce that he had picked UCLA as the college of his choice and left shortly after for California.

The St. John's athletic administration would not officially award Lapchick's job to his assistant during the season, which had to make Carnesecca wonder about his future. Carnesecca was loyal to St. John's and had attended its prep school as well as the university. He had worked hard alongside Coach Lapchick and was acknowledged as an authority in the new scientific approach to basketball. But what if he didn't get the job?

To balance the attack on the university, Father Graham made statements supporting Lou Carnesecca, admitting St. John's was fortunate to have such a well-respected young coach, "whose previous service at St. John's left no doubt of his devotion to students and the sport."

O

Knowledge of Lapchick's medical situation carried weight in the decision to enforce his retirement. When added to his age and rumors that he had lost control of the techniques of coaching, St. John's believed it had enough ammunition to pull the trigger. Lapchick was old by 1960s standards, obviously in poor health, and if allowed to continue coaching, might jeopardize St. John's hold on Carnesecca. From the school's point of view, retiring Lapchick was the logical decision. However, Lapchick was an icon in a sport that was by far the major one at St. John's. For St. John's to allow him to leave under clouded circumstances was at least questionable.

The perception was that after twenty years of loyalty to St. John's, Lapchick was forgotten. Leaving so unceremoniously, and with only outsiders to honor him, was disappointing. When Lapchick asked for one last year because of the suddenness of his dismissal, St. John's could have complied. Instead Lapchick would leave quietly, and this left a bitter taste in everyone's mouth.

While attempting to salvage his job, Lapchick focused on what he did best: coach. In spite of the emotional turmoil, he turned his thoughts to the basketball season. With Bobby McIntyre and brother Kenny, the team had two excellent scorers returning along with point guard Jerry Houston. Ex-Marine, Bobby Duerr gave them a strong forward who stoically played defense, scored when needed, and rebounded, too. For his efforts Duerr received little fanfare, but he never complained. He was an ingredient needed by every successful team.

Ken Wirell was also back and became a much-needed sixth man. But the exciting addition was sophomore Lloyd "Sonny" Dove. "Sonny" may have been a nickname from his youth, but "sunny" was more descriptive of his personality. The slim, 6'7", fluid, bouncing sophomore forward was a highly recruited all-city player from St. Francis Prep who was happy to be at St. John's. He gave the team a good shooting forward who could sky for rebounds. The pieces for an excellent year were in place.

But like with every team he coached, Lapchick wanted to get things in order for the season. The experienced coach, who read players well, started the season on a humorous note. The two McIntyres were surfers and had quietly spent the summer in Hawaii enjoying their sport. While Carnesecca knew of their passion, Coach Lapchick only got wind of it in the fall and had no opportunity to discipline them for engaging in a potentially career-ending sport.

By the end of the first week of practice, Lapchick signaled Bobby McIntyre over to center court. He never liked confronting someone with bad news but preferred to throw out some rope and have the individual hang himself. The younger McIntyre had no idea his coach knew of his surfing and was floored when Lapchick started to discuss the subject. "Hey, Kid, why do you surf?" Lapchick asked. Like any cornered youngster, Bobby thought fast and began a long-winded explanation of the benefits of surfing and why it was profitable for an athlete to be so engaged.

"Coach, my legs are stronger, and I've found our practices have been a breeze because my wind is so much better." The 6'7" forward went on as Lapchick's gaze narrowed by the minute. He continued to listen, never saying a word, allowing the rope to tighten around McIntyre's throat. Five minutes into the harangue, McIntyre sputtered out of gas, but not before Lapchick had a chance to see through the facade of nonsense his player had pumped out. At that point the coach cleared his throat and laid one on him. "Kid," he said, "you're full of shit." Stunned by his coach's perceptive reaction, McIntyre was reduced to silence and walked away feeling "as if I were about a half-inch tall." In spite of what the administration believed, the players never doubted who was running the team. As the team prepared for the season, someone was needed to pull them together, someone strong enough to communicate orders on the floor and follow directions.

Jerry Houston, the 6'1" Bronx senior, the uncomplicated but dedicated floor leader, would be the most important ingredient of Lapchick's final team. He possessed qualities that excited coaches. He loved the game, as Lapchick did, and, like a loyal soldier, carried out orders. Houston admired his coach and felt strongly about his predicament. He was ready to do whatever it took to send him out a winner. If the administration and the student body couldn't be moved, Houston thought, then the basketball court was still a place where the team could demonstrate for its coach.

Houston got to know Joe Lapchick when he watched St. John's Hughie Kirwan, a Vinegar Hill neighbor, play in the Garden. After setting a New York City scholastic single-game scoring record of 69 points, Houston was offered a scholarship by St. John's.

The new recruit met Lapchick in Alumni Hall in 1961 and was immediately impressed. It was memorable, and Houston still treasures it. "This was the man I had heard and read about, who had coached the Knicks and St. John's," he recalled. "Lapchick had such great success and experience."

When they met, Houston recalled Lapchick extending his big hand to greet him. "I felt the strength and size of his hand," Houston recalled. Lapchick said he had heard good things about him. "He was low-key, cordial, but I felt a genuine warm feeling from the man."

Although a New York all-star, Houston questioned whether he was capable of playing for St. John's. But, as the year progressed, his insecurity vanished. His desire, coupled with ability and sincerity, made him a necessity for Lapchick's last team. When it came to clutch play, Houston delivered. He felt his college play was the highlight of his life. But the real chance to pay back his coach would start during the Holiday Festival.

Chapter 18

A Gratifying Night

Michigan's Cazzie Russell was everybody's All-American but an opposing coach's nightmare. The 6'5", 220-pound forward could score, handle the ball like a guard, rebound, and exude star charisma. "So good," Lapchick thought, "he was going to be an all-time great." On January 2, 1965, in Madison Square Garden, the muscular Russell led a heavily favored Michigan team against St. John's in the Holiday Festival final. Michigan was trying to match its football team's Rose Bowl 34–7 trashing of Oregon State the day before.

Besides Russell, the tournament had included some of the nation's best All-Americans. Princeton had led Michigan in the semifinal only to fall apart when Bill Bradley fouled out with five minutes left, and now both Bradley and Dave Bing of Syracuse settled for watching the final from the stands. Garden TV announcer Bob Wolff had just arrived from the West Coast, where he covered Michigan's Rose Bowl win. While Michigan tried for sports history, St. John's hoped to be competitive with the Big Ten power. In the opening round, LaSalle gave the Redmen a tough fight before losing, 78–71, but the Cincinnati Bearcats in the semis went down to the wire before Lapchick's luck took hold, 66–64.

Michigan was big and strong like Terminator warriors. St. John's forward Ken Wirell remembered that most of the Michigan players, from the pair of 6'7"s, Bill Buntin and Oliver Darden, to Jim Soens and Russell, all had cubic-inch strength, the volume of a Paul Bunyan.

The team averaged 90 points a game, with Russell canning more than 26. Many sportswriters privately felt Coach Strack's undefeated Wolverines would maul the less-physical Redmen. However, by the 1960s, basketball was becoming more scientific, and St. John's was prepared.

Double-up half-court pressure was the latest defensive rage. St. Joseph's defensive specialist Dr. Jack Ramsey, a future NBA coach and TV commentator, shared his knowledge during a summer clinic, which Lou Carnesecca sponged up. The aggressive strategy caught opposing teams by surprise and upset their game tempo. It started with two players trapping the ball handler, often causing him to panic and pass recklessly. The defense continued to trap the ball while the other three defenders looked to pick off bad passes. If the defense succeeded, the offense usually unraveled and melted into a heap of confused players.

After studying the new defense, the enthusiastic St. John's assistant was convinced of its potential and shared his belief with Lapchick. Months of hard work produced "The Bush," a lethal weapon Lapchick's Redmen would unleash to "ambush" its opponents.

Michigan's strength dominated the first half, and St. John's, through the fine shooting and rebounding of Dove, trailed at the half by only five, 39–34. But after Michigan warmed up in the second half, it demonstrated why the team was highly rated. As the old pro watched from the bench, he appreciated Michigan's power. "I was admiring the way they were taking us apart," Lapchick later said, "and hoped the kids wouldn't look bad." But, with 9:35 remaining, Lapchick called time-out, the Redmen trailing 68–52.

The players slumped into their seats as Lapchick tried to revive their fight. He let them drink water and towel off before he got to what was on his mind. Lapchick wanted them to know he didn't think the game was over, and he only had sixty seconds to convince them. "You can do it, you still have time," were his first words, which he delivered slowly, with that vintage Lapchick smile and a controlled level of confidence in his voice. He knew only too well how players gauge a coach's response to adversity during a time-out.

"He wasn't excited," Dove remembered, "but calm; the way he was talking you couldn't tell whether we were down by 50 points or 1." Lapchick made sure Houston and Kenny McIntyre understood what he wanted. "There was always an air of confidence about him," Dove insisted. "And he had a way of passing it on to his players." For a few seconds, the coach turned to his assistant to discuss strategy. "Now Lou? What do you think?" Lapchick questioned Carnesecca. "Coach, it's time for The Bush." The ambush was ready. Lapchick calmly set the defensive strategy and sent the team onto the floor armed with the weaponry and confidence they needed, ready to see if all the practice would pay off.

Most coaches admit the last thing they want is an overconfident team, one that believes a game is over when it's not. A team that is leading comfortably and relaxes too soon lacks the resolve to resist a passionate rally, as Michigan found out that frosty January night in the Garden. The Redmen, prepped for their defensive attack, clawed at the Wolverines, making them look as if they were in the midst of winter hibernation. "It wasn't so much what *we* did," Lou Carnesecca remembered, "but what *they* did. They forgot to shoot and started throwing the ball away."

While racing up the court, Houston recalled looking to the bench and seeing how excited Lapchick was getting with each basket. With his confident look and broad smile he seemed to be saying, "I'm proud of you guys, and I know you're giving your best." Just knowing he had such thoughts spurred the team on.

The aggressive defense caused Michigan to become careless with the ball, treating it like a foreign object. Crosscourt passes rarely thrown came winging from Russell and Darden. With fewer than four minutes left in the game, Kenny McIntyre, who had played poorly in the first half, hit four straight jump shots that got the standing-room-only crowd of 18,499 screaming fans on its feet and into St. John's rhythm. With 2:25 left, the sandy-haired shooting guard's last shot tied the score at 70–70. The Big Ten champs called time-out to regroup.

With 2:08 on the clock, Dove drove right and hit an eighteen-foot jump shot that gave St. John's the lead, 72–71. Buntin's free throw knotted the score, but then Jerry Houston, "Mr. Clutch," took over. While St. John's exercised patience down the stretch, Houston, at the 1:37 mark, pivoted on the right side of the court and drove baseline for the go-ahead score, 74–72.

A minute later, Russell hurried up court only to charge into Bobby McIntyre and foul out. With a 2-point lead and twenty-eight seconds left, Houston was deliberately fouled and again found himself in a crucial spot. Official Vic Degravio handed him the ball for two shots and stepped aside. The senior wiped his hands on his socks, took a deep breath, and fired a free throw that bounced off the front rim to the left.

Lapchick knew with less than a half minute remaining, Michigan had time to tie the score, which automatically added pressure to the second free throw. Going through Houston's mind was that this shot could nail it down for his old coach. He wanted nothing more. Houston bounced the ball three times, took a deep breath, looked up, and fired a bull's-eye, giving St. John's a commanding 75–72 lead. After a series of desperation shots, a tap-in proved to be Michigan's only field goal in the last ten minutes. As the buzzer blared, the Garden scoreboard read 75–74, and the crowd gave Lapchick and his team's performance an extended ovation. Michigan never got back on track after its 16-point lead, scoring only 6 points the last nine and a half minutes. The crowd had witnessed a historic comeback, one that would be talked about for years.

St. John's had done the impossible and defeated the number one team in the country. With the crowd's encouragement, the Redmen's press exposed Michigan's slow feet and weak ballhandling, and, unnerved, the team's poor play had snowballed. Acknowledging the retiring coach's accomplishment, the crowd poured onto the court, lunging to reach Lapchick and carry him around like a victorious Roman general. When the hysteria subsided, Lapchick and his team lined up to collect the winner's cup and gold watches. Photographers and sportswriters made the rest a glorious page in St. John's history books.

Sportswriters surrounded Lapchick as he made his way through the pandemonium of the locker room. They didn't know whether to question him or hug him. "Boy, oh boy, what guts," were the first words from the excited coach. "Wasn't this some comeback?" summed up Lapchick's reaction to the unbelievable finish. Lapchick had experienced, as the *New York Post*'s Jimmy Cannon later described, "A gratifying night." Morrey Rokeach of the *Journal American* wanted to know how Lapchick rated the come-from-behind victory. "The highest step on the ladder of my career," but when asked how the team rated with his previous teams, he called it, "Comparable, but not quite as good as the 1959 Tony Jackson–led team." Even on the high end of a glorious victory, Joe Lapchick was fair and honest.

As he turned away from the knot of reporters, two former Knicks elbowed their way into the happy, wild, and steamy room and mugged him. "Congratulations," Carl Braun whispered into his former coach's ear. Harry Gallatin's big country smile said it all as a pair of huge hands collided in a bear trap of a handshake. "I wish my players could play that hard," the newly appointed Knicks coach said to his old mentor. At that point, the sportswriters spun back into Lapchick's line of vision.

"How old do you think I am now?" Lapchick confidently addressed them. He tried enjoying the monumental win, but his impending retirement robbed him of some of its joy. He wanted to coach, his body language screamed out. The Michigan victory reminded him how much he would miss it. It stirred feelings that told him he wasn't finished and still had some pop left. Basketball was Lapchick's passion, and the victory only energized his survival instinct. He was Joe Lapchick, and deep inside he hated being put out to pasture. He was fighting with the only weapon he knew—basketball. Joe Lapchick made everyone know of Carnesecca's contribution to the Michigan victory. St. John's would not have won without the successful advantage gained from The Bush.

The Michigan victory demonstrated something about the aging coach, something difficult to put into words. Joe Lapchick's quiet volcanic passion for the game willed a victory in his last Holiday Festival. His players were motivated to play above their ability and not let down the man they had grown to love. Houston and Dove felt the emotional stress from all that had transpired at school since September. But while Lapchick led by example, there was another element that crept into the picture and that was verbalized by the *New York Times* sportswriter Dave Anderson. He realized Lapchick's farewell efforts had become "the whole story" of the tournament. The sports media was pulling for a "Miracle of Forty-Ninth Street."

Lapchick's survival instincts had gotten him out of jams before. He had overcome the intimidation of coaching educated college men whose cultural roots embarrassed his blue-collar upbringing. He was not going to buckle and cave in now. He could overcome what was working against him. He was Joe Lapchick, and he would end his career with pride. He coached as he always did; he spoke the way he always spoke. He was truly "Mr. Basketball," and he wasn't going to beg for his job.

Chapter 19

The Last
Hurrah

L apchick's final team at times performed as
if it were the best he ever coached. The players continued to win key
games by playing above their heads. They did not stack up against the nation's best and yet responded at tournament time, causing their coach to
say they "played with ice water in their veins." As January slipped into
February, and campus life quieted down, there was a sense of a team destined to answer the bell for him. But there were others who tried to show
their appreciation for Joe Lapchick in a different way.

Early in January, after the Michigan win, two St. John's seniors, Tim
Kelly and Steve Lucas, had an idea. "Why not raise some money for
Coach?" Tim said out loud while eating lunch in the student cafeteria.
Steve enthusiastically seconded it. After clearing it with Dean Salerno and
the president, Father Burke, the "Joe Lapchick Student Appreciation
Committee" was formed. They hoped to present Lapchick with a new car
and membership in a local golf club. Kelly taped a picture of a deluxe
LeSabre Buick on the bulletin board in the dean's office. "Our goal,"
Kelly reminded readers of *The Torch*, "is to have Coach Lapchick ride out
of here in a new car."

Large coffee cans wrapped in red crepe paper with "Joe Lapchick
Appreciation Drive" penciled on them appeared around the campus. The
drive lasted three weeks. When it became obvious that the student drive
had fallen short by $1,500 of the funds needed for a new car, no one from

the university stepped up to complete the dream. So instead, the students bought "the most expensive set of golf clubs," and a black-and-white TV and would present the gifts to Lapchick at the spring sports banquet. "We loved Coach," Lucas later said.

Kelly's piece in the *The Torch* made clear the purpose of the fundraiser was to "remind Coach Lapchick of the appreciation of the students." When the readers were told to turn to page eight for the campaign's ground rules, bold headlines told them more about the retiring coach. "Joe Lapchick is Mr. Basketball," Walter McLaughlin is quoted. "He is the spirit of sports at St. John's," Father Graham reminded students in the school paper.

"We have all benefited greatly from his long and colorful career." Kelly also advised students to accept the university's right to ask Lapchick to leave "according to contract."

Lapchick realized he never bothered to build a financial nest egg. The university's pension seemed meager. However, when Lapchick was sent complimentary copies of *The Torch*'s story, he never projected any anger and thanked the students. "St. John's has been darn good to me," he wrote diplomatically. "I am appreciative of all their efforts that make my stay a most pleasant one." While trying to maintain a strong front, Lapchick never lost sight of preparing his team for its last game at Alumni Hall. To him, that would be a momentous occasion.

○

Rich Lapchick talked persuasively with his mother at the breakfast table the day of the Massachusetts game. "Mom, you have to come to Dad's last home game. The cheerleaders want to present you with a bouquet of flowers and, besides, it's his last home game," he said with the kind of smile mothers find hard to resist.

Bobbie Lapchick looked up from her coffee to acknowledge her son's suggestion. She was everyone's prototypical mom with her combed back hair streaked with gray that she didn't bother dyeing. Like her husband, she was in the habit of coming to breakfast formally dressed. Bobbie had all the protective and loving motherly instincts sons appreciate.

She had attended only one of her husband's games his first year at St. John's, and the team had lost to CCNY, which was coached by Joe's

Celtics teammate Nat Holman. Joe is so superstitious, she thought. He would be upset.

"What do you think?" Bobbie asked her husband, who didn't appear in the kitchen until after Rich had left for school. "Rich wants me to come to your game tonight, Joe." He looked up from the *New York Post* and smiled. "Bobbie, you have to be there; it'll be fun. What do you have to lose? I'm going to retire, and besides, everyone will get a kick out of it." Bobbie liked the idea. It would be nice to see his last home game. Who knows, she thought, maybe I'll bring him luck.

The couple left for the game at his usual departure time, and at half-time the mothers of the senior players and Bobbie were honored with flowers. There was a brief mention of her husband's last game, and then the Redmen settled down to defeat the visiting Massachusetts Minutemen.

As she waited for her husband after the game, she noticed the big smile on his face when he exited from the dressing room. "Bobbie, cancel all your plans. You have become my good luck charm. I'd like you to come to the NIT," Joe urged her. Bobbie didn't realize it, but she was in for a bumpy but pleasant ride.

○

Defeating nationally ranked Michigan in the Holiday Festival placed Lapchick and his Redmen on a collision course with destiny. There are times in sports when the confidence level of coaches and players is such as to assure victory. Joe Lapchick and his Redmen were on one of those journeys. The Michigan victory was the first half of the adventure. But there were more goals to fulfill, an additional field of dreams that sports people like to think about.

As the field for the NIT was completed with St. John's [17–8] included, visions of a double victory danced in the heads of the media. Although it had been done before by Lapchick's 1958–59 Redmen team, nothing would make his sportswriter friends happier. But there were roadblocks to an NIT dream. The tournament was filled with quality teams, and the likely bracket called for St. John's to play Army and Villanova, two teams the Redmen lost to during the season. St. John's also drew former Holy Cross and Boston Celtics superstar—and now coach—Bob Cousy's high-scoring Boston College team in the first round, and, if successful, they would likely face New Mexico State, the nation's top defensive team in the quarterfinal.

There were no cupcakes for the retiring coach; his work was cut out for him. But besides his inspired team, Lapchick's greatest assets were Madison Square Garden, its crowd, and the sports media, which created a special chemistry. He won all his big tournaments there and knew his sportswriter friends would give St. John's all the encouragement they could handle. But he didn't want his team caught in an emotional farewell tribute, which would create unnecessary pressure. In preparing for the tournament he preached, "Don't win for me, win it for yourselves."

But despite Lapchick's talks, the sports media presented the NIT as a golden opportunity to send their friend into retirement as a winner. The coach didn't encourage it, but he didn't discourage it either. The Redmen took the floor against the Boston College Eagles and beat them, 114–92. The game set the tone for the rest of the tournament. Lapchick, ordinarily a conservative tactician, allowed the team to run with one of the best fast-break teams in the nation. After the victory, it did not take long to sense St. John's was on a predestined mission. New Mexico State was next, which proved stingy with points as anticipated, but again the Redmen adjusted and pulled it out, 61–54. They were rolling now, and the Garden crowd and the media helped build momentum. As predicted, the semifinals included Army and Villanova. Tates Locke's Army team had beaten St. John's earlier in the season and always provided forty minutes of physical basketball. St. John's struggled but held on to to win, 67–60. The Redmen were in the final.

Waiting for the Redmen was Villanova, one of the best teams in the country with Coach Jack Kraft's challenging zone defenses. Attacking unusual defenses was not Lapchick's strength, but determination can overcome major hurdles, and on Saturday, March 20, 1965, Joe Lapchick was not going to be denied his moment with basketball immortality.

O

"I'll be home for dinner," Joe Lapchick shouted up the stairs to Bobbie, as he headed out the door for what would be his last official basketball practice. "Maybe we'll go for a fish dinner," he suggested, which they liked doing on Fridays during Lent. As he drove his Oldsmobile down

Wendover Road at 10:30 A.M. the traffic was light. As he waved to his next-door neighbor, his mind drifted to the finality of the day.

Taking the Saw Mill River Parkway out of Yonkers, he realized how set in his ways he had become. He and his entire family had lived their lives in the Terrace City, and even after he left the Knicks and returned to St. John's, he spent twenty years in one school while coaching more than thirty years in New York. He knew there would be a stack of mail waiting for him to answer before his noon practice. As he turned to glance at a passing car, he looked at the large brown grocery bag sitting on the passenger seat. No one in the world, he thought, could figure what it was doing there. He was sensitive to partings, and thought a large suitcase would be a melodramatic reminder that he was "cleaning out his locker." The sound of it seemed ominous.

But today was the day that all the accumulated paraphernalia would be stuffed into that brown bag, and if anyone sees it when he leaves, it could be mistaken for garbage, he thought. As he approached Union Turnpike, he remembered the running gag he had with sportswriter Lennie Lewin about traveling light—a gag that never quite ended. He remembered the time he won the bet when he pulled an envelope out of his jacket pocket with nothing but a toothbrush in it. He never did carry much when he traveled with the Knicks. Well, when I leave today, it'll be the way I came in, with no baggage, he thought.

"Morning, Coach," Jim Fitts, the senior security guard, called out as he always did when Lapchick entered Alumni Hall. "How you doing, Jim," the old coach answered. He turned down the hallway and crossed paths with track coach Bill Ward. "How are you going to do against Villanova?" he wanted to know. After they chatted a few minutes, Ward wished him well, and Lapchick continued to his office.

Making his way downstairs, he noticed Vinnie Colluro and other managers playing a three-man game on the main gym floor, and made a mental note. The next friendly face he saw was that of his able assistant. "Lou, let's practice in the auxiliary gym not to disturb the kids playing on the floor." Carnesecca looked a little surprised. "Hi, Coach. No problem, I'll clear it."

As he laid his brown bag and car keys on the desk, he noticed the anticipated stack of mail. He sat down and ripped open the first envelope, which had a familiar out-of-town address. It was from an old sports cartoonist friend, Alan Maver, from Berkley, West Virginia, wishing him good luck. The old coach unfolded a cartoon that would run in his paper. Its headline read: "Going Out in Style," and it predicted he would win his fourth NIT. "You always was, and will always be, a gentleman," he wrote. "We miss you out here and always enjoyed your games with the Celtics." So did I, Lapchick thought.

An alumnus wanted an autographed picture for posterity. Lapchick reached into the desk's bottom drawer for the color photo from the public relations department. It was nicely done, he thought. Lapchick's sincere smile made the memento a keepsake. The coach thanked "Frank" in a large Victorian script, the way all Lapchick's brothers and sisters wrote, and signed it.

The large script caused his thoughts to drift back to his mother's poetry, which she enjoyed writing, and the Czech songs the family loved singing at holidays. "Why am I thinking about that?" he wondered.

Near the bottom of the stack was a Western Union telegram from Denver, Colorado. "Dear Coach," it started, "Vince Boryla, that skinny-legged rascal," Lapchick shouted out. The old Knick was wishing his old coach "the very best" for his last game with Villanova. "My prayers will be with you." That was nice of Vinnie, Lapchick thought, before his crew-cut assistant interrupted him. "We're ready to go, Coach,"

Lapchick left the brown bag, his unfinished mail, and any sentimental thoughts in the office and dressed for his last practice. His red pullover coaching shirt had become a favorite. As he laced his sneakers, he thought how attached he became to certain items of clothing or pens, pencils, coffee mugs, and a million and one other items as he got older. That was the way he felt about St. John's. It had become another layer of skin, one he wasn't anxious to shed. He felt a sudden bubble in his stomach, a nervous twitch that reminded him of what was happening over the next twenty-four hours.

The press attended Lapchick's final strategy meeting in the players' dressing room. Gene Roswell of the *New York Post* was finishing a feature he started with the tournament, and Sam Goldaper from the *Herald Tribune* was up front chatting when Lapchick entered the room. The players, he thought, seemed calm, noticeably subdued, almost laid-back, with no show of emotion or talk about winning for him, just a locked-in focus that would have worried Villanova's coach Kraft.

When they got on the floor, the starters worked a few minutes against the Wildcats' zone, and after a series of attempts at breaking it, Lapchick was satisfied. A few other basic maneuvers, followed by spot shooting and rotating free throw shooting, rounded out the workout. Kenny McIntyre was in the middle of setting a tournament record for consecutive free throws. He looked relaxed as he ran off another two dozen.

At 1:22 P.M., Lapchick looked at his watch and blew his final whistle, ending practice for what he believed was the last time. "That's it boys." He told everyone the time to meet at the Garden for the next day's 3:00 P.M. game. "Remember, we're wearing red away uniforms," the coach reminded them. As he mumbled a few words to the press, his mind was distracted by thoughts of his first practice in DeGray Gym. "Nearly thirty years ago," he said to no one in particular, and he wondered where the years had gone.

"I'll never be late for practice again," Jerry Houston ragged his coach as both walked off the court with Lapchick jokingly holding his floor leader in a headlock. Houston and his coach were confident they would never get the chance to be late again. The point guard continued into the players' locker room, only to be greeted by a scrawled directive on the blackboard: "One more to go. Win it for Joe."

Lapchick made his way down to his office where he showered, dressed, and began to pack his brown grocery bag. Sneakers and towel were stuffed in first. Next were old mail and phone memos from the office. An old photo of his family was taped to the back of the locker door, which he removed, looked at, and slid into a manila envelope to keep it dry. He threw an old calendar into the garbage. He took a couple dozen photos from his desk and placed them neatly with the family picture, away from the damp towel. His whistle lay on the desk. He stared at it, wondering if he would ever use it again. He walked over, picked it up, and dropped it into the bag.

As Lapchick walked out, baseball coach Jack Kaiser made small talk about the coming snowstorm. "I'm sure we'll play tomorrow," Lapchick reminded Kaiser. No NIT has ever been canceled." Tomorrow was the day. As he walked to his car, he noticed long lines of students buzzing around Alumni Hall's lobby, looking to buy last-minute tickets. Lapchick hopped into his car and placed the brown bag on the floor in the front. It would keep him company on the drive home and maybe for a lot longer than that. It was beginning to snow lightly as he drove away. He was starting to feel funny. He knew he would have difficulty sleeping.

○

The St. John's players floated past the NBC cameramen tuning up for their nationally televised NIT finale. The tournament continued to capture excitement in spite of NCAA competition. Maybe it was the Garden mystique, the New York media, or just the tradition associated with it. The NIT still turned heads and sports pages. Houston and Dove followed the McIntyres down the runway. Lapchick signaled Houston outside the locker-room door with a long index finger. "Jerry, I want you to have this." Lapchick handed him a neatly wrapped box. Houston unwrapped the small package and inside was a set of vintage NBA cuff links. "I know you will not be singled out by the tournament," Lapchick mumbled, "but I wanted you to know we would not be here without your leadership and sacrifice."

"Lapchick included a short letter with the gift," Houston said. He unfolded the faded, wrinkled note he still carries in his wallet. "Jerry, a small token of my appreciation for your excellent contribution. I was proud to be with you." Although the cuff links have tarnished, Houston's memory has not. And though the ink on the note has faded, the sentiment of that Saturday afternoon has not; Houston never lets the note get too far from him.

Players filed into the locker room and noticed their last pregame report on the blackboard. Red road uniforms gradually replaced their blue blazers. Above the scouting report was Carnesecca's victory equation: "Guts, Will to Win, And Team Play = Champs!"

While silent emotional sparks ignited the room, there was a calm assurance that the team's final tribute to its coach would be paid. For many of them it was their last game, too. Lapchick gave an upbeat, honest summation, but he didn't want his team too high. "Don't believe that stuff you've been reading about winning this game for me," he pleaded again before the game. "Win it for yourselves." But no one in the room had to be a genius to know the team's mind-set. The players were determined to pay their coach the respect the administration seemed reluctant to offer. "I'll take care of myself," Lapchick insisted, "one way or the other." He had been doing that in gyms for more than fifty years.

Joe Lapchick had suffered through games for years, and as he fidgeted in the dressing room, he seemed relieved that this would be his last. Thinking about the pain he had endured coaching, he longed for a cigarette as he paced the floor. Lapchick had paid his price coaching. Once after a Knicks game in Fort Wayne, Indiana, Lapchick was so stressed he had to be helped to his hotel room because he felt as if he would collapse. Trainer Don Friedrichs looked in on him late that night only to find him hanging by his hands from the top edge of the bathroom door, writhing in spasmodic pain. It was an odd memory on such a day. Today, he had no back spasms, just a strong, calm feeling that something good was about to happen.

Lapchick traditionally remained in the locker room as the Redmen warmed up; he was usually too nervous to go out and chat with courtside crowds of sportswriters and fans who wanted to wish him good luck. He didn't sleep much the last few nights, but he was up for the game. He would more than make it. When it reached three minutes before game time, Lapchick stood erect, walked out of the locker room, and made his last stroll through the Garden runway. As his tall frame approached the playing floor, a long, loud jolt of recognition erupted from the crowd as it welcomed him, and he instinctively tipped an imaginary hat in appreciation.

All 18,499 Garden seats were filled for the final game. Within a day, fifteen hundred St. John's tickets were sold at school. The student body sensed the Redmen would win and that history would be made. They shouted encouragement, hoping all the pieces would come together for the old coach. As the horn sounded, the team gathered for final instructions and the huddled binding of hands and intentions that were sealed with a quick prayer. "Our Lady of Victory, pray for us," was a subconscious urging of outside forces to produce a happy ending. The prayer scene looked like pranksters setting a Guinness world record for stuffing fraternity drunks into a telephone booth. Lapchick almost lost his balance and breath from the team crushing together trying to join hands. As he watched his starting five of Houston and Dove walk from the bench, joined by the McIntyres and Bobby Duerr, he saw confidence mingled with determination on their faces. "They're ready," Lapchick knew. The old coach sat back for his last game.

Referee Johnny Nucatola tossed the center jump, Villanova's Jim Washington's quickness and size beat Dove to the ball, and the last forty minutes of Joe Lapchick's coaching life began to tick away. Never a passive bench coach, Lapchick squirmed almost immediately, standing up, kneeling down, and walking to the water cooler, movements he had made repeatedly over a lifetime, reliving the agony and passion of the past thirty years. After Villanova missed its first shot, Houston crossed half-court, looking to get St. John's off on top. He spotted an opening, beat the ailing Bill Melchionni to the basket, scored, was fouled, and completed the 3-point play. The Johnnies were on the board and had the lead.

While the team's early momentum had the game under control, Lapchick felt tension building in his chest. His insides churned like a steamship's engines, but he knew he'd rather be here than anyplace in the world. It was his last game, and he was trying to enjoy it. As the game progressed, he sensed the players had paid attention and were executing their game plan, which boiled down to patience. The Redmen worked to find openings against Kraft's zone defense. The plan was not to rush shots, but to work the ball until they found the seam of the zone and could get what Lapchick called, "a good shot." With no shot clock, the deliberate strategy kept St. John's on top at halftime, 36–28.

As Lapchick walked slowly from the court, he tried to digest every aspect of the game, breathing in its ambience that would have to last a lifetime. He walked slowly, pausing outside the locker room to review his strategy and hear Carnesecca's. He then entered with the second-half plan. "Jerry, watch those crosscourt passes," and "Sonny, keep Washington off the boards, like you did the first half." The team, wide-eyed, listened to each word. Lapchick again reminded the team to look for good shots, but not to rush. He was satisfied with their performance, but both knew there was a second half. After everyone seemed settled, Lapchick sent the team out to loosen up.

In the second half, Villanova switched tactics and came after St. John's in a man-to-man defense. The Redmen were caught off guard at first and found themselves flat-footed after standing around against a zone. But they continued pounding the boards, played good defense, and maintained a comfortable lead. The team seemed in control of itself and the game. The sellout crowd was a definite "sixth man," actively encouraging every Redmen play. The players were not to be denied the huge gift this old coach deserved. As Lapchick watched, he understood it was more than a championship; to his team, it was a crusade. Lapchick knew enough basketball to sense St. John's was going to win. He felt it in his bones; no one was going to take it away from Houston or Kenny McIntyre. They were on course and playing from a position of strength, a sure way to succeed. The crowd sensed it, too.

Despite a 14-point Redmen lead, midway through the second half Villanova began to chip away. Slowly cutting the lead 2 points at a time, Villanova showed the poise that made it a top-ten team. Successive baskets by Jim Washington, followed by a steal and a layup by Bill Soens set the tone and the confidence level for the Wildcats. But then the game took a dramatic turn in Villanova's favor when George Leftwich glided into position and at the 6:22 mark drilled a sixteen-foot push shot that electrified the Garden and television audience and cut the lead to one, 50–49. Lapchick called a time-out to get a read on how his players were reacting to the comeback, and he was amazed how confident Houston and Kenny McIntyre seemed. The players had been there before and were not going to let each other down.

St. John's had not worked to this point to play dead. Kenny McIntyre spotted his brother, Bobby, heading to the basket up the right side of the court. He made a quick pass to the cutting forward, who caught it on the fly and floated it in for a layup and free throw, putting the Wildcats at arms' length again, 53–49. With fewer than twenty seconds, Villanova's Eric Erickson made a difficult shot that narrowed the score to 53–51. St. John's sat on the 2-point lead trying to "eat the clock" when Houston was deliberately fouled by Erickson. With seven seconds left, and two free throws, Houston had a chance to ice the game.

The senior guard stood at the foul line, behind referee Lou Eisenstein, both dripping wet. Although Houston played steady, he had not scored since the first 3-point play of the game. Now he was asked to lock it up. As players filled in the free throw lanes, and Houston stepped to the line, Washington signaled for a time-out. Houston, making no facial expression, moved slowly with his teammates to the bench. Kraft's efforts to ice him were ignored as Lapchick quickly reviewed the possibilities. But in his mind there was only one outcome, and he couldn't wait to start celebrating. "After Jerry makes the two free throws," the confident coach started, "fall back and let Villanova score, but don't foul." As the Redmen clasped hands for the final time, Lapchick wiped a tear from the corner of his eye. It was strange realizing it was over.

"Two Shots," the official barked as he handed Houston the damp ball and moved to his left. The guard dried his hands on his pants and pumped up the first. All net. Three points, he said to himself. With only a few ticks left on the clock, the second one would ice the game. "Swish." It was over. The team had given the "Old Man" the appropriate send-off, and Houston, again, had been involved in the critical part of the game. It was confetti time.

The buzzer released a flood of tension in the Big Indian, energy that caused him to uncharacteristically dash onto the Garden floor. He hugged the players as if they were his children, and then he was swamped in a sea of gratitude and appreciation from the student body. Joe Lapchick was never so excited; it was a dream come true, the stuff of storybook endings that rarely happen except in those corny 1930s feel-good films, but it was happening to him. He had remained low-key during the game, not wanting his team to get lost in its emotion, but now all hell broke loose.

"Everyone was in a frenzy immediately after the game," the *New York Post* reported. For a frozen moment after the horn sounded, the large student body under the 50th Street basket was stunned, not knowing what to do. Some began to cry, others started screaming, hundreds of them sat back to soak up the scene, as if framing it in their minds. Then, suddenly, the St. John's fans exploded onto the floor like pellets from a shotgun, like swarming locusts seeking out the Redmen team and "Mr. Basketball," their hero.

The crowd found him somewhere near half-court and hoisted him up as he tried reaching out to shake Bobby McIntyre's hand. In a few seconds, both were lost in a sea of euphoria. When the mob scene subsided, the McIntyres and the rest of the team carefully lifted their coach for a brief victory lap around the court. Why not? He had carried them for years. Among all the praise was the fact that Lapchick's St. John's teams had won an unprecedented fourth National Invitation Tournament, a feat that would never be matched. As he was carried around the court, waving to hysterical fans, he repeatedly shouted to himself, "What a way to go!" He would repeat that expression throughout the night.

The game ended in a dead heat with Lapchick's coaching career. The scoreboard continued to post the 55–51 final score. Like a sharp knife cut, the end of his coaching career wasn't felt at first. It took time to reach his senses. Lapchick was basking in victory, not wanting to face its solemnity. He reran the results in his mind while blotting out that there would be no more. This was it. There was no better ending to a career than the one he just experienced; it was the way to go.

"How does it feel knowing you've coached your last game," Sam Goldaper asked. "No more worries," was the first reaction from the leathery ex-coach. Then, with a mischievous smile, he said, "Starting today, I am a professional bum." As he chatted with sportswriter friends, out of the corner of his eye he spotted the tall shadow of a young man who obviously, by his extraordinary size, played basketball. He had come into the dressing room to congratulate the team and his friend, Sonny Dove, on their NIT victory. "Hey Lew," Lapchick yelled over, "you're in the right dressing room." Lew Alcindor looked startled, smiled, and hurried out.

As sportswriters encircled the victorious coach, on the other side of the locker room *The Torch* editor questioned a dazed Bobby McIntyre. "Why did you guys play so hard for Coach?" The sweaty player tried to think among the merrymaking, and then answered honestly. "We respected him so much," he started, "but we never played for him, we played to show him." "What do you mean?" the inquisitive scribe asked. McIntyre knew the student editor probably couldn't understand what he was about to say, but he gave it a try. "He would say things to you, and you would think, 'I'm going to show that sonofabitch.'" But he thought some more and clarified it. "After a game if you played well, and won, and while you're sitting by your locker saying to yourself, 'I really showed him tonight,' he would come by, tap you on the back and say, 'Nice game, kid,' and that made it all worth it." McIntyre was describing what separated Joe Lapchick from all the pretenders who call themselves coaches. This was a man who inspired through the reputation and manner he projected, and all the attempts to explain why he couldn't go on doing what he excelled in seemed absurd to the young athlete.

After literally lacing up sneakers for more than fifty years, Lapchick now had to walk away from the only life he knew. He could successfully sell cars, give speeches, or represent a corporation, but he knew how quickly fame disappears, like a puff from an Old Gold. Lapchick knew how much he would miss basketball. A late-winter snow was blanketing the city, but the warmth in Madison Square Garden would have melted a blizzard. As Lapchick was called out to accept the victory trophy, the Garden crowd, all 18,499 of them, gave him a frenzied five-minute ovation. It would be his last.

That afternoon, Lapchick took a long time to leave Madison Square Garden. As he and Carnesecca crossed the Garden floor, a cleaning man he had known for years called down from the mezzanine. "Good luck,

Joe." Lapchick shaded his eyes and squinted to pick out the voice, then waved to the well-wisher. A *Life* magazine photographer caught Lapchick's final image in this building, which housed many good memories. Both would soon be torn down. With his tan tweed overcoat draped over his left shoulder, he raised his right hand and stretched out his long arm, providing a classic farewell. Walking down the stairs past the courtside seats to the runway, an exit sign caught his eye. And, as if on cue, Joe Lapchick quietly made his last departure into the late afternoon snow.

As Lapchick pulled his coat collar up to ward off the steady falling snow, his thoughts were riveted on the finality of it all. It was over, and he had done his best. It was a great run. His team of scrappers sent him out a winner, something he had been and always would be. The old coach didn't hear the horns honking as he and his assistant slushed across the street and headed to Leone's to put the victory into proper perspective. His family and friends would be there, ready to help him begin a new life.

O

What if the university could have foreseen Lapchick's miraculous season? What if it knew the team would defeat Michigan and capture the NIT? Would that have changed the retirement ruling? Lapchick was in poor health and probably couldn't have coached more than another year or two anyway, and the university would have walked away looking better. His satisfaction was going out a champ. As one sportswriter put it, Lapchick left with "the Holiday Festival tucked into his hip pocket and the NIT championship sparkling in his eyes." He was a proud man, proud of the 1965 finish, and no one could ever take that from him.

Time, however, has a way of easing pain and diminishing memory. With time, Joe Lapchick's "forced retirement" was only remembered by the sports media as his "retirement." Future sportswriters would have conveniently forgotten just how the last year for Joe Lapchick evolved. The irony of Lapchick's dismissal is that Carnesecca was the right choice to follow him. He was outstanding over the next twenty years and would rewrite St. John's record books. He made the university's decision seem prophetic. No one, however, would ever deny that Joe Lapchick had helped his old school by the polish he had applied to his knowledgeable assistant.

In some ways, Lapchick's problem was that he was ahead of his time. He utilized assistants the way today's major programs do. Assistants concentrate on game preparation as well as scouting and recruiting. The head coach pulls everything together, creates the winning atmosphere, and makes critical decisions. He also generates team discipline and makes sure it's maintained, and he functions as the key figure during games making substitutions as well as calling time-outs. There was no doubt Joe Lapchick controlled his team from the bench as Bear Bryant, Vince Lombardi, Bob Knight, and Digger Phelps did. To a novice, coaching is magic formations and slick plays, which in reality all coaches borrow from each other. But it was Lapchick who acted as the carrot players chased trying to satisfy him.

A strategy is only as important as the coach's ability to convince a team that it can work. It's the application along with the necessary motivational skills that makes winners. Lapchick was a master at motivation, a coach respected by other coaches. And the 1964–65 team sustained proof of his coaching ability. No preseason judge of basketball would have rated the Redmen among the nation's best. It was a team that played in streaks, but when it had to deliver, it did. The Michigan and Villanova wins were tournament championships against very good nationally ranked teams. Shortly after he left St. John's, the university presented Joe Lapchick with an honorary degree. Lapchick, a man who spent a lifetime catching up with those who had an education, finally felt he was closer to his goal. The gesture was well appreciated and helped to blur bad feelings.

Chapter 20

The Wind Blowing in My Face

"Maybe the biggest lesson of all is the way he handled the time my mother used to call il solo tramonto. *It means "the sun sets." For her it was that time in life when you look back and try to see yourself as you were and as you are, because by that time the sunset takes on another meaning to you."*

—Lou Carnesecca on mentor, Joe Lapchick
New York Post, March 29, 1985

I t was a mild Sunday in March, one that melted much of the winter gleam that surrounded Yonkers. The twilight glow accompanied Joe Lapchick and his son Rich as they drove the Hutchinson River Parkway in the coach's gray Oldsmobile sedan. They were attending the Metropolitan Sportswriters annual dinner at the Hotel Americana in New York, where Lapchick was to be honored. The sportswriters decided to dedicate this dinner to their friend, who would retire after his last games in the 1965 NIT.

After much merrymaking, the guest of honor stood up to say his piece. The pioneer coach offered some sound advice about the course collegiate basketball was taking, and then he folded his notes, removed his glasses, and spoke from the heart. "You have been a wonderful audience tonight and for the past thirty years of my coaching career." He paused, gathering his thoughts as well as his emotions. "If the fun of coaching was playing the games," he reminded his friends, "the added pleasure was sharing them with you." He paused, and then closed with, "May God bless all of you."

But before he sat down, *Daily News* cartoonist Bill Gallo waved Joe Lapchick forward and handed him a large package. As the coach tore off the wrapping, a beautiful Gallo cartoon appeared. It was a touching sketch of a broad-smiling, bow-tied Joe Lapchick with a caption that read, "Thanks, Joe, for everything." Lapchick was urged by Gallo to open the envelope taped to the back of the caricature. Inside a plain white business envelope he found a check for more than $9,000. The old warrior was stunned and couldn't stop the flow of tears that trickled down his cheeks. All he could do was wave to his friends and utter, "Thanks," a word he was never afraid to use. He sat down to a thunderous applause, one richly deserved.

O

Much of Lapchick's retirement was spent sharing a lifetime of experiences with young coaches, whom he referred to as his "adopted children," in a letter he wrote about the satisfaction gained helping others. The number of coaches who found their way to his Yonkers home amazed him. They came to learn, "not how to coach, but rather how to handle problems," of which Lapchick was expert, claiming he had made "thousands of mistakes and learned something from each one." But the coach who made a lasting impression was a serious-minded, former Ohio State forward.

"Of all my memories of people who have helped me," Bob Knight the three-time NCAA basketball champion insisted, "none are greater than those of Mr. Lapchick." The fiery coach often wondered how he ever got to know him. "Why me?" he asked, "I was a rookie coach twenty-two, maybe twenty-three years old, still wet behind the ears, and one of the game's legends treated me like royalty." Joe Lapchick got to know Knight near the end of his career at St. John's. He was introduced to the young West Point assistant at a coaches' luncheon in New York. Lapchick had fond memories of Knight's college coach, Fred Taylor, whose Ohio State Buckeyes were the 1960 NCAA champs. Lapchick hooked his arm around the assistant and squired him around the room, introducing him to New York's basketball elite. "It was the Spindletop Restaurant, a few blocks from the old Garden," Knight recalled.

One of Knight's favorite memories of Lapchick involved a St. John's-Marquette game he was assigned to scout in Milwaukee. "They were staying in the Pfister Hotel, and I decided to have lunch in its coffee shop." Lapchick spotted Knight, invited him to his table, and asked what he was doing in Milwaukee. After Knight explained, Lapchick asked, "What do you need to scout us for?" Lapchick was implying that his team wasn't that good for Army to worry about and that his style was simple to understand. The next morning he invited Knight to travel with the team to Chicago for the Loyola game. While Knight was learning how to beat St. John's, its coach showed uncommon kindness. He not only traveled and ate with the team, but also rooted St. John's on to a big win over Loyola.

When Knight later became Army's head coach, he was a regular guest in Lapchick's home. "I meet with Bobby often," Lapchick explained. "We don't talk Xs and Os, but how to handle personnel." Successful coaching to Lapchick involved knowing how to handle players. "The first thing I did when I became a head coach was visit with Mr. Lapchick," Knight recalled. "Is it important that you're liked?" Lapchick asked. "No, not really," Knight answered. "That's good," Lapchick replied. "If it was, you'd never be able to make the decisions necessary to be a good coach."

"Lapchick taught me to never paint myself into a corner," Knight said. He suggested that a coach make few team rules. Then, if he had to get rid of a bad apple that didn't fit, he could do it simply while another player who might need saving could be helped without the coach contradicting himself. The old Celtic recommended one rule to cover all situations: when a player's actions are detrimental to the team, his school, or himself, he will be dealt with by the coach. The coaching maxim made sense to Knight. "It has been my training rule since the first night I talked to Coach Lapchick." It helped make Knight one of the game's toughest disciplinarians. "In the final analysis," as Lapchick liked to say, it "forces boys to become men."

One day the two were riding an elevator, when Lapchick turned to Knight. "How do you like this suit," he asked. Knight, not particularly a clothes hound, was impressed. Lapchick suggested he visit his tailor to outfit himself properly. Knight then bought all his clothing from Lapchick's haberdasher until he left for Indiana University.

Lapchick also taught the young coach what not to do. Army was playing St. John's in Lapchick's last NIT, and for Knight it was his first taste of the big time. As the teams warmed up, Knight approached Lapchick. "Coach," Knight said slyly, "you guys gotta take it easy on us tonight." Lapchick, who didn't like getting his nose tweaked, smiled and became the teacher again, as he ran an index finger like a razor up and down Knight's cheek. "Bobby, Bobby, don't ever try giving me a barber job." Knight never forgot it, admiring the wisdom of a simple lesson. "Never once after that have I ever said to anybody, 'Now don't hammer us' or any of that bullshit."

Joe Lapchick missed few basketball events at the Garden, but he was often noticed at Army games. "You know where Lapchick always sat in the Garden," Knight reminisced. "By the exit sign in the promenade seats." As Knight walked off the floor at the end of a half, he'd look up at Lapchick, who would stick his thumb under his chin and push it up, as if he were saying, "Keep your head up, keep your chin up high." Lapchick was often found in the Garden runway, consoling the young emotional coach who would get down from a poorly played game or loss. Lapchick was always positive, finding the good in Knight's disappointment. He saw much of himself in the young coach's passion. He knew he had a winner.

Knight understood Lapchick's strengths. "I could draw what he knew about the technicalities of basketball on the back of a postage card," Knight said, "but it would take a frigging encyclopedia to hold all he knew about how to win and how to play." Knight, who knew volumes of basketball strategy, understood technical knowledge alone didn't win games. Lapchick recognized his coaching legacy would never include complex strategy. And yet, his simple style made sense, especially to Knight. "Good shots, careful ballhandling, and good defense" was his description of Lapchick's teams. To Knight, the present Texas Tech coach, "Lapchick's style was classic; the way Vince Lombardi played football."

Lapchick's vocabulary covered all situations, from the tenderest moment to a direct expletive that made a point. Direct, yet caring, but never dull. "He could go from 'f—k that guy,' to the most articulate statement man could make. I loved that part of him." He was a regular guy and yet a philosophical mentor, all at the same time. When Knight spoke of those who most influenced him, he named "Red Auerbach and Mr. Lapchick," but never "Joe Lapchick," out of respect for the pioneer coach that has never diminished.

Knight still remembers Lapchick's home address, telephone number, and tailor's name. His precise recall of events, too, suggested their importance. He treasured minor details of the association—names of hotels, restaurants, and acquaintances. All resurfaced when he spoke about their friendship after more than thirty years. Bob Knight has firmly held onto Lapchick's treasured gambling Scandal Scrapbook. He plans to give it to the Hall of Fame someday. But for now he keeps it nearby, along with the cashmere coat that Evie Levinson sewed. They are warm reminders of his beginning and Lapchick's legacy, a debt Knight will never forget. They represent a rare friendship, but not the only one.

At the coaches luncheon at Leone's prior to Joe Lapchick's final NIT championship in March 1965, Bob Cousy, the young coach of Boston College and former Boston Celtics playmaker and Lapchick's first-round opponent, stood up and told two astounding stories.

In the spring of 1947, Bob Cousy, a freshman at Holy Cross, was thinking of transferring to St. John's. Cousy, one of the country's best guards, was unhappy with his playing time. Familiar with Coach Lapchick, he wrote about his intentions. By today's standards, the initial contact provides a green light for an unscrupulous coach to pounce on a competitor's talent. Lapchick wrote back and reminded Cousy why he was in college. "You are not there to primarily play basketball," Lapchick instructed, "but to get a good education." He went on to praise Holy Cross's academics, as well as the character of its coach, Doggie Julian. The St. John's coach warned that transferring was risky and he could easily lose himself. Cousy stayed at Holy Cross and went on to fame. He wonders how many coaches would have acted the way Lapchick did. "To this day I am grateful to Joe Lapchick for that advice."

After Cousy's first story, he felt obligated to tell the second. During a heated Garden NBA playoff game in the early 1950s, Boston Celtics' Bob Cousy stole the ball at half-court and drove past the Knicks' Carl Braun for what appeared a certain field goal. As the ball passed through the rim, Braun reached under the net and flicked the ball back out, retrieved it, and raced up court as if nothing had happened. Since the two referees were caught out of position, they missed the play. "Then all hell broke loose," Cousy recalled. Coach Auerbach and his Celtics team were furious, exploding onto the court and causing enough bedlam to stop the game. Because the play occurred near the Knicks bench, the team and the crowd knew the Celtics deserved 2 points. But the officials weren't about to accept the Celtics' version, and they approached the scorer's table for clarification. The scorers acted as if they were testifying against a Mafia don. "No, nothing unusual happened," was their response. After the scorer's version of "Three Blind Mice," and with the referees ready to resume play, Lapchick walked toward center court and announced to the officials that the basket was good, "and put 2 points on the board." The Celtics got the points, and later the win, but to Lapchick, being fair was more important. "Trust me when I tell you," Cousy insisted, "there wasn't another coach in the league who would have done what Lapchick did." But Cousy wasn't the last to be mentored by Lapchick.

During his seven years as assistant, Lou Carnesecca adopted much of Joe Lapchick's coaching philosophy while learning how to better handle and motivate personnel. The fundamentals that had won for his mentor served as the basis for much of Carnesecca's success. Lapchick believed that road games should be slowed down and strategy communicated through a strong floor leader. As a successful high school coach, Carnesecca favored a running game, but he became more conservative, less willing to allow the game to get out of control. Both believed "the ball was golden" and should not be given up easily. Lapchick influenced the young coach's passing game out of a half-court offense and man-to-man defense, while staying away from zone variations. Like the old Celtics, Lapchick primarily played five starters, which he felt built confidence, and Carnesecca, too, went no deeper than seven.

Lapchick also offered insights that made Carnesecca a more complete coach. "Joe was a humble man, but he hated 'geniuses' who thought they were better than everybody else," Carnesecca related. "Lapchick loved beating those types and had a subtle way of bringing them down to earth," Carnesecca remembered. "He often did it to me." Once, as they left a banquet, Lapchick handed Carnesecca a card. "Here," he said. "Take this and put it in your wallet. Carry it with you all the time and when you think you're pretty smart, read it." The card said: "Peacock today, feather duster tomorrow." Carnesecca still carries the worn reminder.

"We were on a train," Carnesecca recalled, "heading to play Notre Dame my first year, when I began spouting my imaginary wisdom of the game." The old pro listened carefully, not interrupting the little maestro who acted as if he had helped Dr. Naismith nail up the first peach baskets. After Carnesecca finished, Lapchick gently informed him of the facts of basketball, and softly tempered his remarks, always allowing Carnesecca to speak his mind. "He never talked down to me, he didn't big-time me," the Hall of Fame coach related. "Coach never crushed my enthusiasm. It's the reason why I am richer for my experiences with him."

Lapchick also found time to help his media friends. When *New York Post* sportswriter Lennie Koppett was assigned to cover the Knicks in the late 1940s, and knew little about basketball, Lapchick taught him on their long train rides. As Koppett got to be one of the better writers on the beat, Lapchick occasionally would critique his work, encouraging him to maintain high standards.

Lapchick's era was still the age of gentlemen. He was a New York sports celebrity who trusted the press, while it worshiped him. Koppett knew Joe always leveled with him, whereas most other sports people held something back, or flatly lied.

Sportswriters were aware of rumors that Lapchick catered to the sports media for obvious benefits. Koppett knew, however, it wasn't easily accomplished and saw him differently. "Everyone wants something from the press in the sports business, but we are sensitive and aware of people trying to use us." It is more difficult to make the press like coaches than in an ordinary business. Sportswriters were subjected to people coming at them for exactly that purpose. The idea that by being nice to reporters you received advantages, was, as Koppett believed, "Silly, unless you're real, and that's what made it work for Lapchick." He was media friendly and understood a sportswriter's needs. Whether at Leone's Restaurant, in a locker room, or at home, Lapchick was there for them.

"Joe was what is known as 'a saver,' a sure bet to come up with a story or a column when you had space to fill and nothing to fill it." Sportswriter Phil Pepe recalled how he could bail out a rookie writer in need. A telephone call to his home in Yonkers took care of that. He was always available, willing, interesting, and always quotable. This access was the greatest gift one could give a sportswriter. Pepe summed up Lapchick in a special way: "No newspaper was too small, no story too big, no time too inconvenient for his comment, his analysis, his opinion. And we loved him for it."

○

A *Newsday* feature in the 1980s described Kutsher's Country Club as the "Borscht Belt Dynasty." The three-hundred-acre, 450-room, year-round traditional Jewish resort is located in Monticello, one hundred miles from

New York City. Part of Kutsher's charm was its fascination with sports, and basketball in particular. Over the years, great coaches like Clair Bee and Red Auerbach were closely linked with the resort. After Lapchick's retirement, Milt and Helen Kutsher invited him to be their social director and greeter, a position he readily accepted. Lapchick was asked to be himself, enjoy the club, and simply mingle with guests. Kutsher's had a special meaning to Lapchick, one he described as "Golf, food, and good fellowship." As the Kutshers got to know him, their relationship grew. He enjoyed his gregarious role at their resort and looked forward to his summers there.

On a sunny day in early August 1970, Kutsher staff member Jack Landman met his friend Joe Lapchick on the club's golf course to play the back nine. Both were experienced golfers who regularly shot in the high thirties, low forties range and enjoyed each other's company. They usually played at 4:00 P.M., but on this afternoon by the third hole, Lapchick felt a sharp chest pain, different from his past angina attacks. "Jack, I'm not feeling well. You play; I'll drive." Lapchick tried popping nitroglycerin and digitalis pills, but this time they didn't work. His partner wisely ignored his suggestion, rushed him back to the hotel, and sent for the cardiologist on the grounds, who immediately ordered Lapchick to the hospital where he was placed in intensive care.

On the morning of August 10, the patient was resting quietly when Nurse Stackhouse walked into his private room at 6:30 A.M. to open the blinds and check his vital signs. Stackhouse had heard something about his fame, but being unfamiliar with sports, it never registered. To her, Lapchick was a pleasant patient doing what he was told.

She noticed nothing unusual as she entered Lapchick's room that Monday morning. The first thing she checked was the heart monitor, which registered normal. As she approached the bed, she smiled. Lapchick opened his eyes and asked, "Am I going to die?" Startled by the question, the nurse quickly looked at the monitor and, noticing its regular beat, tried to reassure the patient. Then she leaned over the bed to take his temperature. Almost immediately, Lapchick's eyes rolled back, and the only sound she heard was a loud continuous beep as the heart monitor registered a pencil-thin, horizontal line. The nurse raced to press the alarm for help, but despite the hospital's frantic emergency efforts, Joe Lapchick was gone.

On August 13, 1970, a bright sunny Thursday, Joe Lapchick was laid to rest. The 10:00 A.M. High Mass of the Resurrection at St. Denis

Catholic Church in South Yonkers was well attended. Cameramen and sound crews from CBS and NBC crowded in the balcony with the church's choir to get a sixty-second byte for the 6:00 news. St. Denis could seat six hundred, but that didn't stop cars and spectators from filling the surrounding blocks, causing traffic to jam. Local people who never knew the man wanted to meet him for the first time on his last day.

Joe Lapchick was buried three blocks from where he was born in Yonkers, a short trip from the entrance roof to his old flat in the Hollow, where he played on Mulberry Street and that hadn't changed much in seventy years. A few blocks away was the Immanuel Chapel, where Mr. Kalkhof first taught him to play in the church basement and where he got excited about a game he loved his whole life. After the burial, Mrs. Lapchick invited friends back to her home. All those who attended were reminded that Joe Lapchick had not forgotten them. They were invited by the family to join them for "good food and drink." Lapchick's son made sure of that. As the food was served, Mrs. Lapchick walked around to the dining room table and removed the vacant head of the household's chair, an old Czech custom.

○

When Lapchick died he was still employed by Kinney Shoes, the company he had been associated with from his playing days. After his retirement, he took on greater responsibility at store openings and clinics. The $18,000-a-year contract was more than he ever earned in basketball. Kinney executive Cliff Anderson, his good friend, made sure the Lapchick family was paid for the rest of 1970 and then added the entire salary for 1971. The Kutshers also made sure that Lapchick's $5,000 summer salary was paid for both years. Ironically, when the family estate was totaled, Joe Lapchick unknowingly had left a six-figure balance for Bobbie. All those careful years paid off. Even in death he thought of the welfare of others.

Kutsher's, as Joe Lapchick had predicted, became his life's last round of golf. He often spoke about "playing golf, with a drink in one hand, a club in the other, and the wind blowing in my face." The last scene would have included a twinkle in his eye, standing tall on a golf course on a pleasant day, maybe playing the ninth hole and stopping for a drink, and ready for anything life could offer. He was Joe Lapchick, and he may not have been aware of it, but he was still casting a giant shadow.

O

When I thought about Joe Lapchick's concerns, I felt they were those of a role model, as well as a caring father figure who helped direct confused college students at key moments in their lives. I realized most of us couldn't do anything for him except say thanks. But knowing him, that's all he would have wanted. He never came up short of time, never looked at his watch to tell me he had a more important appointment, because I was that important appointment. Life will never produce a finer person than Joe Lapchick. He will always be thought of in the way he showered his highest praise: A real pro.

Afterword

On a slushy February night of the new millennium, Joe Lapchick was being honored at halftime of the Syracuse-St. John's Big East game in Madison Square Garden. "Ladies and gentlemen," the announcer blared, focusing the crowd on a ceremony beginning on the floor. "We ask that you direct your attention to a special presentation celebrating the one hundredth anniversary of the birth of Joe Lapchick."

St. John's had been blessed with outstanding coaches like Buck Freeman, Frank McGuire, and Lou Carnesecca, but this was Lapchick's night. "No one person is as much a part of this tradition," the voice continued, "as legendary Hall of Famer Joe Lapchick." The three Lapchick children, and grandchildren were greeted at half-court by former athletic director Jack Kaiser and Lou Carnesecca as the crowd was reminded how important Lapchick had been to basketball as well as to St. John's. Dr. Richard Lapchick accepted a large birthday poster signed by the current team. It pictured his father in the red practice jersey he wore near the end of his coaching days. Players who probably knew little of Joe Lapchick wished him a happy birthday.

Younger spectators had little recall of Joe Lapchick. Anyone under forty probably never saw his teams play and might be more familiar with the Lapchick Tournament or his son, Rich, than with the old Celtics star.

It was, nevertheless, a fine gesture by his old school to honor him, and it was well appreciated by his family.

Barbara Lapcek accepted a framed montage depicting her father's career that stirred memories. She wondered how he would have reacted to the tribute. "He might not have liked it." She could hear him saying, "What's the fuss." As a man who didn't like spotlights, he might have felt he hadn't done anything worthy of tying up the Garden. "But then again my father may have thought how lucky he was." At that point, the fans stood up to pay respect to Joe Lapchick. Some, like Hy Gotkin's son, Mark, got goose bumps when the ceremony took a nostalgic hold of him. "I knew what Lapchick meant to my father." Tonight St. John's stood up in Lapchick's "house" and asked the crowd to tip an imaginary glass of cheer in his honor. "A true St. John's legend," the announcer reminded the audience. If spirits have a memory, Joe Lapchick would be standing tall, never forgetting the moment.

○

Several years after Lapchick's death, Bob Knight's Indiana basketball team reached the 1979 NIT final in Madison Square Garden, and he knew Mrs. Lapchick would be there. As his team prepared to battle Purdue, he decided that if Indiana won, he would invite her onto the floor to share his team's award. It was a sentimental moment after the 1-point victory, as Knight went to the announcer's table, interrupted the ceremonies, and asked John Condon for the microphone. "Ladies and gentlemen," the winning coach echoed, "I'd like to introduce the greatest fan that we have here tonight—the wife of the late, great St. John's coach, Mrs. Joe Lapchick." As the Coach's wife was escorted onto the floor, Knight embraced her with the winner's trophy. The respect Knight showed Mrs. Lapchick was small payment to his former mentor's guidance.

For a brief moment, the calendar flashed back to Joe Lapchick's glory days in Madison Square Garden, the arena he most identified with. Seeing Mrs. Lapchick, playing in the Garden, winning Lapchick's NIT was an occasion when the fiery coach's emotions won out. But Knight didn't care about crying in public. He knew that the Big Indian would have been pleased, and more likely, would have joined him.

Index